OXFORD POLITICAL THEORY

Series Editors: Will Kymlicka, David Miller, and Alan Ryan

━━━━━

DISADVANTAGE

OXFORD POLITICAL THEORY

Oxford Political Theory presents the best new work in contemporary political theory. It is intended to be broad in scope, including original contributions to political philosophy, and also work in applied political theory. The series contains works of outstanding quality with no restriction as to approach or subject matter.

DISADVANTAGE

JONATHAN WOLFF
AVNER DE-SHALIT

OXFORD
UNIVERSITY PRESS

*This book has been printed digitally and produced in a standard specification
in order to ensure its continuing availability*

OXFORD
UNIVERSITY PRESS

Great Clarendon Street, Oxford OX2 6DP

Oxford University Press is a department of the University of Oxford.
It furthers the University's objective of excellence in research, scholarship,
and education by publishing worldwide in

Oxford New York

Auckland   Cape Town Dar es Salaam   Hong Kong   Karachi
Kuala Lumpur Madrid Melbourne Mexico City   Nairobi
New Delhi Shanghai   Taipei Toronto
With offices in
Argentina Austria Brazil Chile Czech Republic France Greece
Guatemala Hungary Italy Japan South Korea Poland Portugal
Singapore Switzerland Thailand Turkey Ukraine Vietnam

Oxford is a registered trade mark of Oxford University Press
in the UK and in certain other countries

Published in the United States
by Oxford University Press Inc., New York

ISBN 978-0-19-927826-8

To Elaine and Yifat

PREFACE AND ACKNOWLEDGEMENTS

While working on this book – since 2002 – we have been encouraged by the interest others have shown in our work. Yet the question most often put to us, at least by philosophers, is how it has been possible to write a book collaboratively. What it is about philosophers which makes this, for them, such a salient question we do not dare to delve into here, but it is worth noting that political and social scientists have not thought collaboration at all remarkable. We can, however, report that working together on this project has been a huge stimulus and pleasure. In intellectual terms the advantages are obvious. But there are other benefits too. It is natural that in a long project any author will have moments of doubt and gloom, but in this case we found that at any time at least one of us remained enthusiastic, and so we have never lost momentum. What we would have done if disillusionment struck both at the same time remains, fortunately, untested. We were also lucky not to have had the problem of having to deal with a serious conflict about the content of the book. Perhaps collaboration works best when the authors live more than 2000 miles apart. Whatever the explanation, it has worked extremely well for us. To use a phrase rarely seen in academic circles, it has been great fun.

Some readers may be curious to know which author is responsible for each different part of this book. While it is true that each word must have been first written by someone, each chapter – probably each paragraph – has been worked over and over again by both of us to a point where authorship of everything is truly joint. As a matter of fact, there are arguments and passages that both of us think were written by the other. . . .

We began working on this when we both attended a workshop on inequality organised by Jo at UCL, and we realized that although we were working on different topics there were affinities and connections between our ideas and projects. We first put together a paper of about sixty pages, which, we can now say, thankfully was rejected by a certain philosophy journal, with a cover letter suggesting that such an ambitious project suited a book rather than a paper. So we started writing the book.

The very first draft was discussed at a postgraduate seminar series at UCL in the autumn of 2004. This then provided the springboard for several full-scale drafts and eventual final version. Most chapters, or arguments, of this book have been presented to departmental seminars, colloquia, and conferences. These include the Priority in Practice Workshops, and Philosophy and Law seminars at UCL, the Department of Political Science at the Hebrew University, the Oxford Political Theory seminar, as well as other seminars and conferences in Oxford, the ECPR equality workshop in Granada, the ALSP conference in Dublin, Sapir College, Princeton University, Harvard Medical School, Manchester University, University College Galway, Tartu University, Estonia, Liverpool University, Durham University, the Open University, the University of Pavia, Italy, and Bilkent University, Turkey.

While we shall always remain jointly and severally responsible for our arguments and mistakes, we have benefited tremendously from a supportive community of philosophers, political scientists, economists, and others who have been curious about what we have been up to lately. In particular we would like to thank our students, colleagues, and friends who made many fruitful comments, both verbally and in writing: Faith Armitage, Daniel Attas, John Baker, Brian Barry, Daniel Bell, Fran Bennet, Miriam Bentwich, Sandrine Berges, Erika Ann Blacksher, Alex Brown, Paula Casal, Clare Chambers, Ian Carter, Tom Christiano, Miriam Cohen Christofidis, Elizabeth Cripps, Geert Demuijnck, Nir Eyal, Cecile Fabre, Brian Feltham, Marc Fleurbaey, Steve Gardiner, Axel Gosseries, Alon Harel, Simon Hampson, Daniel Hausman, Noam Hofshtater, Richard Hull, Attracta Ingram, Anat Itay, Dale Jameison, Alya Khan, Kathy King, Cecile Labord, Catriona McKinnon, Jeff McMahan, Andy Mason, Saladin Meckled Garcia, David Miller, Veronique Munoz Dardé, Orit Nuttman-Shwartz, Yair Odem, John O'Neill, Shepley Orr, Mike Otsuka, Avia Pasternak, Anne Phillips, Roland Pierek, Tom Porter, Sanjay Reddy, Ingrid Robeyns, Bo Rothstein, Shlomi Segall, Saul Smilansky, Zofia Stemplowska, Georgia Testa, Alex Voorhoeve, Adam Swift, Christine Sypnowich, Leif Wenar, Stuart White, and Andrew Williams. There must be many others too, and we apologise for omitting their names. Our research assistants in Israel and the UK, Miriam Bentwich, Anat Itay, Noam Hofshtater, and Avia Pasternak, helped us tremendously.

We would like to thank Nuffield College, where Avner spent a most fruitful year of sabbatical, and the department of philosophy at University College London, for allowing Jo a sabbatical term, and the Arts and Humanities Research Council for funding a second term (which was officially granted to support other projects, but the AHRC deserves thanks for contributing to a period of research leave in which substantial progress was also made on this book).

Special thanks are due to Dominic Byatt, editor for politics at Oxford University Press, who encouraged us and supported this project, and to David Miller and three anonymous referees for their profound and challenging comments and criticism, which have led to many improvements in the final version.

Finally, we would like to thank Elaine, Yifat, Max, Daniel, Hillel and Shiri, for their patience and help. We hope we haven't been too unbearable during these years.

Part of this research was conducted with the financial help of the Israel Science Foundation and the Max Kampelman Chair for Democracy and Human Rights.

Jonathan Wolff and Avner de-Shalit

CONTENTS

Introduction

1. The Story of Leah

Leah[1] was born twenty-five years ago, the youngest of five children, to an immigrant couple from North Africa. Penniless on reaching Israel, they were allocated a small government flat and a plot of land – half an acre – in a small town in the south of Israel . With no education or any knowledge of farming, they found themselves competing for menial jobs. Leah's family was religiously orthodox, so put her under pressure to marry when she was eighteen. This she did, and never finished high school. In Leah's town the men worked and the women stayed at home to look after the children. Leah was expected to fall pregnant immediately and fulfil her maternal role, but alas, in the first year she did not conceive, and so her husband left her.

The social pressure and 'shame' were unbearable, so Leah decided to consult a kabbalist mystic, known for 'curing infertile women with his spells'. Her problem, she was told, was that she was unlucky because of her name, and that if she changed it to 'Lucky', her life would turn around. Leah listened, changed her name, and met a handsome young man the next day. Thinking this a sign from heaven, she immediately accepted when the man offered to marry her. She even became pregnant and gave birth to a baby girl when she was twenty. However, several days after the birth the man confessed to Leah – by now Lucky – that he could not cope with fatherhood and fled. After several weeks, when he failed to return, Leah asked for a divorce, which was granted.

Now Leah – Lucky – was a single parent, twice divorced at the age of twenty-one. Her father decided to take an extra job to relieve the family's poverty. He obtained work as a security guard at the entrance to a supermarket. This was a highly dangerous job, since this was the time of the *Intifada* (Palestinian uprising) and involved a serious risk of death. A significant number of security guards were killed challenging intending suicide bombers, who then blew themselves up at the entrance, also killing the guard. Consequently, only people who were desperate for money applied for these positions.

At the same time, her father decided that he could not cope with the 'shame', and made it clear that she must marry yet again and settle down. There was, he said, a respectable person in town, who was ready to marry her, and rumour was that he was rich and could support her. Leah/Lucky did not even meet him. Instead, she went to another 'kabbalist', who was 'known to bless people whose life had gone wrong'. She asked him if she should marry the respectable candidate. This kabbalist gave Lucky/Leah the nod, and so she married this man, who turned out to be thirty years older than she was. Nobody had checked whether he was, in fact, rich, or even whether he was working. When they were married, he told Leah's parents he was moving into their house. Only then it was revealed that he had been unemployed and had no savings. He was not a crook – in fact he genuinely did not understand what the fuss was about. All very well, but Leah-Lucky was now married to this person, whom she regarded as good-for-nothing.

What do we feel when we read about cases like this? Many people will feel angry or frustrated. How dare these men play with Leah's life in this way? How can we tolerate social structures that force women into such dependent and confined lives?[2] But we also feel that in a deep sense, Leah/Lucky is disadvantaged. Her life is a harsh and miserable mess; she must struggle with poverty; she cannot afford anything beyond the basics; she cannot spoil herself; she says she cannot take care of her child because she is moody and gloomy all day and because she is very, very poor; and she cannot reciprocate her parents' support and love. She is humiliated by the community, by the men who have power over her, and by her indigence. She had no proper education. She cannot be autonomous. Yet she does not live in the gutter, like a character in a Dickens story, or in the filthy conditions depicted by Engels in his study of England in 1844. But still, she has never had genuine opportunities to achieve what she had good reason to want to be or have. She says she had potential and is probably never likely to fulfill it.

There are many people like Leah, although, thankfully, not in her precise circumstances. What they have in common is that they are disadvantaged in a number of ways; that consequently they are highly vulnerable; and, quite often, attempts made to improve things do not help or even make things worse. Part of the aim of this book is to produce an account of disadvantage which is rich enough to capture the ways in which the lives of Leah and others have gone wrong, and to consider the sorts of steps that societies can take so that their situations can be improved, and that others can avoid their fate. This is part of a broader set of aims: to try to provide one account of the nature of a society of equals and of how it might be possible to go about moving society in such a direction.

2. *A Consensual Starting Point: Priority to the Least Advantaged*

Our aim in this book is to provide practical guidance to policy makers by providing a version of egalitarian theory which can be applied to actual social policy. An initial difficulty is that within academic political philosophy there is much disagreement about how an egalitarian theory is to be formulated, and so any selection of a particular version of egalitarianism is likely to meet opposition not only from non-egalitarians, but also from most other egalitarian theorists. Hence no social policy founded on such a basis will carry wide conviction.

In reply, we observe that while philosophical disagreement certainly has its place, for the purpose of social theory it is necessary to see how a broader consensus within egalitarianism can be generated. If theorists fail to meet this challenge they risk leaving social policy in a theoretical vacuum, or perhaps in chaos where any theory is treated as if it is as good as any other. Hence there is every reason to investigate whether a broad consensus is possible. And, indeed, it seems to us that some, although not all, of the major philosophical disputes among those in the egalitarian tradition, very broadly construed, will leave little trace on policy dilemmas. Consider, in particular, the dispute between those who argue that economic goods should be distributed in such a way as to make everyone equal; those who think that there should be absolute priority for the worst off; those who think there should be some sort of weighted priority for the worst off; and those who think that what matters is that each should have enough (what are called 'sufficiency theories').[3] These may seem to be radically distinct in their implications, and indeed in theory they are. However, provided that there are people in society who have not yet achieved sufficiency, and provided we have in mind limited, or at least finite, budgets and financial resources, then all of these views appear to converge on the same general policy prescription in the short to medium term: *identify the worst off and take appropriate steps so that their position can be improved.* This consensus point – which might even be shared by some right-wing political parties – will be the focus of our analysis, and it is for this reason that the book is called *'Disadvantage'* and not *'Equality'*. We do not claim that there is consensus on the view that the worst off should be helped at all costs, or that governments can ignore others, but merely that government's most urgent task is to consider the claims of the least advantaged first. Of course there is convergence on this only insofar as it is kept vague and uninterpreted, and there is room for serious disagreement on how strong the priority to the worst off should be. An extreme view is that the worst off should have absolute priority in the sense that their claims silence those of all others, while a much more modest view would be that if we can bestow a similar benefit on two people we should, other things being equal, give it to the one who is worse off. Nevertheless, this general convergence is enough to get us started. While we will argue for our own interpretation of priority to the worst off in Chapter 9, many of the policy recommendations which follow from this interpretation are also compatible with alternative interpretations of the strength of priority.

3. The Nature of Disadvantage

If government is to take steps to improve the lives of the least advantaged, it needs, first of all, an understanding of what it is to be disadvantaged. It is, currently, very common to think of disadvantage in terms of poverty, and poverty in terms of low income. Obviously there are very good reasons for this, in that income allows one access to a great deal of what matters in life, and is also relatively easy to measure. However when we think of cases like that of Leah/Lucky, the immediate problems she faces are not confined to lack of money, although this is, as we saw, a considerable part. In addition she has been subjected to the power of her father and community, shabbily treated by a succession of men, and denied a proper education. She is currently very depressed, and lacks employable skills and opportunities. Hence her disadvantage is multifaceted, and for reasons such as this we will argue later that disadvantage is plural in nature.

Clearly providing Leah with more money, and boosting her purchasing power, would have a number of positive effects. In the short term it would make her life more comfortable, in that she could purchase better food, clothes, and leisure opportunities for herself and her child. Looking further ahead, she could enroll in college and gain skills and self-respect, and thereby also develop, and try to realize, her potential. Hence money is an extremely valuable means to other things that make life go well. Yet it is limited too. Perhaps her father will not permit her to go to college. To do so perhaps she would have to leave home, and thereby abandon her social network, which could be a traumatic experience. Even if she does gain skills she may face racial or sexual discrimination in the workplace.

In short, redistribution of money cannot in itself end oppressive social structures.

The question of whether egalitarianism should focus on matters of distribution alone, or whether issues of social structure should instead be its focus, has, for reasons like this, become an important matter of recent debate. Our view is that this is a misplaced dispute, and suitably understood, issues of both distribution and social structure can be accommodated into a single view. Explaining this debate, and our resolution of it, will be helpful as a way of outlining the general pluralistic theory of disadvantage which we will argue for in the following chapters of the book.

One view of the demands of egalitarianism – which we can call the 'distributive' idea – is well put by G. A. Cohen. He writes: 'I take for granted that there is something which justice requires people to have equal amounts of, not no matter what, but to whatever extent is allowed by values which compete with distributive equality'.[4] On this view a society of equals is one in which people have something in equal measure; perhaps wealth, happiness, or standard of living. By contrast a relational, or social, view of equality takes the task of an egalitarian society to be not so much to distribute goods the right way but to create the right types of classless relationships between people; avoiding oppression, exploitation, domination, servility, snobbery, and other hierarchical evils.[5]

As should be clear, we are very sympathetic to the idea of social equality, and agree that some recent theories of equality have not paid sufficient attention to the relations between citizens in a society of equals. Instead some strands of egalitarians have concentrated essentially on the way governments treat their citizens, rather than the way in which those citizens treat each other. Yet it is important not to make the opposite mistake of ignoring the economic realm. Hence Tawney wrote:

Though the ideal of an equal division of material wealth may continue to elude us, it is necessary, nonetheless, to make haste towards it, not because such wealth is the most important of man's treasures, but to prove it is not.[6]

Now if we are to take Tawney's rhetoric literally it is hard to agree that it is worth the effort of implementing material equality in order to prove that material goods are not the most important thing. But we should surely agree that we are unlikely to achieve relational equality if we do not also try to address material inequality. Ending oppression quite obviously is an important goal, but it means much less if the emancipated do not have the means to achieve fulfilling lives.

Thus it seems necessary to consider what is right in both distributional and social theories of equality. Rather than seeing material equality and relational equality as separate goals, we try to draw them together into a single model. The important point for us is that social equality is not – or at least not only – some mysterious good in itself. Unless it can be shown that social equality – such as relations of community and solidarity between people – is good for the people who live in that society, it is very hard to see its point. Hence we need to identify the goods which, once realised by equal relations, contribute to individual well-being. Social equality and inequality, then, is something which makes individual lives go better or worse, by affecting their sense of belonging to society, or connection with others; what we shall later call 'affiliation'. Accordingly we do not object to the idea that a society of equals is one that distributes goods the right way, but we must insist that it is vitally important that the idea of 'distribution' and the idea of 'goods' both need to be taken very widely. Not all goods are material goods. Quite possibly the most important ones are not. And it is important to note, as Tawney points out, that when we leave the sphere of material goods 'to divide' is not always 'to take away'.[7] That is, we can provide more of these goods – a feeling of being valued, for example – for some without taking from others. Thus distribution – and redistribution – on this rather communitarian view, concerns not only the possession and transfer of material wealth, but the diverse ways in which people's lives can be affected by government policy, by the nature of the society they live in, and by how they regard and treat each other. This will include anything from the changing of tax bands, to the closure of a bus route, to the active discouragement of bullying in the workplace. All of these can have costs and benefits – sometime only costs, and sometimes only benefits – and we intend to count all such costs and benefits as part of the way goods in society are distributed. In our view any change in how people's lives are going – to put it broadly – is to be thought of as redistribution.

The concern to unite distributive and social equality permeates the whole of this book. Indeed, the distinction between distributive equality and social equality often seems artificial, or too theoretical, since in reality they cannot always be distinguished that way. Consider, for example, having good friends. Obviously nobody 'distributes' friends, but it is plausible to claim that one's job, salary, status, access to leisure, and education – all of which are distributed – could easily make an impact on whether one has friends and who they might be. So in an indirect way, access to having friends is distributed and therefore is part of what constitutes the distribution of some good. But obviously, friends and friendship (and how friendship is conceived and perceived) determine also relations within society and are therefore part of what may help to build and constitute social equality.

Moreover – and going back to the question of why we chose to call this book 'Disadvantage' if it is about equality – framing our theory around the concept of 'disadvantage' follows our assumption that the distributional and social approaches need not be at odds with each other. By designating those who lack access to some goods (for example, those lacking employment) 'disadvantaged' we immediately locate these people in relation to others; but moreover, we also hint that by lacking or losing such access their disadvantage may well have been created by others, or, if not, is at least tolerated by them. We therefore analyse their situation within the context of a community of people who may or may not care about each other. We also assume that their situation is not a natural outcome of some inevitable 'law of nature' (for example, that there will always be some people who must be much worse off than others) but rather has to do with the social and political institutions in which they happen to live. Indeed, when focusing on the disadvantaged we immediately have in mind those who fall within groups which can plausibly be thought of as among the *least* advantaged, or less euphemistically those who are the most disadvantaged: the chronically unemployed, the rough sleepers,[8] the illiterate who dropped out of school very early, those fourteen-year-old girls who become teenage mothers, and so on. It seems fair to claim that there are a number of groups who suffer very serious neglect in the contemporary shrinking welfare state. Although it is rare for such groups to be utterly abandoned by the state; it is nevertheless not uncommon for states to offer only limited assistance to the very worst off. The cost of taking care of these people and bringing them above a certain threshold is said to be enormous, while the chances of getting satisfying results are slim. On the other hand, investing the same money in other disadvantaged groups who face less severe problems – say, those who have only recently lost their jobs, or the homeless who are not rough sleepers – is likely to yield better and quicker results and does not involve such huge sums of money, so governments, local authorities, and even charities can think that their funds are best deployed in this way.

But is this a question merely of distribution, of who gets what? It seems to us that it is a larger and more profound issue. Redistributional policies which do not adequately reach the very worst off are likely to have destructive effects on social attitudes. Where there is a policy to offer only limited support to the least advantaged, we see around us a growing number of drug addicts, rough sleepers, teenage pregnancies, and so on. Perhaps when this phenomenon started people were genuinely very moved. But it seems fair to say that Western societies are becoming apathetic. Although many may express sympathy for the plight of those in such bad situations, it is sometimes thought that leaving such people to fend for themselves is part of the harsh reality of any modern economy. As many who have travelled to countries where extreme poverty prevails tell, the sight of the masses lying, often hungry, in the streets shocks first, but after some time 'one gets used to it'. But we should not allow ourselves to get used to it. In other words, we want to claim, the state of the least advantaged is a mark of shame and speaks poorly of Western societies. It should be a call to action not only because some people get or own less than others but also because it implies that social relations have deteriorated to an inhuman state. Now it may seem that saying this ignores the fact that helping the very worst off can be extremely expensive and only marginally effective, and that in these comments we appear to commit ourselves to a very strong and implausible ideal of 'absolute priority to the worst off'. We do, in fact, have some sympathy with such an 'extreme' idea, once it is correctly understood, but we accept that some ways of understanding absolute priority do not generate reasonable social policies.

4. Disadvantage, Pluralism, and Risk

The insight we wish to develop, we have indicated, is to understand well-being in such a way that everything that affects people for good or ill can figure in an understanding of their level of advantage and disadvantage. Accepting that there are many determinants of well-being, so understood, and that they are not all reducible to a common currency, leads us to the claim, for which we will argue in detail in Chapter 1, that advantage has to be understood in a *pluralist* form. We are far from the first theorists to suggest this. There are two highly developed versions of a pluralist approach in contemporary political philosophy which have influenced the path we have taken. One is the 'complex equality' approach taken by Michael Walzer and David Miller, who separately and together argue that different principles of justice, and even forms of argument, apply in different circumstances, in various spheres, or for different goods.[9] The second is the 'capability' approach as developed by Sen and Nussbaum, according to which, in order to understand how well or badly someone's life is going, we need to attend to what they can 'do and be'; their 'capability to function'. This means that to assess an individual's well-being we need to attend to a variety of such things as life span, bodily health, bodily integrity, affiliation, control over the environment, and many other categories. We are happy to take the pluralist approach in general, and Sen and Nussbaum's theory in particular, as the starting point for our theory. In Chapter 2 we add significant modifications, based both on our theoretical reflection and an empirical research. In subsequent chapters we also incorporate some ideas from Walzer and Miller.

Our main revision to the 'capability approach' is the idea that what matters for an individual is not only the level of functionings he or she enjoys at any particular time, but also their prospects for sustaining that level. To put this in another way, exceptional risk and vulnerability is itself a disadvantage, whether or not the feared event ever actually happens. A casual employee, who may be put out of work at any time, is in quite a different situation from someone on a permanent contract, even if she is in receipt of the same wages and never actually unemployed. Furthermore, disadvantaged people often find their functionings insecure in a way which the better off do not experience. So, for example, somebody who has just been made homeless might be healthy like any other person, but since he is exposed to bad weather and to violence in the streets, his health and bodily integrity are not as secure as those of others. Furthermore, the steps people take to protect themselves against risk can have severe costs. To take an extreme example, it has been argued that in the Chicago heat wave of 1995 more people died in higher crime areas than in lower crime areas. The apparent explanation is that those in fear of crime were afraid to open their windows while asleep at night, or go out on the streets during the day, and so stayed at home in literally stifling conditions.[10] The issue of risk and vulnerability is discussed in detail in Chapter 3.

5. *The Indexing Problem*

We have suggested that there is a broad consensus on the claim that governments have a special duty to help the least advantaged. We have also claimed that disadvantage is plural in nature, and irreducible to a single currency. These two ideas may seem innocent enough when presented independently, but together they generate a problem. How, then, in a pluralist view, can we identify the *least* advantaged? This is the 'indexing problem'. Are the least advantaged those in poor health? Those with low income? Those who are socially isolated? We define disadvantage as a lack of genuine opportunity for secure functioning. But how can we compare lack of opportunity for different secure functionings? Which deficiency is worse? We discuss the methods and problems of comparing disadvantages in Part 2. However, following our analysis of many samples of empirical research, we come to the conclusion that there is a sense in which there is no need to attempt to settle the question of which is the most important functioning. For the most serious disadvantage occurs when for some reason several disadvantages cluster together. We have seen, for example, that poverty leads people to take risks to some functionings which can make them poorer still, put them in prison, or damage their health. For example, one recent study points out that women in low income families in Israel cannot afford contraception and so have a much higher unwanted pregnancy and abortion rate than those who are wealthier, thereby putting strain on their physical health, emotional well-being, and finances. This is not to mention the anxiety caused by taking such risks. Disadvantages and risks compound each other and cluster together.[11]

From this we derive a powerful policy proposal: a society of equals is a society in which disadvantages do not cluster, a society where there is no clear answer to the question of who is the worst off. To achieve this, governments need to give special attention to the way patterns of disadvantage form and persist, and to take steps to break up such clusters. The theoretical conclusion of this book, then, is that if by improving the lives of the least advantaged, governments can achieve a general declustering of disadvantage to the point where we can no longer say who in society is worst off overall, then they have every reason to claim that they have moved society significantly in the direction of equality. Moreover, we suggest that a good way of doing this would be to search for what we call 'corrosive disadvantages' (namely, disadvantage the presence of which yields further disadvantages) and 'fertile functionings' (i.e. those functionings the securing of which is likely to secure further functionings) and to pay special attention to these. Such a strategy would make policy as cost effective and efficient as possible. In Chapters 7 and 8 we discuss our own findings about the questions of which disadvantages are corrosive and which functionings are fertile.

6. Methodology

It is a fair question to ask what we believe a philosophical investigation about disadvantage and its indexing can contribute to a policy oriented study. Consider once again the story of Leah. For suggestions about how things would have to change in order to improve her life, we would do far better, it could be claimed, to ask a therapist or a social worker than any kind of theorist, but among theorists a social policy specialist is much more likely to be of help than a political philosopher, however well-meaning. More generally, it might be argued, policies can be inferred fairly directly from empirical studies. On this view political philosophy operates at another level; perhaps inspirational rather than practical.

This would be a reasonable observation for much of contemporary political philosophy but, by contrast, we think that a more constructive engagement is possible. So let us say a few words about our approach.[12] First, unlike several philosophers, we do not believe that political philosophy should aspire to a level of theoretical abstraction which detaches it from the empirical world. To explain, in the last thirty years or so, possibly under the influence of the style of argument in contemporary epistemology, moral and political philosophy has taken an increasingly abstract style, making much use of bizarre examples, and surprising counter-examples.[13] It is true that the pay-off can be impressive. By this method theories can be shown to be vague or inadequate, laying open the path for more precise modifications or replacements. But the cost is that political philosophy, and especially now egalitarian political philosophy, has seemed oddly disengaged from the real world. If, as egalitarians allege, the real world is so full of unjustified inequality, it is surprising that many political philosophers prefer to use examples which have so little contact with the real world. Accordingly our approach is to maintain contact with empirical reality, and its complexities, throughout. Indeed we believe that this approach has a number of purely theoretical advantages and, as we shall argue in later chapters, reveals a number of inadequacies with current egalitarian theory.

However, at the same time, policy makers cannot meet the challenge of designing policies for rectifying disadvantage without a proper philosophical and conceptual discussion of what disadvantage is. Furthermore questions of priority setting between different calls for resources requires a philosophical consideration of the various techniques in which disadvantages can be indexed.

To be sure, the idea of linking theory and practice is hardly new. Marx's notorious 11th *Thesis on Feuerbach*, that the Philosophers have only interpreted the world, whereas the point is to change it, is much quoted in this context. Actually, we feel, this is both rather generous and rather ungenerous to philosophers, at least if extended to contemporary analytical political philosophy. Among political philosophers there has been, on the whole, little interest in interpreting the world. By contrast there has been no shortage of interest in generating principles to legislate how the world should be. What we have lacked is any account of how to get to where such philosophers wish to go, *starting from here,*[14] which is of course what the government needs to know. We hope that this book is a step in that direction.[15]

In that respect it is important to mention here – although we return to this throughout the book and appendix – that as part of this project we conducted in-depth interviews to examine our philosophical intuitions and theories. It may, in fact, be somewhat misleading to call these 'interviews', rather than semi-structured discussions, as they can be distinguished from more standard forms of 'interviews' in two ways. First, we were interested in the reasoning and the rationale just as much as the views and positions people held. Second, we did not regard it as a process whereby we, the scholars, learnt the attitudes of the people. Instead, we addressed this as an exercise in joint learning, in which both sides learn from the other – ourselves from the interviewees and the interviewees from us. In particular many learnt a new way of thinking about their roles and responsibilities or about their situation as disadvantaged people. In that way it was rather a *consulting* process. We see this as part of a process which we call '*dynamic public reflective equilibrium*', which is explained is more detail in Chapter 2. In a nutshell, the idea is that instead of using the well known 'reflective equilibrium'[16] technique alone – trying to balance a particular philosopher's theory and intuition – we brought these interviewees into the process. Accordingly we did more than simply learn about people's attitudes and views. Instead, we consulted our interviewees about our views, and we learnt from them. In this process we revised and modified our theory according to the theories and intuitions expressed by the interviewees.[17] The subjects were not chosen at random. Rather we chose 'experts' of two types; first those who are involved in forms of service delivery and support to the disadvantaged, and second, those who have been on the receiving end of such services, i.e. disadvantaged people themselves.

Why do we think these interviews have played an important role? Imaginative though they are, philosophers are an unusual sociological and psychological group, and we can hardly expect their concerns, and still less their intuitions, to be representative, at least without further investigation. Therefore these discussions, we hope, corrected biases in our own concerns and perspectives. The rewards, we believe, of this encounter with reality are considerable and enrich our practical and theoretical understanding of disadvantage. They also helped us to consider the types of policies which may help reduce disadvantage in a number of ways. We discuss this in detail in Chapter 2, and in Part 3.

The relevance of these remarks for the present enquiry is that at all stages in this book we rely both on philosophical reflection and on empirical research, including, by means of our interviews, some consultative methods. In doing this we are neither handing authority over to the philosopher who then tells people what to think, nor handing authority to the people who then tell philosophers what their theories should reflect. Rather we are trying to fashion a version of egalitarian theory that is responsive to the concerns of a wide range of individuals, and thereby has some chance of gaining their allegiance. Hence both philosophers and the people have some authority, which for reasons we have explained we see as part of a continuous process.

7. From Theory to Policy Recommendations

Our hope for this book is that it will address the concerns both of political philosophers and of those who work in the theory and application of social policy. But of course, this might raise a problem: the contrast, or at least a possible gap, between the account of the ideal world – what a society of equals would look like in glorious detail – and what we suggest policy makers should do tomorrow. Now it may be hard to see what the problem is here. If we set out the ideal of a detailed account of what a society of equals would be, isn't it obvious what would take us in the right direction along the royal road to equality? The answer, though, is that it may not be obvious at all. For one thing, if we take the steps in the wrong order, it could do more harm than good. Consider, for example, an egalitarian theory such as Ronald Dworkin's, in which an attempt is made to combine individual responsibility with egalitarian distributive justice.[18] In such theories, against a background of equality of resources people are to be held responsible for the consequences, including the costs, of their choices.[19] This is presented as a version of an egalitarian theory which attractively preserves the values of choice and freedom, compensating for lack of luck, and therefore now often referred to as 'luck egalitarianism'. Suppose we are convinced and now wish to take the first step towards implementation. It is very likely to be much easier to implement the 'responsibility' element than the 'equality of resources' element, but if we take this route to implementation, for which, of course, there is no license in Dworkin's own work, we find ourselves not half way to Dworkin's egalitarian ideal but rather in laissez-faire capitalism. Holding people responsible for all the costs of all their choices without first equalising their circumstances, does not look much like an improvement from an egalitarian point of view.

A similar but distinct problem is that implementing new policies may increase people's feelings of oppressive treatment, powerlessness, and stigmatization, even when the steps are taken for their own good, and on their own behalf. Many welfare policies, such as free school meals and food vouchers, can have these effects, although of course the problem is often in the implementation rather than in the policy itself. In the effort to help people, governments can make them feel picked out, picked on (made to undergo tests that others do not), and patronized. Creating a society of equals will be hard work, and quick fixes can backfire. With the best of intentions we may go backwards, not forwards. This type of problem is considered in detail in Chapter 10.

8. *The Book's Structure – a Brief Summary*[20]

It may be worth saying just a little more to explain how the elements of this book fit together. The book falls into three parts.

In the first we set out our account of the nature of advantage and disadvantage. We argue that disadvantage is plural (Chapter 1) and, in the first instance, is a matter of low functioning (Chapter 2). However, we argue that a further essential compounding aspect of disadvantage is that an individual's functionings are or become insecure involuntarily and in a manner which other people do not have to experience (Chapter 3). But individual responsibility needs also to be taken into account, and so we conclude by offering our analysis of disadvantage in terms of lack of genuine opportunities for secure functionings (Chapter 4). Therefore the government should guarantee genuine opportunities for secure functionings.

The book's second part looks at the difficult theoretical issues involved in taking our theory and providing something that can be of use in guiding policy. For the state to rectify such disadvantage, and assuming that the state's resources are not endless, it has to decide which functionings are more important; in other words it has to index disadvantages. This appears highly complex but we argue that the complexities would be mitigated if disadvantages cluster, in the sense that some people suffer multiple disadvantage, and therefore it is rather clear who are the least advantaged (Chapter 5). After considering the question of how to measure performance on (secure) functionings (Chapter 6) we present evidence that disadvantages do indeed cluster, and therefore it is possible to identify groups as among the worst off (Chapter 7).

The book's third part then looks at how the theory can actually be applied in practice, and so is policy oriented. If this is the case, we contend, then the government should first and foremost de-cluster disadvantages. In order to do this, it is best for the government to pay special attention to those disadvantages which are corrosive – in the sense that they are responsible for the clustering – and those functionings which are fertile – in the sense that securing them is likely to secure other functionings (Chapter 8). Next we explore the question of whether the government should pay attention only to the least advantaged, or whether it should also devote its attention to other groups (the 'strength of priority' question) (Chapter 9). Finally we explore some complications of social policy in a pluralist view, where making people better off in some respects might make them worse off in others, and especially others which might undermine the goal of social equality. We propose ways in which individual disadvantage can be addressed without undercutting social equality (Chapter 10).

Who then, is this book for? Given our own background it will be of no surprise that we hope that this book will be of interest to political philosophers, especially those concerned with current theoretical debates about equality. This book is intended to be a contribution to these debates in a number of ways, but it should have particular appeal to those political philosophers who wish to see philosophy informed by sustained engagement with empirical reality.

Another audience for this book follows naturally, and this is the group of social policy theorists and practitioners who are interested in political philosophy and wish to find deeper justifications for the policies they favour. We are delighted to note that there is growing interest among politicians and government officials in the question of how political philosophy can be applied to the real world. There is significant growth in conferences and books devoted to these topics. Thus, we hope to reach those people involved in developing strategies for service delivery in social policy, who are at the cutting edge of the implementation of change, and who show an interest in finding a theoretical framework and vocabulary to describe, assess, choose between, and attempt to justify various proposed policies.[21]

Finally, we do hope that those in government who have the task of raising and then disbursing extremely large amounts of money in pursuit of just social policies will read this book. We realise that this hope may be vain but it is, at least, a hope. Throughout the book we will argue that if the government's goal is to take steps towards building a society of equals then some steps will be more effective than others, and that particular types of research will be needed in order to decide how best to spend public money. We do not rule out the possibility that this could ultimately require significant reassignment of resources from one government sector to another.

PART 1

The Secure Functionings Approach

Introduction to Part One

As explained in the Introduction, our aim in this book is to come to an understanding of what needs to be done to bring society closer to the goal of a 'society of equals'. As will be clear from that discussion, we take the immediate task to be to identify those who are among the least advantaged and for governments to take steps so that the lives of such people can be improved. Our first step is to approach the issue of analyzing disadvantage by means of a discussion – even if a brief one – of the contemporary philosophical literature which addresses a question variously known as 'equality of what?' or the question of the 'currency of egalitarian justice'. We also raise some questions about the methodology employed in this discussion.

This literature begins with the assumption that in an egalitarian society people are to be or become equal in some respect, and then tries to identify or isolate that respect. In our terms, of course, this project is to try to identify the account of advantage and disadvantage most appropriate for thinking about the project of creating a society of equals. As should be apparent from our discussion of distributive and social equality, we believe that this debate needs to be widened in order to capture all relevant elements of disadvantage, but to show this it will be helpful to start within the existing literature.

Typically those engaged in this topic set out their favoured theory of the currency of justice – the currency of advantage and disadvantage[1] – and defend it by providing counter-examples to competing theories, which they then show can be handled by their own theory. Hence some theories of advantage will be shown to have the counter-intuitive consequence that redistribution is required (or not required) in unlikely circumstances, and an alternative approach is presented which seems not to have such unpalatable consequences. Hence the debate proceeds in a fashion which is familiar within a certain style of analytic philosophy: counter-example and reformulation.

While accepting the uses (and limits) of this methodology we also believe that it could be used in a more fertile way than it has to date. The philosophical literature is full of examples – someone wanting to build a monument to his God;[2] someone with an expensive taste for claret;[3] someone too lazy to walk to Berwick Street Market;[4] someone, inspired by reading Hemingway to wish to travel to Spain to indulge his new-found taste for bull-fighting[5] – but very few taken from real social policy fields. Of course, we would not want to deny that such thought experiments have their place. However, our view is that when attention is turned to relatively mundane real-life policy issues the standard methodology of counter-example and reformulation of theory yields much richer rewards, and that the elements of a complex theory of advantage and disadvantage emerge.[6] Our hope is to demonstrate this over the chapters of Part One.

CHAPTER 1

The Pluralism of Disadvantage

1.1 Towards Understanding Disadvantage

To get started let us review the task that confronts us. A theory of disadvantage is needed for our project, and it appears that it must meet two constraints. First it must provide a realistic and practically applicable account of what it is to be well-off or badly-off – advantaged or disadvantaged. Therefore it should be able to reflect the intuitive judgements we make about who in society is well-off or badly-off, at least to the extent that this is properly a matter of government or social concern. Similarly it should also enable us to provide an account of when a disadvantage has been rectified. We shall call this combination of demands the 'realism constraint'. Second, it should allow us to identify the least advantaged, and, ideally, to place each member of society on a scale of relative advantage and disadvantage, as well as being able to identify absolute disadvantage. This is the 'indexing constraint' which gives rise to what we call the *indexing problem*.

From the start it appears that there is an intuitive tension between these constraints. Realism pushes towards complexity, indexing towards simplicity. How this tension is to be managed is not, at first, clear. It would be very appealing, however, if it were possible to derive a plausible account of disadvantage which naturally allows all sources or forms of advantage and disadvantage to be placed on a single scale. In such a way the indexing problem would automatically be solved. We will, however, argue in this chapter that this option is not possible, and that the indexing problem is serious and unavoidable. To argue this we need to investigate leading versions of theories which attempt to understand disadvantage in a way which would, if acceptable, provide a single scale.

There are several possible candidate theories of this sort. One is the theory of subjective preference satisfaction, which uses standard economic theory to construct a utility function for each individual, and then further theory is used to solve the problem of 'interpersonal comparisons of utility.'[7] Those taking this route adopt what will here be called 'welfarist' approaches to understanding disadvantage.

A different approach is to understand advantage or disadvantage in terms of command or possession of resources, all of which can then be compared and given a monetary value, by means of market, or hypothetical market, pricing.[8] In such a theory an index of at least relative advantage and disadvantage becomes a trivial matter. Despite their substantial disagreements, this 'resourcist' view has in common with subjective preference theory the thesis that all advantages and disadvantages can be reduced to a single good or source. Accordingly we will refer to such theories as '*monist*' theories. As can easily be appreciated, the great advantage of a monist theory is that on such a theory the indexing problem disappears. Where such theories may well come under more strain is whether they are able to meet the realism constraint; we will return to this.

Not all theories of advantage or disadvantage are monist. Some theorists deny that all forms of advantage and disadvantage are comparable in the way a monist theory supposes. Monism implies that for any two goods, either one has to be ranked ahead of the other, or they are tied as equally valuable, and the agent concerned should properly be indifferent between them.[9] However, someone who has to choose between, on the one hand, a well-paid job which requires relocation, and on the other the companionship of family and friends, which mandates remaining in his or her home town, may not see things in such simple terms. If it is thought that the options are incomparable, in that it is neither true that one is better than the other or that they are tied as equals, then this is to adopt a 'pluralist' theory of advantage and disadvantage in which goods are diverse in their nature.

Now it might be said that there is no reason why all goods of the same type are comparable in the sense of being rankable on a single scale. For example, a Ferrari and Rolls Royce are both cars, but it is not hard to understand someone who says that they cannot be compared. Much, then, depends on what 'goods of the same type' means. But rather than try to solve that problem we will adopt, initially at least, a minimalist criterion of pluralism in which goods are plural if (but not only if)[10] they cannot be compared. Consequently if it is true that a Ferrari and a Rolls Royce cannot be compared then, at least in one respect, they offer different goods: perhaps exhilarating speed and stately comfort. Pluralist views come in many varieties and strengths, but their central core is simply the denial of monism; the denial of the view that all goods could, in principle, be placed on a single scale.

Pluralist views may often seem more realistic than some monist views, but this comes at a cost, in terms of difficulties with indexing. The problem is obvious. If two goods, or two forms of advantage and disadvantage, cannot be compared, then they cannot be placed on a common scale, and so it will become impossible, in many cases, to say whether one person is worse off or better off than another. One way of attempting to overcome this is to appeal to 'lexical priority' among goods, in which one good always takes priority over another in case of conflict. Rawls's theory of justice, is an example, in which, among other things, and in particular circumstances, liberty is given lexical priority over other goods such as income.[11] This is a pluralist view which does allow comparison and ranking. However within the sphere of economic or distributive justice, Rawls's view is less clear. On one reading, at this level the theory takes the form of a monist view in which there is just one good to be distributed – money (in the form of income and wealth[12]). An alternative reading adds a further good, 'the social bases of self-respect', which cannot be compared to money in any straightforward sense. This latter reading suggests that Rawls' view contains pluralistic elements even within a broader lexical priority. We will return to this possibility later.

This brief discussion should illustrate the apparent tension between realism and indexing. Realism may seem to exclude monist theories. In the interviews that were conducted for our project, virtually every interviewee, when reflecting on the nature of advantage and disadvantage, appeared to suggest a pluralist view in which different categories simply could not be compared.[13] Nevertheless given the immense difficulties this presents for indexing disadvantage in order to identify those who are among the least advantaged in society, there is very good reason for attempting to see whether a monist theory can be made to work. An advocate of monism could hope that the interviewees' rejection of monism was related to the fact that they were not confronted with the task of trying to think through questions of indexing, and if they had been they may have been prepared to think about the issues in a different way, supposing, say, that governments should confine themselves to a more limited enquiry.

Unfortunately, however, we believe that the task of constructing a monist theory which also meets the realism constraint is hopeless, and therefore requiring governments to think in monist terms would lead to unacceptable social policies. Indeed, our view is that a very simple argument shows the grave implausibility of monist theories. In the interests of realism, we shall argue, it is necessary to adopt a pluralist theory, and so if this requires much further thought regarding indexing, so be it: we will have to grasp that mettle. Our simple argument is that the only plausible forms of monism must adopt what we call 'the compensation paradigm'.

But the compensation paradigm is unacceptable. Therefore monism is unacceptable. The next section provides the details.

1.2 The Compensation Paradigm

1.2.1 Refuting Monism

Our rejection of monism begins by reflecting on the implications of such theories when it comes to remedying the injustices which are commonly agreed by egalitarians to be in need of attention. Any theory of distribution will need to be able to identify particular situations as failing to live up to the distributive norm set out by that theory and to recommend steps to be taken to rectify this deficiency if the desired outcome is to be achieved. But what steps? What sorts of action are called for to remedy such injustice or disadvantage?

This issue is discussed less often than one might expect, but when it is it seems to be suggested, or at least implied, that remedy should take the form of 'compensation'. However it is not always clear what is meant by 'compensation'.[14] Sometimes it appears to be little more than a place-holder for the idea that 'something must be done'. But when spelt out in more detail compensation is generally viewed in cash terms, or at least in terms of material goods, the provision of which is regarded as 'making up for' something else which is lost or lacking. We can see that there are two quite separate possible rationales for offering compensation in such a form, corresponding to the two major currents in contemporary egalitarianism of welfarist and resourcist theories outlined above. According to the version of welfare theory under discussion here, to be disadvantaged is to suffer from lower levels of preference satisfaction than others, and so disadvantaged people need compensation to bring them to an appropriate level of preference satisfaction. As all forms of preference satisfaction are comparable, then in straightforward cases any lack of satisfaction can be made up for, in principle, by other sources of satisfaction, and given its versatility money will always be suitable, if provided in sufficient quantity.

In reply, however, it will be said that there are cases where something is so detested, or 'dis-preferred', that no amount of anything else could make up for it. Perhaps no amount of money would entice me to play Russian roulette with a gun with only two chambers. This is not because life and money cannot be compared, but rather because my life could be so important to me that no amount of money could make up for such a high risk of death. Therefore non-substitutability does not imply incomparability.[15]

These reflections force a distinction between what we could call '*comparison monism*' and '*substitution monism*'. Comparison monism is the view that all goods can be put in a single scale of comparison. Substitution monism claims that any good can be substituted for enough of any other, at least before a 'saturation' point kicks in and additional units bring no further satisfaction. The Russian roulette example shows that comparison monism does not entail substitution monism. If money has no saturation point, at least within the range we are likely to be considering,[16] then according to substitution monism money can, in principle, compensate for every other loss. Although comparison monism has been the main topic of philosophical interest, substitution monism is the view we need to consider from the point of view of social policy, when we want to consider what can be done to address a particular disadvantage.

If it is accepted that no amount of money can compensate for a high risk of death, then that is already to deny substitution monism. Now this may seem a cheap victory for pluralism, as it might be said that nothing can compensate for a high risk of death. One possible response to this is to point out that people are often prepared to undertake very risky surgery in the hope of prolonging their life, or greatly improving their health, and so it is not true that nothing can compensate for a high risk of death. However, a better way of putting the objection is that every theory will be in difficulty when it comes to valuing life and high risks of death. We accept this, and so in the argument which follows we will not primarily rely on such cases in our argument against substitution monism.

We have seen how substitution monism seems implicit within preference based theories of advantage and disadvantage. The same issues apply to at least some resourcist theorists, according to which to be disadvantaged is to lack an appropriate level of resources, whether internal (e.g. talents) or external (e.g. wealth) irrespective of the effects of this on that person's welfare. On such a view a disadvantaged person should be offered additional resources (normally external resources) of sufficient cash value to make up for this lack. Interestingly, then, despite their position in the debate as competitor theories, both strands can agree with the policy of offering cash compensation for disadvantage, albeit for different reasons and under different circumstances. This convergence may explain why the question of whether compensation is the right approach is rarely raised as a live issue in the existing literature.

However, when we turn our attention to real social policy we find much less focus on compensation so understood. Consider, for example, support for people with disabilities. While it is true that people with disabilities sometimes seek support from the state in cash form, this, first, is only one of many measures sought, and second is seemingly rarely if ever claimed as compensation for the special miseries of disability, although the idea that it is required to allow people to overcome a lack of internal resources is more plausible. Even so, financial claims of disabled people will normally be based on one or both of two specific reasons. The first is poverty, the consequence of the difficulties disabled people often face in earning an adequate income. The second is the special expenses of medical or other equipment or personal help required simply to get by, which may soak up a large proportion even of an income that would otherwise be adequate. Yet aside from cash transfers there are many other strategies that societies adopt for addressing disability. These include medical intervention, support by means of provision of equipment and paid carers, and technical, social, and cultural change.

Or consider cases of severe environmental injustice, in which people have to be evacuated from their homes, for example because of contamination caused by a chemical spill. These people often report that they lose not merely in financial terms, but also, and perhaps primarily, suffer profound feelings of dislocation (literally); the loss of a sense of place, which impacts upon their self identity. Such loss, therefore, cannot be removed or properly 'compensated' by cash transfers. What they need is for their original home to be cleaned up, restored, and made habitable again, or the closest possible substitute. As a preliminary argument, then, we should note that both leading forms of monistic egalitarianism typically at least implicitly recommend a strategy which in reality is rarely thought of as appropriate as a complete account of how to address disadvantage. This is a consequence of their monism.

In response it could be argued that welfare theory or resources theory, or indeed any other form of monism, is not committed to offering cash compensation and nothing but cash compensation, for there may be reasons why other measures may be better. For example, some forms of collective provision may be a more efficient means of delivering welfare or resources than individual cash compensation,[17] or other strategies could be cheaper.[18] Rather, our claim is that according to substitution monism, there is no principled objection to remedying all forms of disadvantage by means of cash compensation. Yet we believe there are such principled reasons, and therefore substitution monism must be rejected, and replaced with what we could call 'substitution pluralism'.[19]

To put the argument somewhat more formally:

1. In the case of some disadvantages it is appropriate to remedy them with money.
2. If substitution monism is true, and money is appropriate to remedy some disadvantage, then it follows that money, in principle, can remedy all disadvantage.[20]

But

3. There are cases where money is not an appropriate form of remedy for disadvantage.

Therefore

4. Substitution monism is false.

Premise 2 reflects the idea that on a genuinely monist view the only salient difference between disadvantages is that they are 'bigger' or 'smaller'. Since money is scalable in exactly the same way then there seems no reason to deny that money ought always to be an appropriate remedy if it ever is. To deny that this follows by pointing out that disadvantage has more structure or points of differentiation – for example by saying there are many types of resources and these are not all substitutable – is simply to abandon monism.

If this formal argument is accepted as valid, and premise 2 also accepted, then the weight of the argument now comes down on premise 3, namely that there are cases where money is not an appropriate form of remedy for disadvantage. The question now is whether this can be demonstrated.[21]

It may well be that the examples of disability and environmental injustice given above already adequately demonstrate that the remedying force of money is limited. But to pursue this further, consider disabled people who protest that they are excluded from the workplace, because of its material configuration and difficulties in travelling, and thus they lack opportunities open to others. Imagine now that two social policies are possible. One is to convert the material environment so that all can work.[22] The other is to pay cash compensation to those who cannot work. And let us suppose that it is cheaper, all things considered, to pay compensation, and that the people with disabilities say that they would prefer this. How should we respond? Those who believe in a preference based theory, or, it seems, a resource based theory, seem committed to the conclusion that cash compensation is obviously the right thing to provide. If, however, we have at least some reservations about such a policy then this seems inconsistent with both theories. For example, one could argue that the essence of the disadvantage of inability to take one's part in the workplace – however we analyse this in detail – is something over and above the disadvantage of low preference satisfaction or lack of resources. We shall consider the essence of disadvantage in general at greater length in Chapters 2 and 3, but at the moment suffice it to say that this particular disadvantage implies that the disabled people lack the chance to develop valuable social relationships, or skills, or to see themselves as people who make a contribution to the lives of others. This in turn cuts them off from a source of self-respect which is normally consequent on such activities, whether or not they are aware of this.[23] And this, it would seem, would be a reason for rejecting cash compensation as the appropriate remedy, even if it is acceptable to the people themselves.[24] If this argument is accepted then this is enough to reject the compensation paradigm, and with it any monist theory.[25]

Now the obvious response is to insist that nevertheless cash compensation is the right policy in this case. Prima facie, there seem to be powerful arguments in its favour: after all, in terms of preference satisfaction everyone is better off (the disabled have what they prefer, and the taxpayer has a lower burden.) However, this argument is not decisive as it assumes precisely what is at issue: that preference satisfaction is the appropriate measure. How, then, can we try to settle the matter? One thing to consider is the rhetoric in which people sometimes reject offers of financial compensation: that they do not want to be 'bought off', for this is 'cheapening' or 'degrading'. Yet it is hard to understand this complaint on either the welfare view or the resource view. On this view buying off – giving more money either as a resource in itself or as a means to preference satisfaction – is simply what you do to address disadvantage. The buying-off objection seems to be that the real claim, whatever it is, has been missed, or even in some way corrupted by the attempt to pay cash.

Indeed, cash transfer can miss the point to the extent that it is counterproductive and even insulting and frustrating. To see why, consider a case of a person who injures herself tripping on a broken paving stone in a badly lit street. When lying at home with her leg in bandages she decides to write to the local authority to demand that they fix it and put up proper lighting. She does so because she is concerned about the hazard this presents to other people. The local authority receives the letter and decides to compensate her financially for her five last days of work and the pain. There are at least three ways in which the local authority misses the point. First, this person's act was future oriented, in order to prevent the repetition of such an event, while their compensation is past oriented. Second, she did this from altruistic motives, whereas they treated it as if she was doing something out of self-interest. Thirdly, she was acting as a good citizen, that is politically, and they turned it into a legalistic issue. Hence the local authority has attempted to individualize a complaint which was made in the public interest. This is, then, one powerful understanding of what it is to be 'bought off'.

However this example will lead to the response that the buying off objection does not show what we claim: that it is an inappropriate way of treating individual disadvantage. Rather, it could be said, buying off is a mechanism by which a general complaint or claim is neutralized through paying enough to silence its most vocal advocates (rather like bribing the lawyer in a class action suit) and hence is a form of corruption. This is an important point, for as we shall argue later, many claims made by individuals are made as members of an affected group – a group some-times as large as the whole population – and so paying money to that individual does not settle the claim. Yet even when the claim is made by and for an individual alone, the 'buying-off' objection can still apply. There are cases where cash payment will not meet the claim without loss. Consider an employee who has been harassed and victimized by their boss. Probably some people might claim that for a large enough salary any of us would be prepared to put up with this. Yet in accepting such payment it is hard to resist the thought that one has demeaned or cheapened oneself in the process, perhaps by bartering away one's self-respect. To make sense of this there must be more than one determinant of what makes people's lives go well or badly.

We should make clear, however, that we are not arguing that it is always wrong to offer compensation. Compensation *is* a common prac-tice, and people expect to be compensated in some cases in which they were wronged, or made disadvantaged. This is manifested most com-monly in tort law, but also in industrial relations. For example, if I am made redundant but am likely to find a good job within, say, six months, it is probably acceptable that I should be compensated by six months' salary. Our argument is not that cash compensation is never appropriate but rather that it does not always remove the disadvantage suffered. The strictly limited nature of this claim is worth emphasising. For the pur-poses of this argument we do not need to make strong claims concerning comparability monism: that there are goods which are incomparable in the sense that it is impossible for a given individual to compare them. On the contrary, in some cases we do encourage comparisons between different goods. For example we will argue here that it is better to change the social and material environment to provide people with particular opportunities than to give them cash compensation which would provide opportunities of a different sort. This, indeed, is to make a comparison. Rather our point can be put in a different way: that if someone has a claim of a particular type then there are at least some cases where no amount of money will 'discharge' that claim.

What, then, does it mean to discharge a claim? This is clearly a central idea for this argument, although it is tricky to spell it out. First we can illustrate some ways in which a claim is fully discharged. If John inadvertently causes Rachel financial loss, paying her an equivalent amount, perhaps with interest, is likely fully to discharge the claim. There is nothing left for Rachel to complain about. And the same is true, in some cases, where Smith destroys some of Jones's property and so Smith pays Jones its full financial value or, even better, restores that property to its original state at Smith's own expense. In cases where Jones has no sentimental attachment to that property – say it is held purely for commercial reasons – and there is nothing special about it, it appears that cash compensation once more fully discharges the claim. Yet for a contrasting example, if Smith publicly humiliates Jones, by spreading lies about Jones's private life, paying Jones compensation seems not to discharge the disadvantage Jones has suffered. An equally public statement of apology and retraction also seems necessary. And, importantly, this still seems so even if Jones would have preferred an even larger sum of money and no apology. Jones may find this acceptable, but in some sense he should not. That, at least, is our claim.

For another illustration consider the following 'before and after' argument. A man worked for a company where his employment contract provided him with health insurance, at the firm's expense. Being young and healthy, he didn't bother to examine the finer details of the policy. Unfortunately, a year after entering the job he was diagnosed with cancer, and had to take six months off work to receive drastic chemotherapy. When he finished this therapy he looked at his insurance and saw he was covered for a huge sum of money. Naturally, he was very pleased.

But obviously, he was not, or at least did not feel, *compensated* for the cancer or for suffering because of his chemotherapy sessions. The payment did not *rectify* the scar that was left due to the chemotherapy, or remove the anxiety associated with the cancer. Nevertheless he was much better off with the payment than without it, although the money did not rectify anything. His memories and pains, and the anxieties he experienced, are there forever, and these sufferings are not, in our sense, discharged by the payment of money. Consider the following: given the choice *before* being ill, would he have decided to go through the cancer and the treatments? Would he have chosen to have cancer in order to receive the money afterwards? Would he have been indifferent towards the cancer if he had known he would receive the money? We doubt it. It seems safe to conjecture that few would choose this, unless they were in special circumstances. But nevertheless even if he would have chosen it, and even if he is happy with the result, there seems something disturbing about making this sort of 'deal', which is absent in cases of cash compensation for the destruction of ordinary property, say.

What this story shows, we believe, is that while it may be that for society sometimes the best that can be done is to offer compensation, from the point of view of the victim or the disadvantaged this does not discharge or take away the disadvantage suffered. Elizabeth Anderson has argued that remedies should match the problem addressed.[26] This is close to what we wish to suggest, although in slightly modified form. Remedies should allow the individual to overcome their disadvantage, but the 'currency of advantage and disadvantage' is not always the 'currency of appropriate government action'. Those who lack a job should be given a job, or a means to it, which in some cases may even be money to fund a training course.[27] We would not wish to rule this out, and, we think, neither would Anderson.

To summarise the argument, we have suggested that plausible forms of substitution monism must adopt the compensation paradigm in which every disadvantage can, in principle, be remedied by provision of compensation in the form of financial payment. But, we have suggested, this paradigm is false. Not every disadvantage can be overcome by the provision of money. Therefore substitution monism is false. Now, there are several responses to these arguments. A monist may simply repeat that he or she fails to share our intuitions, and that provided enough money is paid, then everything can be compensated and the disadvantage is discharged. A political version of this defence is that even if there is more to disadvantage than can be incorporated into a monist theory, for reasons of public policy a monist theory, and with it compensation, is acceptable. We have given our reasons on the other side.[28]

1.2.2 Refuting Lexical Priority

However, a reader who is sympathetic to our arguments so far may nevertheless point out that a refutation of substitution monism does not rule out the possibility of solving the indexing problem. We need also to consider views which order goods into lexical priority. According to such views, goods form a hierarchy. If good A is lexically prior to good B, individuals are to be ranked, in the first instance, according to their score regarding good A, and no increment in good B can make up for a lack of A. Indeed many of our examples appear to confirm the Rawlsian thesis of the lexical priority of first, basic liberty, and second, opportunity, over wealth and income. Those who suffer from discrimination in the job market should not (only) receive financial compensation but rather also be provided with the basic liberty which protects them from discrimination. Those who lack the education which gives them opportunities should receive it, rather than financial compensation. The great advantage of such a view is that while it is pluralistic, it nevertheless contains enough ordering within it to enable us to index advantage and disadvantage.

This is obviously a very elegant solution, and we can acquire a renewed admiration for Rawls' thought by understanding that meeting the twin goals of realism and solving the indexing problem is a major motivation for his particular formulation of his principles of justice. However, we also have to see the limitations of his view as well. First, it is not true that liberty and opportunity have absolute priority on Rawls' view. This is only true when we have reached a particular level of material wealth. The implications of this for the structure of the theory are clearly brought out in the following remarks from *Political Liberalism*:

The first principle covering the equal basic rights and liberties may easily be preceded by a lexically prior principle regarding that citizens' basic needs be met, at least insofar as their being met is necessary for citizens to understand and to be able fruitfully to exercise those rights and liberties.[29]

The consequence of this is that it is not true, for Rawls, that one type of good always has lexical priority over another; the context also needs to be taken into account, which will make it harder to judge when or whether a substitution of one good for another is acceptable.

Second, and perhaps more important, by assuming a simplified model of the social world in which, among other things, no one suffers from disabilities or problems of special health needs, Rawls sidesteps some areas where issues of non-compensation may arise. The justification offered for this is the suggestion that it is important to get the central cases right before dealing with special cases which may be distracting.[30] However it is also the case that when such assumptions are relaxed, insisting on lexical priority becomes more complex.

Let us consider how issues of disability could be dealt with within a Rawlsian framework. Given that post *Political Liberalism*, there are four principles of justice, it appears that there are four options that could be considered without fundamentally changing the theory: that disability calls for remedy at the level of basic needs; at the level of basic liberties; at the level of opportunity; or at the level of income and wealth. Each provides its own interesting route to an account of how a society of equals should treat issues of disability. Yet understanding this also shows the limits of any view that tries to place goods in lexical priority. To illustrate, let us assume, as some disability activists do, that the disadvantage of disability is at least analogous to discrimination: people with unusual body types face a whole range of barriers to living a life with the opportunities open to others, ranging from an exclusionary material environment to hostile social attitudes. This, let us suppose, is akin to sexual or racial discrimination. On such a view the disadvantage is loss, or even violation, of basic liberty. The argument made earlier was that such a loss could not be repaired by the grant of extra money in the form of compensation, which is a claim that both pluralists and those who believe in Rawlsian lexical priority can accept. However, let us consider a different proposal: that instead of changing the physical environment and attempting to change social attitudes, the government offers disabled people an improved package of basic liberties in order to compensate them for their disability. Perhaps disabled people are offered enhanced police protection, a 'fast track' to legal services, and a greater publicly funded budget if they want to run for office: not because they have particular needs in these respects, but to compensate for discrimination. The question, then, is whether the extra liberties make up for the loss of others.[31]

If it is said that these extra liberties do not make up for the loss of liberties – that they do not 'discharge the disadvantage' – then pluralism has been accepted within one level of lexical priority. This will then make the indexing problem reappear at that level, and so lexical priority no longer solves the indexing problem. Alternatively it could be said that the provision of extra liberties of a different type does indeed compensate for the loss of other liberties. But this seems very implausible. Each basic liberty seems desirable in its own respect, and not substitutable in this way. This, then, would appear to violate the realism constraint. And, of course, the same argument can be made whether disability is treated as needing attention at the level of basic needs, basic liberties, opportunities, or income and wealth. Whatever level we settle on, the lexical view appears to entail that any disadvantage disability leads to or constitutes can be addressed by giving more of whatever else is also at that level. Yet realism suggests that the lexical priority view must collapse into a more complex form of pluralism. Consequently substitution monist views of disadvantage and those which assert a lexical priority among goods cannot be sustained if the realism constraint is applied. This, then, appears to be a general argument for pluralism. However there are many possible pluralist views, and it will be a further, complex issue to determine how such a pluralist view can or should be formulated.

It may seem, however, that the argument provided so far proves too much. It appears to rest on the assumption that if a lack of x cannot be made good by a greater provision of y, then x and y are different dimensions of disadvantage. While superficially appealing, this claim seems to have the unwelcome consequence that disadvantage is radically plural indeed. Arguably, for a connoisseur of cheese, no amount of Roquefort can make up for a shortage of Brie. Or even of Gorgonzola.

Yet do we want to say that such shortages represent, at least for such a person, different dimensions of disadvantage? Strictly that might be the right conclusion to draw. However, for political and practical purposes, we can cluster different items together, seeing some substitutions as much more acceptable than others. Generally a lack of Gorgonzola is better made up for by the provision of some other sort of cheese, or even some other food, than by, say, a new pair of gloves. But a pair of gloves can be a better substitution for a lost hat than for a lost book. It comes closer to discharging the disadvantage.

As we have suggested, we have no need to make the extreme claim that there can never be what might be called fully compensating substitution. Money can often serve as a substitute for other goods. There are cases where cash can fully make up for the loss of something else: perhaps for the loss of a job which is valued solely as a source of income, and not, for example, as a source of self-respect, activity, and companionship. This is independent of reasons of efficiency and non-intrusiveness to prefer cash compensation to other forms of remedy, even when there are other arguments to favour the latter.[32] It is so because it must be the case that in varying circumstances some goods will be more essential than others for well-being, for developing a decent human life, and if this is so, in some contexts substitution will be acceptable, whereas in others it may not.

In sum, when we argue that disadvantage is plural in nature we mean only that there are some cases where a shortfall in one dimension cannot be adequately remedied by greater provision of another good, even when this good is recognized as valuable by the compensated party. We do not intend our view to have greater metaphysical commitment than this. This is a form of partial incommensurability, which is compatible with partial commensurability. We accept that cash can be converted into other things of value and that people often make choices and substitutions without any sense of loss. Some commensurability is a fact of everyday life. But so is some incommensurability.

1.3 Conclusion

This chapter began by raising two constraints on an egalitarian theory that aims to make an impact on the world: the realism and the indexing constraints. It then set out to argue that disadvantage is plural in the sense that it is not always the case that a disadvantage in one respect can be discharged or overcome by greater provision of a particular universal currency such as money or preference satisfaction. Our argument for this is that there are clear cases where the attempt to provide money either valued in itself or as a means to preference satisfaction seem to miss the point of the claim made. This, we think, is an important result, even though the conclusion itself is not novel. We argue for this conclusion simply because it strikes us as true and supported by good reasons. Realism suggests that disadvantage is plural. However, as we have indicated, such a view has considerable costs. We have said that one vital task of government is to identify those among the least advantaged and to take steps so that their position is improved. Yet if disadvantage is plural it is unclear who the least advantaged are. This problem, then, is a main motivation behind our research, and is therefore something we will grapple with in this book. However, before we can do this we need to deepen our understanding of disadvantage. This is the task of the next three chapters. We then return to the indexing problem in Part 2.

CHAPTER 2

Functionings

If, as we have argued, disadvantage is plural, what are its dimensions? Consider, for example, lack of access to a workplace or lack of education. What precisely is it about these things that makes them disadvantages? Can we arrive at a comprehensive account of the various forms of disadvantage? Our task in this chapter is the relatively narrow one of considering how to construct such a list of disadvantages, as a first step towards a more complete philosophical theory of disadvantage. In the remainder of Part 1 – Chapters 3 and 4 – we will look at further dimensions of disadvantage, and in particular at issues of risk and opportunity. Together with the current chapter this will provide us with a philosophical theory of disadvantage. Nevertheless we need to keep the analysis of disadvantage distinct from another issue which we shall take up in Part 2: how can we put our philosophical theory of disadvantage to practical use. While the prior task of delineating a pluralist account of disadvantage is relatively narrow, the question is not simple at all.

2.1 Sen's Theory: The Capability Approach

A very convenient route into our investigation into the categories of disadvantage is the well-known 'capability' approach, put forward by Amartya Sen and further developed by many other scholars, most notably Martha Nussbaum.[1] We will develop our own account through partial agreement and partial disagreement with the capability approach, especially as presented by Sen and Nussbaum.

According to the capabilities approach, advantage and disadvantage is not a matter of possession of resources, or of preference satisfaction, but rather of what a person is able to do and to be. As Nussbaum writes: 'We ask not only about the person's *satisfaction with* what she does, but about what she *does*, and what she *is in a position to do* (what her opportunities and liberties are). And we ask not just about the resources that are sitting around, but about how those do or do not go to work, enabling [the person] to function in a fully human way'.[2] This implies not only that people should have access to whatever they (have good reason to) want to be or do, but also that they should have the freedom to choose among these options. In other words, social policies should be evaluated according to the extent of freedom (negative and positive) people have to achieve doings and beings that they (have reason to) value. Sabine Alkire adds: 'Rather than aiming to equalize the income of an elderly farmer and a young student, for example, policy-makers should aim to equalize the capability each has to enjoy valuable activities and states of being.'[3] Now Alkire's claim about equalization is a further step, on which, at this stage, we are neutral. But the important point is that the analysis of advantage and disadvantage is made in terms of 'valuable activities and states of being', not resources or preference satisfaction.

These 'beings and doings' that one has a reason to be or do are called by Sen and others 'functionings'. Now, what are capabilities? Sen writes: 'if the achieved functionings constitute a person's well-being, then the capability to achieve functionings (i.e. all the alternative combinations of functionings a person can choose to have) will constitute the person's freedom – the real opportunities – to have well-being.'[4] We can therefore think of capability as a set of vectors of functionings, reflecting the person's freedom to lead one type of life or another.

While useful, the term 'capability' is not perfect. First it is not always used consistently. Sometimes the term 'capabilities' is used as 'freedoms' for functionings; whereas other times it refers to potential combinations of functionings not yet achieved.[5] Furthermore the word 'capabilities', as Alkire aptly puts it, 'does not immediately conjure the image of intrinsically valuable human ends; it seems to be engaged in observing possibilities rather than looking forward to valuable actualizations of functionings'.[6] But since indeed the point is not only to create opportunities for the sake of creating opportunities, but to allow for the fulfillment of a life worth living, a good life, we prefer to use the terminology *'(genuine) opportunities for (secure) functionings'*. We shall explain why we need to introduce the qualifiers 'genuine' and 'secure' in subsequent chapters.

2.2 Categories of Disadvantage

So far we have argued that disadvantage is plural, and registered our broad agreement with the capability approach. We will reserve the details of our disagreement for Chapters 3 and 4. First, though, we need to see if it is possible to draw a list of the categories of advantage and disadvantage.

At this point we want merely to attempt to provide a basic list. It is 'basic' in the sense that we postpone the question of the relative weights of the different categories and the question of the circumstances under which governments have a duty to take action to address disadvantage. Although these vital issues are at the heart of this enquiry, there are other questions that must be dealt with first.

For simplicity, our question at this point is *'what categories of functionings exhaust those necessary to construct a full philosophical theory of advantage and disadvantage?'* By this we assume that functionings are, in a way, the opposite of disadvantages. In other words, being disadvantaged in a particular way is primarily a matter of not being able to achieve the functioning. Yet even this question must be prefaced by two prior questions: 'who decides which functionings constitute an optimal human life?' and 'how is such a decision to be made?'

Given the extensive philosophical work already attempted within the capability approach it would be absurd to do anything other than attempt to build upon the existing literature. Indeed our task has been made considerably easier by Sabina Alkire's remarkable survey of no less than thirty-nine lists of basic needs or basic functionings provided by theorists from different disciplines.[7] We shall take as our starting point Martha Nussbaum's well known list. While Alkire finds Nussbaum's list in some respects unsuitable for her purposes, and while scholars of the capability approach have distinguished between Sen's and Nussbaum's approaches,[8] we find it intuitively very powerful, building on related ideas from Aristotle and early Marx concerning what it is that makes a life fully human.[9] In addition, Nussbaum's list is a good starting point because it is meant to be part of a policy oriented research project – in her case the 'formulation of basic political principles of the sort that can play a role in fundamental constitutional guarantees'[10] – and because of its grounding in cross-cultural empirical and theoretical work. The latter, in part, leads Nussbaum to claim that even people who otherwise have very different comprehensive conceptions of the good can reach the same conclusion about what functionings are included in this list, as an 'overlapping consensus'.[11] Nevertheless, we want to examine its validity both analytically and empirically. Thus after reviewing Nussbaum's account we shall extend it further, based both on theoretical reflection and on our own empirical research, which will be described shortly. But first, here is the list:

1. *Life*: Being able to live to the end of a human life of normal length; not dying prematurely, or before one's life is so reduced as to be not worth living.
2. *Bodily health*: Being able to have good health, including reproductive health; to be adequately nourished, to have adequate shelter.

3. *Bodily integrity*: Being able to move freely from place to place; having one's bodily boundaries treated as sovereign, i.e. being able to be secure against assault, including sexual assault, child sexual abuse, and domestic violence; having opportunities for sexual satisfaction and for choice in matters of reproduction.

4. *Sense, imagination, and thought*: Being able to use the senses, to imagine, think, and reason – and to do these things in a 'truly human' way, a way informed and cultivated by an adequate education, including, but by no means limited to, literacy and basic mathematical and scientific training. Being able to use imagination and thought in connection with experiencing and producing self-expressive works and events of one's own choice, religious, literary, musical, and so forth. Being able to use one's mind in ways protected by guarantees of freedom of expression with respect to both political and artistic speech, and freedom of religious exercise. Being able to search for the ultimate meaning of life in one's own way. Being able to have pleasurable experiences, and to avoid non-necessary pain.

5. *Emotions*: Being able to have attachments to things and people outside ourselves; to love those who love and care for us, to grieve at their absence; in general, to love, to grieve, to experience longing, gratitude, and justified anger. Not having one's emotional development blighted by overwhelming fear and anxiety, or by traumatic events of abuse or neglect.

6. *Practical reason*: Being able to form a conception of the good and to engage in critical reflection about the planning of one's life.[12]

7. *Affiliation*: Being able to live with and toward others, to recognize and show concern for other human beings, to engage in various forms of social interaction; to be able to imagine the situation of another and to have compassion for that situation; to have the capability for both justice and friendship. (...) Having the social bases of self-respect and non-humiliation; being able to be treated as a dignified being whose worth is equal to that of others.[13] Being able to work as a human being, exercising practical reason and entering into meaningful relationships of mutual recognition with other workers.

8. *Other species*: Being able to live with concern for and in relation to animals, plants, and the world of nature.

9. *Play*: Being able to laugh, to play, to enjoy recreational activities.

10. *Control over one's environment*: Being able to participate effectively in political choices that govern one's life; having the right of political participation, protections of free speech and association. Being able to hold property not just formally but in terms of real opportunity; and having property rights on an equal basis with others; having the

right to seek employment on an equal basis with others; having the freedom from unwarranted search and seizure.

One might wonder whether in order for a life to be 'not deprived' one must enjoy all of these functionings, most of them, or perhaps just some of them. This question has been widely debated[14] and Sen himself suggested several times that some of the capabilities are more 'basic' than others, and that the basic capabilities are relevant at least for deciding a 'cut-off point for the purpose of assessing poverty and deprivation'.[15] We approach this question with the help of our interviews, as described in detail below, and so will discuss it in the context of the question of the relative weightings of the categories and indeed whether any categories should be given a weighting of zero. But for the moment we side with Nussbaum who claims that a life that lacks any of these functionings is in some important sense deprived, when we define lacking them, or even *finding one of them insecure involuntarily* (we explain this idea in the next chapter), as a form of disadvantage. As mentioned before, this is distinct from the question of when, if at all, governments have a duty to act, which needs to be settled at another level, and so will also be dealt with later.[16]

2.3 Evaluating Nussbaum's Account

Faced with a list such as Nussbaum's it is common to find oneself with a number of reactions. First, one can hardly help being impressed with the vision and thought that has created such a rich and plausible account of human well-being. Second, one might wonder about the inclusion, or at least relative importance, of some of the categories. Third, one might wonder about the exclusion of certain other possible elements. But finally, and most importantly, one might wonder about its authority. What right does a philosopher have to set out a list of categories of human well-being?[17] This objection could take a number of forms. Perhaps no one has the right. Perhaps philosophers are particularly ill-suited to the task, and are bound to have an intellectualist bias.

Of course, academics in this area hardly aspire to the 'pure'. Nevertheless their own life experience typically gives little reliable insight into the nature of disadvantage. Hence, as a matter of general reassurance, and, perhaps, to correct unnoticed bias, there seems an important need to validate the list perhaps by means of a cross-check with more empirical forms of enquiry: consultation with people from a wide variety of walks of life, analysis of surveys, and the like. Indeed engaging in these more empirical forms of research will allow us to achieve what we referred to in the Introduction as 'dynamic public reflective equilibrium' using both philosophical theory and public consultation to arrive at a more democratically supported, and therefore, in some sense, legitimate, view.

Let us very briefly review the idea of 'dynamic public reflective equilibrium'. That moral exploration involves a process of 'reflective equilibrium' is now widely accepted. Essentially, reflective equilibrium means 'that we "test" various parts of our system of moral beliefs against other beliefs we hold, seeking coherence among the widest set of moral and non-moral beliefs.'[18] One part of coherence is logical consistency, another is simplicity, and a third is intuitive plausibility. By constantly moving forward and then retracing our steps, by continuously revising and modifying our theories and intuitions, we try to find equilibrium. These revisions are crucial. Reflective equilibrium means that if a theory is very appealing in that it fully explains and justifies a number of intuitions, but at the same time contradicts some other intuitions about particular cases, it is often the case that we will change the other intuition – the 'instinctive belief' – rather than modify the theory. Yet we might also or instead modify the theory if that particular intuition has such weight for us that we are prepared to give up other beliefs for its sake. Failing to recognize both possibilities implies dogmatism.

There is the question, of course, of whose intuitions and whose theories should be weighed against one another, and two models of reflective equilibrium have been suggested in response. The first explicit version was offered by John Rawls[19] whose model is of a private reflective equilibrium, in the sense that both the intuitions and the theories are those of the philosopher. As Miller puts it, 'the reflective equilibrium that emerges is an equilibrium only for the person who has engaged in the thought-process Rawls describes'.[20] How do we know that this process is a success? A successful process is one that yields a consistent and coherent theory, which ties in with the philosopher's intuitions. Sometimes these intuitions happen to be shared by many others, but the point of the 'private' reflective equilibrium is not to convince the reader of a philosophy that a theory fits the *reader's* pre-existing intuitions, but rather to convince the reader that the philosopher has managed to develop a very accurate theory whose principles of morality harmonize with philosophical intuitions that are themselves reasonable. In other words, a successful theory meets the condition that: *if* the reader shares – or can be brought to share – the intuitions which are contained within the author's reflective equilibrium, she is also likely to accept the moral principles put forward, and consequently the theory.

An alternative and more promising (in the context of politics) model of reflective equilibrium – what can be called 'contextual reflective equilibrium' – is suggested by Michael Walzer in three of his books.[21] Although, to the best of our knowledge, Walzer has never claimed to be using a mechanism of what is called here 'contextual reflective equilibrium', we nevertheless think this is a proper reading of his suggestions regarding political philosophy. Walzer argues that social criticism is to be applied to a particular community and its morality. The philosopher understands and examines the values of a society and then proceeds to theorize about them. This is an interpretative rather than inventive learning process.[22] The philosopher examines the behaviour and expressed views of the individuals who make up the community, and interprets them in terms of what she understands the community's values to be. The philosopher does not invent morality, but holds up a mirror to her community. The mirror is a critic as far as it holds up a standard of 'profound social idealism'.[23] The philosopher serves to reveal all of the lies that a society tells itself. This is a 'reiterative' activity[24] in the sense that the philosopher is not interested in having the last word, but sees the theory she puts forward as providing fresh input to the moral discourse, pending re-evaluation. 'The critics who aim to get things right aim at a rightness that is relative to their critical occasions. They want to produce a strong argument and a local political effect, but also (. . .) an object of reflection and debate'.[25]

In Walzer's model, however, the intuitions considered are those of the philosopher and the community's intellectuals, while the *theories* are those of the philosopher alone. It is at this point that we put forward a third model, namely the model of 'public' reflective equilibrium, where the theories considered are also those of the public, as well as the philosopher, and where the philosopher engages in and conducts the process of finding a reflective equilibrium. Few deny that a theory of political philosophy should relate to real cases and be relevant to real life. We seek a methodology for achieving this aim. To do this, it should also arise from practice. The best way to do so would be to start with the general public, activists and individuals who are engaged in moral reasoning and political activism and their dilemmas, alongside the theory and reasoning of the political philosopher. Hence, a theory of political philosophy should be derived from wider sources, i.e. not only the detached philosopher or anthropological explorer, but the public as well. It should be a theory that reflects the actual philosophical needs of the public, of people who seek to convince others by appealing to practical issues, and not necessarily the philosophical needs of the philosopher, who convinces colleagues by appealing to consistency and simplicity. Naturally, the philosopher should not take the value of the public's propositions for granted. People's intuitions, arguments, claims, and theories should also be scrutinized. However, the fact that they need to be critically examined does not affect the main point: that people's intuitions, claims, and theories should be a fundamental point of input for a political philosophy of democracy which seeks policy change. Indeed, one might argue that if a theory does not tie in with the way citizens behave and think, then the theory needs to be modified. Of course one could equally conclude that the people are wrong but in a democratic society it might be absurd always to assume that the people are wrong and the philosopher is right. There comes a point when it is worth listening to the people.[26]

Of course it would also be absurd to presuppose that citizens will speak with one voice, or even that a particular person will always provide consistent views. A profusion of contradictory messages is only to be expected. How to manage such diversity becomes a question of vital importance, and one which will concern us throughout this book. The philosopher's claim to authority to settle such disputes may seem deeply suspect. But it is clear that the fact that the public contains many voices is not a reason for ignoring it, or, in our case, declining to explore Nussbaum's categories through public consultation.

2.3.1 Method of Consultation

In order to provide a test or cross-check for Nussbaum's categories, we engaged in a process of evaluation, in which there were four steps:

- Step (1) Our reflection upon Nussbaum's list began in a traditional way: by considering how well it covered the position of people within our experience whom we would have considered disadvantaged in some way, and discussing such cases between ourselves, with other political philosophers, and with people in social policy fields, including both academics and service providers. We also considered a series of existing empirical studies.
- Step (2) This preliminary investigation led us to propose a number of further categories of functionings, as we shall explain shortly.
- Step (3) We then tested our categories in a more formal interview setting, conducting initially thirty-eight, and later an additional sixty, in-depth interviews in Israel and England. The nature of the interviews is explained in Appendix 1. We wished to accomplish a number of tasks within the interviews, and the investigation of this chapter – arriving

at a list of categories of disadvantage – drew on only part of the interview. The first phase was simply to ask the interviewees what they considered the basic categories in terms of essential functionings, without providing any prompts. In the second phase we presented a showcard, listing Nussbaum's categories as well as the further categories added by us, and asked the interviewees to comment.

- Step (4) We then asked the interviewees whether they felt that the showcard missed out any important category of functioning. On the whole we received support for the categories, but also have been led to add a further category as a result of the interviews. Reflecting on the information we received from these interviews, and interpreting the interviewees' input, we revised again the list of functionings. This will be explained in detail in the following sections.

At this point one could challenge our method[27] by claiming that it is not clear whether the interviewees understood us correctly, and whether we understood them. Such a claim can be based on the assumption that it is not clear whether we and the interviewees, especially if they were from a different cultural background, meant the same thing when we used concepts such as 'affiliation', 'rational reflection,' and so on. This is a powerful, and perhaps rather obvious, challenge, which has been put to us by many colleagues and students. If this is correct, then it puts in doubt all empirical social research, from surveys to interviews. However, in the present case our method allows considerable flexibility, and we and our research assistants discussed these concepts and their meanings with the interviewees. Since we were open to be influenced by the interviewees, we were not assuming particular conceptions and understandings of these concepts; rather we wanted to reach full understanding on both sides – interviewer and interviewee.

Another challenge which might be raised at this point is that there is something circular and self-fulfilling about our method, in that in order to find disadvantaged people and learn what their disadvantage meant to them, we had already to have in mind a preliminary conception of disadvantage. This could be right, had it not been the case that the disadvantaged people we interviewed were people who would fall under the category of disadvantage under almost any definition of disadvantage. One has to be really original, or very eccentric, in order to believe, for example, that homeless people, or those who are chronically unemployed, are not disadvantaged. Moreover, we conducted these interviews not in order to identify particular disadvantaged people, but rather to know what the essence of disadvantage was – in other words, what is common and what differs over a wide range of cases of disadvantage.

2.3.2 *Evaluation, First Phase*

The first phase of evaluation was, as we mentioned above, to reflect upon Nussbaum's list in the light of the experience of people whom we know, and to discuss the categories with people active in social policy fields. It bears keeping in mind that much of Sen's original inspiration is to consider the analysis of disadvantage with respect to the developing world, and in at least some of her writings Nussbaum has followed him in this concern. Although we too are interested in these issues, the point of the current enquiry is to explore disadvantage in the developed world. Indeed, reflecting on forms of disadvantage in the developed world can provide an interestingly different perspective.

Consequently our initial view is that while Nussbaum's list is indeed admirably comprehensive and inclusive, nevertheless there is room for extension. One way of putting our concern is that Nussbaum's list of functionings is surprisingly over-influenced by what can be called 'the language of justice': who gets what in the process of distribution; and in the 'language of liberalism': what one is entitled to. This emphasizes the person as a receiver, seeking to expand his or her possessions and as an individual promoting his or her material well-being. Keeping in mind that Martha Nussbaum's philosophy in general is very sympathetic also to the 'ethics of care', and not merely to justice,[28] it seems to us that extending the list in the way we want to offer below should not violate the spirit in which Nussbaum's list was drawn. Indeed it may well be that what we have to say on this topic is already implicit in Nussbaum's account, spread, perhaps, between category 5 'Emotions' and category 7 'Affiliation'; however, they seem hidden, as if absorbed in other functionings, emphasizing the liberal, autonomous individual who cares for her entitlements rather than the active member of a community who participates in social and political activities. Hence we feel it is worth drawing this out as a point of special focus.

Although the ethics of care has been identified with feminist political philosophy[29] we find its importance lies in the shift of focus from the person as a recipient, as a passive, self-centred claimant always with an eye on what he or she gets, and how he or she benefits from social relations, to a more comprehensive and diverse view of the person, who is sensitive to others and who is a giver. In that sense, we would like to suggest, the ethics of care goes hand in hand with a republican view according to which what matters when we come to compare the well-being of people is not only what one is entitled to, but also to what extent one is able to contribute to society and one can participate in the collective shaping of the public; that is, in politics This view considers individuals as members of a community who care about the community and about their participation in it not less than about their possessions, entitlements, and so on.

What became clear in our initial discussions, and, as we shall see, even more so in the interviews, is that while it is true that in order to flourish as an individual one needs to have one's self-referring functionings developed and sustained – one needs to see that one gets things for oneself – it is equally true that one also needs to be a person who has feelings for others, and is able to express them in appropriate ways. Being able to care for others is part of being a person, at least under normal conditions, and therefore part of one's well-being. Notice that we do not promote the ethics of care as an *alternative* to justice. We agree with Onora O'Neill that 'when the "voices" of justice and care are presented as alternatives between which we must choose, each is viewed as a complete approach to moral issues, [whereas] the two in fact focus on different aspects of life. Justice is concerned with institutions, care and other virtues with character, which is vital in unmediated relationships with particular others.'[30]

Our point is that one should have the chance to express oneself, and one's connections with, and care for, others, through appropriate means. Take, for example, the importance of being able to show gratitude.[31] People often seem to have a pressing need to reciprocate, not necessarily in the vulgar meaning of giving back something of equal value; indeed, often this is something we cannot even measure. It is the very idea that if I received from you something one day I can reciprocate by doing a favour to you, or by showing my gratitude, even if I am poor and you are very rich. In fact, when a poor person offers a gift to a rich person, the assumption is not that the rich person needs the gift, or that this gift's value is the instrumental value of this commodity to this rich person. On the contrary; the assumption is that this is an important act for the poor person regardless of the subjective value of this object for the rich person. Showing gratitude to others, 'paying one's respects', and showing joy at other people's joy all form part of a flourishing human life. This is seen in many lists of needs reported in surveys and interviews.[32]

Narayan et al. quote a poor person from Ghana who remarks that being poor is when 'you know "good" but you cannot do good' because you do not have the means.[33] Elsewhere they quote people referring to 'inability to reciprocate with gifts' as a severe disadvantage, both for its own sake and because it has harmful consequences, from humiliation, loss of honour, to social exclusion.[34] Perhaps it is right to say that in rural developing countries failing to offer gifts leads to social exclusion, whereas this is not the case in developed countries; but the loss of honour and a sense of humiliation, in the very basic sense that one cannot express one's respect or love, is universal. One thing, for example, that upsets some severely disabled people is the inability to perform simple services that typically express one's respect and friendship for others, such as making a visitor a cup of tea. This lack can cut deep into self-respect.

We therefore conclude that engaging in such expressive activities as *doing good for others*, and *being able to show gratitude*, and even being able *to follow the elementary norms of etiquette*, are important functionings, and that those who cannot afford to do good to others, who cannot show gratitude, and so on, because they lack the (financial or physical) means or the time to do so, are disadvantaged. The interviews have confirmed our view that it is important enough to require separate emphasis. As one of the interviewees said: 'Doing good to others allows one self-esteem. Being human means not only to receive; one wants to give.'

Our next modification may seem more surprising: *the possibility of being able to live in a law-abiding fashion*. Consider, for example, a hard-working person, doing an unskilled job in a Western country, struggling to nurture a family. He is probably earning the minimum wage, or even less than that. If he is concerned about his children's well-being and if he wants to guarantee for them clothes they will not be ashamed to wear, and good nutrition, and perhaps to have a modicum of social life, he might have no option but tax evasion, buying goods he knows are stolen, claiming benefits while working, and the like. He might hate what he has to do both because of the risks and because it makes him an outsider. The latter links living within the law with social relationships and social exclusion, about which we elaborate below.[35] However, at the moment we want to claim that a society that is constructed in a way that in effect forces some people to break the law in order to lead a materially decent life is especially incompetent or unjust.[36]

Now it may be replied that almost no one is literally forced to break the law, and this is shown by the fact that many very poor people live perfectly law-abiding lives. No doubt it is true that some very poor people declare to the authorities all their earnings, even from casual work, never buy anything they suspect to be stolen, or evade paying a bus fare even when they know they will not be caught. We do not know how common such impeccable behaviour is among the very poor, but this is, in fact, beside the point. The sense of 'force' we use here is not 'absolute compulsion' but rather 'in the circumstances necessary to achieve a minimally decent standard of living'. Accordingly, it is consistent with this to be able to remain within the law, if one is prepared to abandon the prospect of a minimally decent standard of living, as, no doubt, many law-abiding poor people do.

Another objection to the inclusion of this category is that there is no need to postulate this particular separate functioning, since having functioning X should imply being able to do or be X legally. However this does not take account of the fact that in order to do one thing – perhaps secure proper nutrition – someone may feel forced to break an apparently unrelated law, such as not paying car tax. Furthermore our interviewees confirmed that 'living within the law' is a crucial functioning and 'not being able to live within the law' is a serious disadvantage. We find this highly important because it is often the case that we hear officials, politicians, bureaucrats, and those to the right of the political spectrum complaining about the poor and the disadvantaged breaking the law, cheating the system, and then asking society to help them. What the interviews show is that at least some of these people are not happy to lead that sort of life, and would rather they could live within the law. It is the system which forces them to do otherwise, and not their corrupt character. Stressing this is one reason to categorize living within the law as a separate functioning. But not less importantly, the depth of this disadvantage can be appreciated by the fact that such disadvantage, virtually by necessity, must remain hidden. For anyone complaining that they have been driven to such a state faces arrest and punishment. Hence it is one of the few disadvantages without an accompanying pressure group. Consequently people who lack this functioning are disadvantaged in three ways. First, they lack the functioning. Second, they may feel very bad about doing so. Finally, they are unable to complain. Consequently we think 'being able to obey the law' is a vital functioning.

At this point we come to a related functioning, perhaps not less important, that of *being able to understand the law*, which was initially prompted by our discussions with people providing services for asylum seekers and other immigrant groups. By this we do not mean professionally understand, as lawyers and judges do, but rather a general understanding that will prevent one from standing astounded and perplexed before the legal system. Indeed a growing number of agencies, such as the Citizens' Advice Bureau, exist precisely to overcome this difficulty. Hence this seems to be evidence that it is a profound disadvantage for some people. Sabina Alkire follows the World Bank report by Deepa Narayan et al., by putting lawfulness and access to judges as part of one's well-being.[37] For the ordinary person, of course, this somewhat misstates the point as access to judges though important is, thankfully, rarely needed. However, knowledge of legal rights and duties is part of what can make day-to-day life run roughly or smoothly.[38]

2.3.3 *The Results of the Interviews*

As mentioned above we tested our account of the categories of functioning by means of interviews conducted in Israel and the UK. There was no deep theoretical reason for choosing these two countries, other than our wish to look at only developed countries for the purposes of this research. In a small study there would be little to be gained by casting the net further, and although these countries were chosen for reasons of convenience they nevertheless provide an interesting contrast, given their differing histories, populations, cultures, current conditions, and political problems. Hence convergence between the countries would be significant, and the range of variation likely wider than in a single country study.

It is also important to note that as we consulted only a small sample we do not claim any statistical significance for our results, but do hope that what we have done should be followed up on a larger scale. However, the populations interviewed were significant. In order to provide a 'concentrating effect' we did not choose people at random but were particularly interested in the views of people with special knowledge. These included welfare service providers – both 'on the front line' and those with management and development responsibilities – but also those on the receiving end. This was a group that was much harder to access, and so represents a slightly smaller proportion of the interviewees. An even smaller sample had experience on both sides; initially as disadvantaged, then as involved in pursuing policies aimed at ending disadvantage.

In phase one of the interviews we asked people for their view of the most important human functionings. Now, at this point of the interviews the interviewees had not been offered any particular frame of reference, and had no common vocabulary. Some had obviously thought a great deal about the issues for themselves and could respond in a detailed, articulate, and prepared fashion. Others were less confident, offering relatively few observations, often drawn from their own immediate experience. Consequently in such cases they tended to concentrate on what they perceived themselves as lacking, to the omission of what they had. For example at this stage of the interview a surprising number neglected to mention having proper nutrition as a basic functioning. It would be odd to conclude that therefore many people think it is not; rather the obvious conclusion is that they had simply taken it for granted.

Allowing, then, an interpretation of the results that sometimes has to 'fill in the blanks', and allowing also that we are not looking for a precise specification of categories so that ideas can be grouped together as 'similar enough to be included in the same category', we can say that there was a broad consensus on a range of predictable items: health; shelter (often elaborated into the idea of a *home*); having paid employment; being educated (often discussed in relation to one's relationships with one's children); and a sense of belonging, whether in society, in a family, or with friends. Much of this was overlaid with remarks about wanting to be valued or, distinctly but relatedly, a sense of being found useful.

One Israeli interviewee, a former soldier, mentioned the importance of 'peace'. This raises a question of levels or categories of functionings. Is living in peace a functioning in its own right, or does its absence put other functionings under threat? The same question could be asked about many other categories, such as health or employment. Not everyone will answer in the same way, and so any particular determination of these issues can look arbitrary. Hence we will not attempt to resolve this; certainly not at this point.

Among other observations of interest, the categories 'access to culture' and 'places to meet people' got more than one mention. Others were more idiosyncratic yet quite understandable: the capability to settle; being able to have or choose one's means of transport; sufficient sleep; and being able to attend schools close to home. Clearly it is likely that these are born of particular experience, yet are not at all eccentric. And it is no surprise that what comes 'first to mind' for many people will reflect their present experience.

However another category appeared in several interviews: *ability to understand and speak the local language*. This is sometimes contested on the grounds that sub-cultures can flourish while speaking a minority language. The obvious counter is that often it is necessary to speak the local language in order to deal with public officials in a more effective way. This then becomes one instance of a broader category or issue, sometimes discussed under the heading of '*soft skills*': essentially the skills one needs to deal with the routine of daily life without frustration. We will return to this in Chapter 9.

Phase two of the interview then moved to an explicit discussion of the categories. All interviewees were shown a card on which fourteen categories were mentioned and briefly explained on a single A4 sheet. The interviewees were asked to comment on each category in turn. Some were reluctant to do this, and for these the interview took a less structured turn. Nevertheless we received a number of interesting reflections from many of the interviewees.

The fourteen categories consisted of Nussbaum's ten, plus three we wished to add to the list for ourselves as explained above, plus one further 'dummy' category, which we will explain below. The three we added were:

1. Doing good to others. Being able to care for others as part of expressing your humanity. Being able to show gratitude.
2. Living in a law-abiding fashion. The possibility of being able to live within the law; not to being forced to break the law, cheat, or to deceive other people or institutions.

3. Understanding the law. Having a general comprehension of the law, its demands, and the opportunities it offers to individuals. Not standing perplexed facing the legal system.

The reasons for including these have been set out above. The category of 'being able to speak and understand the local language' was not included on the showcard as it was a product of the interviews. We will discuss this further below.

The final category (actually number eleven on the list of fourteen) was:
Complete independence. Being able to do exactly as you wish without relying on the help of others.

This category, envisaged as an extreme form of libertarianism,[39] was included for two reasons. One was to make sure we had genuine results, or in other words, as a test for the interviewees, to try to ensure that they didn't just 'nod through' the categories. Hence if the interviewee said much the same about this category as they had said about the great majority of others, this would be an indication that they had not really engaged with the task, and their answers should, therefore, be treated with suspicion. But secondly and more importantly, there is no doubt that the great bulk of work that has been done in social policy fields, and by political philosophers interested in social policy, has assumed what we might call an anti-libertarian, pro-interventionist stance. If, therefore, we found a general sympathy towards the idea of complete independence, especially among those who are receiving benefits from the state, or have done so in the past, then this may require a significant re-evaluation of work in this field. Hence it was intended as a test for ourselves as well as for the interviewees.

We received a great deal of commentary on the categories, only a small portion of which we can reproduce here. In what follows we set out the categories as they were presented to our interviewees, and explore some of the more interesting responses. It is worth mentioning that some interviewees formulated a distinction between what is needed for a barely acceptable life, and what is needed for a good life. This allowed them to assign a priority to different categories, while not denying that the lesser categories were still important.

2.3.4 Interviewees' Responses to Nussbaum's Categories

1. Life: Being able to live to the end of a human life of normal length.

Several of the interviewees commented that being able to live to the end of a human life of normal length is meaningful only if one's life is already good, that is if one has the other functionings. Life for its own sake is not an important functioning, they said. At the same time, most interviewees said that needless to say life is a precondition for other functionings. One pointed out that what parents dread is their children dying early. It is interesting to note that most of those below thirty years of age did not mention life as an important functioning, whereas those who were older did.

2. Bodily health: Being able to have good health, including reproductive health; to be adequately nourished, to have adequate shelter.

One doctor, an oncologist, insisted that in terms of the disadvantage there was no difference between bodily health and mental health, although she did agree that bad bodily health might immediately cause emotional problems. However, when reflecting upon health issues, she claimed that the crucial division should be between short-term problems (that might be severe but nevertheless will end after some time) and chronic problems, where one has to learn to live with one's disability, under which she included, for example, both schizophrenia and children with cerebral palsy. Alternatively, and especially when we have policy and budgeting in mind, she suggested that the categories should be those cases which can be cured and those which cannot. Society had to decide, she said, whether to spend a lot of money on allowing suffering people to live longer or cure problems that need a huge budget, but can dramatically change one's well-being. As an example this doctor suggested a deaf child who could be cured by an expensive operation and technology, the cost of which would be more or less equal to allowing a patient with cancer with an acute metastasis to live longer. On second thoughts she added: 'I am rather glad I don't have to decide in such cases'.

A related disadvantage, which was routinely mentioned by poor people, is weariness: being 'tired' continuously.[40] This, we believe, is distinct from what we could call 'yuppy fatigue' caused by spending too many hours at work. Rather we have in mind a different, inescapable weariness due to continuous worries and anxiety, a need to work around the clock in physically difficult jobs, and so on.

3. Bodily integrity: Being able to move freely from place to place; being secure against assault, including sexual assault, child sexual abuse, and domestic violence; having opportunities for sexual satisfaction and for choice in matters of reproduction.

One of the interviewees, a disabled person, reflected on the list and asserted: 'Numbers 2 and 3 are not important: it is ridiculous to claim that if your body is not perfect you can't achieve a good life.'

This raises the question of the status of the functionings: what do we say of someone who lacks one or more? We return to this important question throughout the book. In the meantime we should note that it may be that the criticism is misplaced: good health and bodily integrity do not require bodily perfection.

One interviewee pointed out the connection between sexual assault as a child and later drug addiction. This, so it was claimed, is often followed by prostitution, leading to an appalling cycle of problems. Reproductive choice was picked up by another interviewee, who was worried about the case of a woman in her sixties who, it was said, had been able to have a child by use of the new reproductive technologies. In sum, although the category 'bodily integrity' does not strike a clear chord with people, the sub-headings make clear that this is a category of enormous importance, and there was little, if any, resistance to the category itself.

4. Sense, imagination, and thought. Being able to use the senses, to imagine, think, and reason – and to do these things in a way informed and cultivated by an adequate education. Freedom of expression, speech, and religion.

One interviewee commented that there was too much packed into this, and that freedom of religion, in particular, should not be included. Others said that of this cluster only education is important. Yet the broad consensus was that this is an important part of a flourishing life. One interviewee who worked with drug addicts pointed out that drug addiction destroys imagination and reason. Another worried that freedom of expression can lead to violation of the rights of others. But in general this was one of the functionings that was constantly mentioned as important.

5. Emotions: Being able to have attachments to things and people outside ourselves; to love those who love and care for us.

This was generally accepted with relatively little comment. Interestingly, those who did discuss it further suggested that one could have a relatively good life without this functioning. But we suspect that at least some of those who doubted this functioning asked themselves, 'do I need emotions?' In some cases emotions might be a burden, especially when one is surrounded by misery and people whose life is a source of constant difficulties.

6. Practical Reason. Being able to engage in critical reflection about the planning of one's life.[41]

Here, more than elsewhere, the suspicion of the philosophers' intellectualist bias raised its head. Some interviewees were bemused about how this could be considered an important functioning when so few people appear able to achieve it. Another pointed out that what seems to be at stake here is an idea of self-determination, yet that need not take the form of second order critical reflection.

7. Affiliation. Being able to live with and toward others, to recognize and show concern for other human beings, to engage in various forms of social interaction. Having the social bases of self-respect and non-humiliation. Not being discriminated against on the basis of gender, religion, race, ethnicity, and the like.

One interviewee, who had formerly been homeless in the UK, asserted that food, shelter, and bodily health were worthless if you did not have a sense of belonging. This belonging can be cultural, or class-related, and it gives you dignity, self-esteem, and most importantly makes you useful. For this reason he also opposed regular welfare policies, which, he argued, maintained people's sense of being victims of society. A rather similar position, though without the radical conclusions, was repeated in an interview with a social worker who takes care of teenage girls at risk. Still, even if this is true it shows that the value of some of the categories is at least in part context-dependent. It does not show that the functionings are without value. Indeed many of the interviewees graded health and bodily integrity among the most important functionings.

The sub-functionings under this heading point in the same direction: to being socially integrated, belonging, being part of a community, understanding local norms and language, being able to contribute. As Maslow famously suggested – referring to needs, though – when physiological needs and safety needs are, by and large, taken care of, a higher layer of needs starts to show up: a desire to belong.[42] On this account belonging is a prerequisite human need that has to be met before one could ever achieve a sense of self-worth.[43] One begins to feel the need to escape alienation, a need for friends and affectionate relationships, even a sense of community. A person lacking these becomes vulnerable to social anxieties.[44] This desire characterizes humans everywhere, claims Maslow; it is a desire to belong to groups: family, nations, neighbourhoods, clubs, work groups, even gangs. This belonging gives us a sense of being liked and loved, and therefore 'accepted', by others.[45]

Indeed, it is very clear from our interviews that this category takes on huge importance for many people, although what precisely they have in mind varies considerably, from involvement in an active community, to having a few good friends. The common denominator, however, may be well expressed by one of our interviewees, an anti-poverty officer at a city council in the UK, who defined 'being valued' as one of the most important functionings. This incorporates both the idea of 'belonging' and 'being understood to be making a contribution'. However we should add one note of caution: some interviewees have found the idea and fact of community to be oppressive.

What is the causal connection between poverty, or any other form of disadvantage on the one hand, and lack of affiliation on the other hand? One interviewee, a social worker who works with teenage girls who had to flee from their homes because they were at risk, notes: 'Even [these girls'] ability to have housing or food depends on their ability to develop relationships with others.' That is, without affiliation – in effect, people to rely on – everything else becomes insecure.

Yet the causal connection is plausibly said also to go in the other direction, from the enjoyment of other functionings to a sense of belonging. Sen, famously, quotes Adam Smith on the importance of the right clothing in order to be able to appear in public without shame.[46] This was confirmed by an interviewee who works with disabled children, who said that those who are well-dressed sit differently in their wheelchairs to those who are obviously from poor families. Sen offers this as an example of a commodity that may be variable, unlike perhaps nutrition.[47] However, one of our interviewees provided an interesting echo and possible correction to Sen: even proper nutrition and bodily health is necessary if one is to avoid shame in public. Here she had in mind homeless teenagers who often suffer from appalling nutrition and hygiene leading to very obvious health problems which can leave the individual suffering from sores and lesions on the face and arms. While it is common to see people in large cities in dirty clothing – for example builders or art students – if such a person is also looking poorly nourished and ill then it is far more likely that the conclusion drawn will be that they are homeless. But furthermore people can be ashamed simply to appear in public looking so ill. It is not implausible that this is far less socially relative than Smith's own example. We would also like to suggest that 'walking about' works on both a literal and a metaphorical level. It is not only the actual appearance in public, but the fact that people suffer shame because they lack what is considered to be part of a decent, moral, or appreciated life.

It is clear that the relation between poverty, or other forms of disadvantage, on the one hand, and lack of belonging, on the other hand, is complex. One of our interviewees, another anti poverty officer at a local council in the UK, said she did not think low income communities were more deprived in the sense of belonging. For example, some such organizations offer education services organized by workers for workers.[48] Another of our interviewees, a formerly homeless person, described his childhood as life in a 'drunken family'. However, despite being very poor, and living in slums, they did benefit from a supportive community, and did have a sense of belonging. Alas, this was ruined when the government tore down the slums and gave them new housing. This was a blow to community life, and as a result his family became homeless. This story is a case where a family became disadvantaged because of the loss of community; however, the impact can be in the other direction as well. Many disadvantaged people we interviewed told us that once they became disadvantaged they lost social solidarity, which, ironically, they needed more than ever. Indeed, this loss of solidarity is often noticed when we see how homeless people are treated. For a different example, a few cancer patients reported that some people 'suddenly ignored' them, perhaps because they did not know how to cope with their friends or relatives now being very ill. More common are such cases with HIV carriers.[49] We will return to the causal connections between different forms of disadvantage in Chapters 7 and 8.

8. Other species. Being able to live with concern for and in relation to animals, plants, and the world of nature.

Most of our interviewees thought this was not a very important functioning. One, who works with disabled persons, laughed in embarrassment and justified her position that this was a luxury, and at any rate, not an important functioning. A disabled interviewee said this was not a condition for a good life. On the other hand, another interviewee suggested that relationships with other species were extremely important, although not many people acknowledge this, adding that as long as they did not acknowledge this there was nothing to do about it, so the state was not obliged to see that people achieve it. Indeed the state's policy in the UK was set out by a third interviewee, who pointed out that the expense of keeping a pet is not taken into account when calculating household need. A fourth interviewee, formerly homeless, noted that for homeless people relationships with other species, especially dogs, are most important, as it teaches them to take responsibility (for the dog) and this is the first step towards rectifying their situation. Indeed it is very common to see homeless people taking great care of dogs.[50]

9. Play. Being able to laugh, to play, to enjoy recreational activities.

This was generally accepted with little comment, except the remark that 'people's lives do not have to be full of leisure', and that 'drug addicts forget how to play'. At the same time it was not mentioned as a most important functioning.

10. Control over one's environment. Being able to participate effectively in political choices that govern one's life. Being able to have real opportunity to hold property. Having the right to seek employment on an equal basis with others.

No one rejected the idea of control over one's environment, but the way this was developed raised criticism. Involvement in politics cannot be essential, it was said, as many people have no interest in politics. This may be true but brings out the difficulty of conveying the options properly in the interview setting. For the proper contrast would be, not those who take no interest in politics, but those who are not permitted to take an interest in politics. This, no doubt, would be much more troubling.

Interestingly, many among the poor (although also among the non-poor) mentioned being *completely* dependent on others (and thus lacking control over one's life) as a great disadvantage.[51] The poor often describe being completely dependent as worse than extreme poverty.[52] The fully dependent would be single mothers who are out of work, the disabled, and the very elderly with no assets, and would include both those dependent on the state and those who are dependent on relatives or friends, or on charity.[53] In one interview, a social worker suggested that the fully dependent are *the* least advantaged, especially when they are so disadvantaged that they do not even know how to complain or report to the authorities about their situation.

The category of private property provoked comment. Interestingly, Nussbaum herself reports that in earlier versions of her list she did not include it, largely because her own broadly feminist political views had persuaded her that private property is controversial and should not appear on a universal list. However she was persuaded otherwise by her experience with poor women in India, for whom private property was both an important aspiration and capable of having a transforming effect on their lives.[54] Interestingly a number of our interviewees sided with the early Nussbaum.

This may have been expected from those who had lived on a Kibbutz, but several interviewees from the UK made the same point. It is certainly worth considering this objection further. In some societies it may be that possession of private property is part of what it is to be a fully functioning human being, whereas in others this is not the case.

2.3.5 The Additional Categories

Naturally we were particularly interested in what our interviewees made of the additional categories. The first of these, category 11, was our 'dummy libertarian category' introduced both to see if it provoked a different kind of reaction and to see if people, especially the disadvantaged, were particularly attracted to it.

11. Complete independence. Being able to do exactly as you wish without relying on the help of others.

Roughly we are able to divide responses to this into three categories. A number of people, as we expected, simply rejected it. A second group had a more complex response summed up by one who said 'independence is important but it is defined incorrectly on the sheet as [...] everyone is dependent to some extent'. In discussion many of these people endorsed an ideal of autonomy, which could have been expressed in terms of category 6 – practical reason – or category 10 – control over the environment. For example, one interviewee said that elderly people find independence very important. This, most likely, expresses an opposition to the idea of an enforced dependence, especially where greater thought would allow a greater measure of independence. The third, much smaller group gave enthusiastic endorsement to this category. This included one disabled young man, as well as one person who approved of a stoic or Buddhist idea of independence. However this was the view only of a very small minority. Our conclusion is that among our sample there is no compelling reason to include a category which goes beyond that already incorporated into categories 6 and 10.

The way in which the interviewees responded to this question gave us confidence in our method. Although some interviewees were not at all happy with the list of functionings presented, almost all of them commented on each functioning in a way in that showed genuine engagement. No one simply agreed with everything, which had been our fear.

12. Doing good to others. Being able to care for others as part of expressing your humanity. Being able to show gratitude.

This received enthusiastic endorsement, although it was also rejected by a small number as unnecessary for a good life. It was also suggested that it was very important for poor people, even if those in serious distress are not troubled by their inability to care for others. Perhaps the general attitude was summed up in the comment that 'it is not necessary for life, but it enriches one's life'. One interviewee pointed out that the homeless have particular difficulty with this, yet they do express their care for others when they have the chance, if not always in the most beneficial way, such as through sharing drugs and alcohol.

13. Living in a law-abiding fashion. The possibility of being able to live within the law; not to be forced to break the law, cheat, or to deceive other people or institutions.

To our surprise this category was rejected by two lawyers, working for NGOs, who pointed out that many people who break the law are nevertheless able to lead good lives. Others pointed out that people often choose to break laws, still others that sometimes one ought to break the law. Once again, however, the interview setting may not have been ideal for conveying the real meaning of this category, which is to be able to lead a decent life without having to break the law. This was understood by one interviewee, who claimed that drug addicts in the UK have to break the law in order to get help. Others made similar points. For example, an interviewee who works in a city council in the UK said: 'When it comes to living lawfully, low income individuals and families are especially deprived in this sense – we look very critically on benefit fraud, but we kind of expect the rich to get away with avoiding taxes.' Another interviewee, a former prisoner who has also overcome poverty, described the time he started living a lawful life, how excited he was when he first started paying for the tube and for the bus, and how excluded you are when you are not living legally.

14. Understanding the law. Having a general comprehension of the law, its demands, and the opportunities it offers to individuals. Not standing perplexed before the legal system.

One interviewee who works with disabled people suggested that the least advantaged among them were – among other things – those who did not understand their rights and the law. To extend the category further, this is mentioned also with regard to everyday economic interaction. Disadvantaged people claim that a banker will not listen to a person who can't even open an account because his earnings are not secure, or because he does not have any income. But, these people add, isn't it the case that an affluent person will find it easy to arrange a meeting with the bank's local branch administrator?[55] One of the interviewees, an Israeli lawyer who works with an Israeli NGO that offers legal services to Palestinians in the Occupied Territories, said that the least advantaged among those he worked with were those who either could not afford any legal service, or did not know the law, and did not realize that the law could often protect them. An interviewee who works with low-income families in the UK said: 'Low income individuals have much less access to the law. Rich people can afford having lawyers who will explain the laws to them. Low income people have to deal with the incomprehensible Inland Revenue and Tax Return forms.' Another lawyer we interviewed, who worked with poor families, the unemployed, and other economically weakened groups, said that the most urgent policy change in Israel was to follow the example of the UK and make the legal system more accessible to people. The problem, he said, was mainly of language (see the next section where we discuss the functioning of knowing the language) in its broad meaning, and this can be overcome by legal aid as in the UK.[56]

2.3.6 A Further Category

At the end of the second phase we asked the interviewees if there was a missing category. In some cases their views on this had already become clear, and indeed well before the interviews were concluded we came to the conclusion that a further matter was sufficiently important to merit consideration in its own right: the *functioning of being able to communicate, including being able to speak the local language, or being verbally independent.*[57] This arose in various interviews. A volunteer at an asylum centre in the UK, who has been there for several years, referred and time again to the issue of language – how important it is to be able to speak the language of the place you are in. This is so essential, she claims, that she believes studying English – which is optional – should be mandatory for refugees. The ability 'to really understand' what the culture is about, how to get by, are preconditions for all other functionings, at least for newcomers, she argued. Another interviewee who works in Israel with new immigrants from Ethiopia, some of whom live in poverty, claims that one of the indicators for knowing who are the least advantaged among them, is whether they can master the language. She claims that this is part of their sense of belonging to a place. They were uprooted from their natural environment in Ethiopia when they emigrated to Israel, and part of their absorption is to be able to speak Hebrew. A lawyer who worked with socially weakened groups in Israel claimed that one of the indicators for the least advantaged among those he worked with was whether they were 'verbally independent'. Lack of such a skill, he claimed, made it almost impossible for them to reach whatever goal they aimed at.

The experience of new immigrants to Israel – a country that absorbs new immigrants by, among other means, offering a free yearly course in Hebrew – serves as another example. In the 1950s, when the majority of the population of the young country was composed of new immigrants, not knowing the language was not an obstacle. Today, when there still is a flow of newcomers, but when they find themselves in a society where the language is established and mastering it is taken for granted in job interviews, or in everyday interaction, and so on, not knowing the language is a great obstacle. So much so that in November 2005 it was reported that alcoholic immigrants to Israel from Russia found it more difficult to participate in courses to curb their addiction, because the courses were based on the participants deliberating about their drinking habits in Hebrew. One of these newcomers was so eager to get rid of his drinking habit that like Ulysses, he asked to go to prison for eighteen months so that he would be forced to go through this course, but he found he did not follow discussions as his Hebrew was still very poor.

But it is not only newcomers or refugees who face this problem. Many people do not speak or write fluently even in their mother tongue, and get easily frustrated when they are not properly understood. This came out in some of the interviews.[58] This is a rather important point because often when people cannot express themselves and get frustrated, it ends up in violence.[59]

In another interview, with a person who for several years has been a health issues officer at a city council in the UK and who specializes in low-income communities, the issue of being able to express yourself and communicate also came to the fore. According to this interviewee, having no access to the authorities makes one deeply deprived and disadvantaged, and this is often because one does not know how to express one's situation, which could be the result of a failure of one or both of linguistic or communication skills.

Although we feel that we have gathered a wealth of information, we also concede that our list is provisional and we expect it to be developed and refined in the course of future theoretical and empirical research. Indeed we will shortly indicate some possible rationales and directions for change. However we are confident that the empirical and theoretical work on which we draw, as well as that which we have done ourselves, provides a good grounding for future work. At least the method of determining the functionings, which we put forward, overcomes the problem to which many scholars have pointed, namely the worry of biases in the selection of functionings. Such a bias might result from the social, or gender, or economic positioning of those determining the functionings.[60] Our method hopefully avoids this because it is based on a plurality of sources.

We should also clarify that the functionings are not intended to provide a philosophical analysis of 'the human good'. Rather they are thought of as components of well-being; dimensions by which people can be advantaged or disadvantaged, both relatively and absolutely.[61]

2.4 Conclusion

Our aim in this chapter has been to devise a list of functionings, as part of the task of setting out our own particular pluralist account of disadvantage. We first reviewed Martha Nussbaum's often quoted list, and then suggested a method for determining such a list, one which involves consulting the public. By carrying out this exercise we extended the list. This, however, raised a question with regard to priority or hierarchy among the functionings, and indeed we suggested that it is reasonable to claim that some functionings are more important than others. We will return to this particular question in Chapters 5 and 6. We now move to analyse the concepts of functioning and disadvantage.

CHAPTER 3

Risk

3.1 Introduction

In the last chapter we attempted to set out a provisional account of the basic categories of advantage and disadvantage. So far, though, we have done very little to explain how we understand the essence of being disadvantaged, beyond expressing our general sympathy with the capability approach in which it is customary to distinguish functionings – say, being well-nourished – from the capability, in this case, to achieve nourishment, also sometimes understood as the freedom to achieve nourishment. Sen's lead on this matter has been followed, seemingly with little question, by many others.

Whatever the advantages of the shift from achieved functionings – and we believe them to be considerable – it cannot be denied that introducing the idea of capability massively complicates the picture of disadvantage. Functionings are more or less observable; capabilities are not, at least in any straightforward manner. Schematically it is not difficult, in principle, to imagine how to represent an individual's state of functioning. We can imagine any individual's functioning state to be represented by a bar chart which expresses how well that person is doing with respect to each of a number of different functionings. The simplest form of this would express each person's functioning level as a percentile ranking with respect to how that person compares with others in his or her society. Hence each bar in the chart would be given a value between 0 and 99. This we will call a 'functioning map'. But can we represent an individual's 'capability state'?

One important complication is that capabilities are counterfactual – what someone could achieve, or even could have achieved, had different choices been made. Yet a second difficulty is that a person's set of 'capabilities' is the alternative combinations of functionings that it is feasible for this person to achieve.

Interestingly, this has the very important implication that to achieve one functioning an individual may have to sacrifice another. This is a point to which we shall return below. The more immediate issue, though, is that there is something of a conceptual difficulty in talking about a person's capabilities in the way in which this is often done. We know, roughly, what a functioning is (reading, say) and in some cases there is a clear matching relation between particular functionings and particular capabilities; literacy is the capability to read. However, given that a capability set is, in effect, the set of *sets of alternative functionings* one is able to achieve, it follows that with the same resources (capabilities) one might be able to achieve quite distinct sets of functionings. Suppose someone has money for a ticket to the theatre, or for a good meal, but not for both. Now we ask whether this person has the capability for the functioning of play or the functioning of using one's imagination. Even though there is a sense in which he or she does, there is also a sense in which it is quite misleading to say so because purchasing the ticket means giving up dinner and therefore the functioning of being satisfied and well nourished and the functioning of health.[1] To portray this accurately a level of capability enjoyment cannot, then, be represented by a simple bar chart, as one might attempt to represent a set of achieved functionings. Rather an indefinite number of bar charts is required, representing the different possible levels of functionings an individual could achieve, given the resources at their disposal in the context of the social structure in which he or she is placed. While this produces some conceptual clarification, it seems to render the idea of capabilities problematically complex for public policy (a problem to which we shall return).

Given these difficulties, it is worth asking what it is that motivates the shift from achieved functionings to capabilities. Sen provides an example of an affluent person who fasts, perhaps for religious reasons.[2] He may have the same functioning achievement in terms of eating or nourishment as a destitute person who is forced to starve, but the first person's 'capability set' is different from the second person's set: the first can also choose to eat while the second can't. In other words, the rich religious faster has the capability for nutrition, and thus lacks the functioning only through choice. Hence our political response to the two cases should be quite different.

This is, on the face of it, plausible and attractive. Yet when we examine the literature very few examples seem to be given to motivate the distinction other than that of the affluent person who chooses to fast. It is worth pausing here. As noted the shift from functionings to capabilities is highly significant. Yet affluent fasters who put their health at risk are rare,[3] and do not feature highly on the public policy agenda.

(We put aside issues of eating disorders, which raise quite different concerns.) But if the only reason for shifting from achieved functionings to capabilities is so that we do not have to provide wealthy fasters with food vouchers we might wonder whether it is worth the effort. Are there other cases? Perhaps we could add George Orwell, down and out in London and Paris, but a telegram away from sanctuary at the Ritz. Are there more pervasive cases in social policy? Politically the important cases where people can be the author of their own diminished functioning are those people who put their life and health at risk through poor lifestyle choices, and even more so, those who refuse paid employment. Yet these are subtle and difficult issues, which surely we do not want to settle on the basis of our intuitions about a rich religious faster or even George Orwell. Indeed we will discuss these types of issues in detail in the next chapter. In the meantime we conclude that the move to capabilities is rather less well motivated than often thought.

Nevertheless, we do not recommend that achieved functionings should be the the sole measure of well-being. Instead, the main purpose of this chapter is to make a different argument. In their zeal to emphasize freedom to achieve functionings, capability theorists have failed to bring out a somewhat different issue of great importance: the freedom to *sustain* functionings. To explain, let us start with two examples from Sen.

The first is from the southern edge of Bangladesh and of West Bengal in India, where the Sundarban ('beautiful forest') grows.[4] This is the habitat of the Royal Bengal tiger, which is protected by a hunting ban. The area is also famous for the honey it produces in natural beehives. The people who live in the area are extremely poor, but survive by collecting and selling the honey, for which they can get a decent price in the city. This, though, is a very dangerous job. Every year some fifty or more are killed by tigers. The second case is of Mr Kedra Mia, a Muslim daily labourer who worked in Hindu neighbourhood in Dhaka, where Sen grew up as a child. While aware of, and deeply concerned about, the risk of going to look for a job in a Hindu neighbourhood in troubled times, Mr Mia had no other choice but to do so to save his family from starvation. Sometime later, very sadly, Mr Mia was knifed on the street by Hindus, and later died.[5]

Although Sen does not emphasize the point, the striking thing about these examples is that the primary disadvantage these people suffer is that they are subject to extreme risks. If there were no tigers, or no Hindu knifemen, there would be nothing to distinguish these cases from perhaps hundreds of millions of others. What makes them special, although sadly not uncommon, is that people accept a high risk of death in order to put food on the family table and by this to fulfil their functioning as parents.

Thus, we believe that without further refinement the capability approach does not capture one significant and pervasive aspect of disadvantage: that very often people are disadvantaged because they are exposed to risks which they would not have taken had they had the option, or are forced to take risks that in one way or another are bigger than others are being exposed to or take.

Some clarification is due. First it is not suggested that human life should or can be risk free.[6] Often being open to risk is an advantage; many people welcome an element, even a large element, of risk as part of a flourishing life. Indeed perhaps almost all of us do. Starting a new relationship carries otherwise avoidable risks; parenthood even more so. But it would be odd to say that such risks disadvantage one; rather they are part of what constitutes a human life.[7] Moreover, sometimes risk is taken in the hope of greater gain. However, note that our account of disadvantage as involving risk concerns those risks which are in some sense taken involuntarily. Often people – perhaps young people more than others – take risks cheerfully. But these are not Sen's cases. In the standard case the risks the honey gatherers are forced to take gave them no pleasure; it wasn't fun, and it was certainly nothing to do with *joie de vivre*.[8] We therefore emphasize that for exposure to risk to become a disadvantage of the sort that should engage egalitarian concerns it has to be involuntary. This excludes from the definition people who, for some voluntary reason, take risks and consequently become worse off, either for the thrill or in the hope of greater gain.

Note that the term 'risk' is used here loosely and broadly, rather than in any disciplinary manner, by which we mean the ways the concept of 'risk' is used in risk management studies, or in some studies of rationality. We use the term 'risk' as it is used in everyday speech: a child crossing a busy street en route to school takes an obvious risk, while a person becoming homeless faces a whole new series of risks.

Furthermore, we should explain what it means to take 'bigger' risks. One risk can be bigger than another in three ways. First, it can be of higher probability, which is to say more likely to happen than other risks. Second, where two risks are of more or less the same probability, one of them could be a risk of a more serious harm. Third, there can be risks which are also pregnant with further risks. The last is a very important consideration. It seems that the fact that a particular risk carries with it further risks is what often upsets and frightens people about this harm. Many people are ready to take a one-time risk; however, they do want to avert continuous risks.

For the purposes of the current project the risks that will particularly concern us are those that are exceptional in that they affect only part of the population. Of course, if the entire population is at risk (say, due to a war or an environmental threat), then they are *all* worse off than they were before. This of course raises the question of whether disadvantage is purely relative to others, or also relative to one's situation before the harm, or to some absolute standard, or some combination. Risks that fall on all can be an extremely serious matter for issues of resource allocation as society may feel that it needs to switch resources from one area to another to cope with such a threat, and this will have further consequences. But in addition to this, there are risks which fall on, or are more serious for, part only of the population, and so it is these which will be the primary, although not the sole, focus of our attention.

Finally, when we say that the disadvantaged individual is 'forced' to take risks, we mean that the risk cannot be reasonably avoided because there is no reasonable alternative.[9] 'Forcing' does not imply that force was used. In fact, the agents can choose to take or avoid a risk, but not taking it would typically confront them with a greater risk, or the certainty of some harm. In other words, the most (often the only) reasonable alternative is for agents to agree to or to acquiesce in something that exposes them to risks to which others are not exposed.[10]

To get a better sense of the issues at stake, consider a case from the field of environment injustice studies.[11] North-eastern Israeli Negev is home to several Bedouin tribes.[12] The Bedouins live in what may be described as a 'town' of tents. North of this area – in occupied Judea, south of Hebron – lie settlements and industries whose sewage, including chemical waste, runs into the open gorge near the Bedouin village. The Bedouin understandably objected to the contamination of their wells. Furthermore their children were exposed to the chemicals in the open gorge, and to avoid crossing it were forced to take a different route to school. This meant negotiating a very busy road, with dangerous heavy traffic. Even in the best of circumstances the Bedouins would have been reluctant to move home as their identity has become bound up with the particular place they have lived in, and so this would undermine their sense of belonging, and hence their affiliation.[13] However, since most of the Israeli Negev is either a military zone and off-limits to civilians, or else Israeli kibbutz lands or nature reserves, they literally had nowhere to go, even if they had been prepared to move. Of course, they could not afford to buy houses in the centre or north of Israel, because they lacked the money and had no property to sell since they lived in tents. Thus, in order to avoid homelessness, the Bedouins were forced to take risks to their health and to their children's lives, and these risks were bigger, perhaps in all three senses identified above, than those faced by others.[14] It seems natural to say that they were disadvantaged in one or more ways, regardless of whether or not they were aware of the risks they were facing. This is also independent of their current level of achieved functioning.

3.2 Insecure Functionings

Examining these examples more carefully reveals various ways in which exposure to risk constitutes or causes disadvantage. Understanding this deepens our notion of disadvantage.

The first way in which someone can be exposed to risk is straightforward and relates to a single functioning: a person is or becomes disadvantaged when a certain achieved functioning is or becomes insecure. For example, someone under the permanent threat of eviction suffers first and foremost because she may actually be evicted, so her achieved functioning (having shelter) is not guaranteed. This could be termed as a threat to the continuous enjoyment of the functioning.[15]

Second, this person suffers because of the stress and anxiety this may cause, and hence the threat is to her emotional well-being, and in extreme cases her mental health, as well as to bodily health. Which may be a consequence of stress. Furthermore, in extreme cases it may affect people's functioning of 'play' through its depressive effects, and other functionings too. Note that anxiety may or may not be in proportion to the 'objective' dimensions of the risk. So, for example, it has often been observed that people are much more anxious about risks of cancer arising from nuclear power stations than they are about what may be larger risks from naturally occurring radon released from granite under their homes. Whether or not this should be condemned as 'irrational' is a complex question, upon which, thankfully, we do not have to rule here. The issue for us is simply that fear and anxiety is a common consequence of the perception that one is at risk. Bearing in mind that often risks do not lead to adverse consequences, whereas fear and anxiety can be omnipresent in someone's life; fear and anxiety may, in many cases, become the most important aspect of insecurity of functioning.

Such fear and anxiety may have further consequences, and lead to a third impact: steps taken so that the risk is reduced by lessening either the probability or the harm. Both of these are likely to be costly, one way or another. For example, someone who fears being attacked on the street, and so has insecure bodily integrity, may choose always to travel by taxi, and suffer the financial costs, or simply not go out, and lose many opportunities as a result. This will, though, reduce the probability of harm. The extent of some harms can be reduced by, say, stringent exercise regimes in the case of health risks. Often the point of this would be, as in the former case, to lower the probability of harm, but strengthening the body can also be a way of reducing the harm What would have been a major heart attack could become a minor one, for example. Again such exercise is often a cost to the person undertaking it, although it could also be a source of satisfaction and fulfilment.

A fourth way in which risk can have consequences is through the steps people take to reduce the impact of a feared event. Insurance is the most obvious example. Typically this does not help to reduce the probability of the feared event, or its extent, but it will allow someone to recover, or to do so more quickly. Similarly, someone worrying that their family income may decline because of the poor health of a family member may decide to take a second job, as a way of preparing for the worst, as we saw in the related case of Leah's father, reducing that individual's opportunities for leisure. This, in turn, might also have an adverse impact on the person's relationships with his or her spouse and children. Conversely one may decide to take steps to reduce one's vulnerability if the feared event happens. Those, for example, who believe that they are at significant risk of developing arthritis may decide to avoid heavy manual work, and take a lower paid, less physical job.

Fifth, a person who believes themselves subject to risk suffers what we could call 'planning blight'.[16] Those facing uncertainty in employment or housing may find it very difficult to plan other aspects of their life; they may put off marriage or having children, for example, until their situation settles.

Finally, an extreme form of planning blight is a type of 'paralysis of the will' where experience of uncertainty in many aspects of one's life can cause a failure to plan even in circumstances where it is rational to do so. The previous example of planning blight concerned what may well be a rational response to uncertainty. This more extreme case is one where much of the world begins to appear beyond one's control, even when in fact this is not the case.[17]

Note that many of the effects will apply with particular force to those who are functioning at a low level within any category. Those, for example, with weak affiliation – say, few friends – are much more vulnerable to a significant further fall in affiliation than those who currently do much better. The death or emigration of one friend will obviously be more telling for those who have come to depend on a small circle. Equally those in poor health may be much more vulnerable to further problems than those in better health. Flu kills the already sick much more commonly than it does those in good health. Hence low functioning often brings with it sharper risks of significant falls. Furthermore, those with low functionings are, as we have already seen, likely to try to take steps to improve their functionings, and this can involve them in greater risk and insecurity.

Hence insecurity will equally affect those who seek to take steps to improve their functionings, just as much as those who seek to sustain their functionings. In this way we can say that although their functionings need not be insecure, people with low functionings very often generate insecurity for themselves in an attempt to improve things.

Analysing this further, we can generalize and categorize three distinct ways in which functionings can be at risk, or, as we might say, three ways in which functionings can be, or become, insecure.

(1) *Risk to a specific functioning.*

A day labourer, or indeed an adjunct professor, lives constantly under the threat of unemployment, and thus lacks security of employment. A rough sleeper person lives continuously under the threat of physical attacks, and thus faces risks to his bodily health and integrity.

(2) *Cross-category risk.*

Often a risk is likely to spread to other functionings in a straightforward manner. For example, anyone relying on their income to buy food will find that risks to employment generate risks to nutrition among other things. Further confirmation of this is revealed in studies which show that poor people are more likely to become disabled than people in higher income groups.[18]

(3) *Inverse cross-category risk.*

Sometimes steps taken to secure one functioning, such as nutrition, may have the effect of putting other functionings at risk, such as life and bodily health, as in the case of Kedra Mia and the honey gatherers. To secure food for themselves and their families they put their own lives in grave danger. Note that unlike ordinary cross-category risk, inverse risks are generally initiated by the agent, who acts in a way that puts one category at risk while trying to secure another. This point develops what we earlier described as an important implication of Sen's theory, namely that the concept of 'capability' refers to the alternative combinations of 'functionings' that it is feasible for a person to achieve, taking into account the means this person has and/or the environment in which she lives. When we analyse the cases above we see that by attempting to secure one particular functioning, a person may find it necessary to take risks in other ways, making other functionings less secure. This is a natural consequence of the fact that a capability set can allow an individual to achieve a variety of sets of functionings, and so in order to secure what they see as most immediately urgent, a person may sacrifice another functioning. For example, as the Bedouins understandably were not prepared to give up their homes, they had no alternative but to take the risks of drinking contaminated water and of their children crossing the busy road and breathing polluted air. So their health and their children's capability to move freely and safely from place to place became insecure. Notice that although in some sense this was a choice they made, in another sense they were forced to do so as under the new circumstances, all other options were not reasonable.

Further examples of inverse cross-category risk are easy to find. Consider the following.[19] It is reported that, due to an economic crisis in Israel, during the year 2002–3, one in five families in Israel became unable to guarantee proper nutrition for their children. The report uses the language of 'insecure capability to have proper nutrition'. This does not necessarily entail hunger – in fact, the functioning which these people rushed to safeguard was well satisfied – but it means that these families bought cheap food rich in carbohydrates (e.g. rice, pasta) rather than healthier, but more expensive food rich in proteins, iron, and calcium. Among these poorer populations the average daily consumption of calcium was 55 per cent, and protein 65 per cent, of those who could afford proper nutrition. Moreover, among those families whose diet contains higher proportions of carbohydrates, the prevalence of diabetes is more than twice as frequent than in families that enjoy proper nutrition. What is even more striking is that according to this report, in order to try and secure their functioning of nutrition, 24 per cent of families in Israel gave up other ordinary basic needs such as medical supplies and continuous electricity and many of them choose not to pay their mortgage debts. In other words securing the functioning which came under threat (i.e. proper nutrition) made other functionings (e.g. to enjoy warmth in the winter) insecure.

Other research confirms this bleak picture. Analysing the income and spending of households in Israel in 2001, the Adva Center for Monitoring Equality in Israel compares an average Israeli family with the average among those families that needed income support.[20] Families on income support had to spend 30 per cent of their income on food, whereas the average family had to spend only 23 per cent of its income, even though average spending on food per person in poor families was only 22 per cent of spending among the general public. In fact poor families had to spend 62 per cent of their income on the basic necessities of food, housing, and clothes, whereas the average family spent only 47 per cent. The consequences are clear: poor families spent much less on health and education. The average spending on health among those families was

52 per cent of the equivalent among the general public; on education these families spent 56 per cent of the average, and much lower figures when compared with the middle and upper classes. Average spending on transport among those needing income support was much lower than the average among the general public.

Interestingly this then generates other risks. Research conducted in England and Wales reveals that despite using private cars much less frequently than people from higher social classes, people on lower income or no income at all are more likely to die from motor vehicle traffic accidents.[21] We presume that this could be due to the fact that these people use older models that were less well designed in the first place, and are now poorly maintained and serviced, so their accidents are more frequent and more serious when they happen. People who are on low income and need cars for transport (other research shows that often public transport does not serve poorer areas as frequently as it serves richer neighbourhoods and towns[22]), in order for example to travel to their workplace, face larger risks to their life and bodily health. This, then, is an example of inverse cross-category risk. To protect basic nutrition, poor people have to take greater risks with transport. Further examples are easily found. We have already mentioned those who feel forced to cheat the system in order to secure a basic standard of living for their families. They put their liberty at risk (in case they are caught) as well as their functioning of living within the law.

3.3 Conclusion

This chapter has argued that one vital aspect of advantage and disadvantage is not only what functionings are achieved, but a person's *prospect of achieving and sustaining a level of functioning should they attempt to do so*. There are at least two key determinants of their prospects: their probability of success, and what they have to sacrifice to achieve that probability of success. A functioning can itself be insecure (lower probability of sustaining it) or the attempt to secure it can render other functionings insecure (increased sacrifice).

Consequently we are now in a position to rephrase the aspect of disadvantage under consideration: *One central way of being disadvantaged is when one's functionings are or become insecure involuntarily, or when, in order to secure certain functionings, one is forced to make other functionings insecure, in a way that other people do not have to do.* Accordingly a policy of rectifying disadvantage would need to pay special attention to the question of how to secure functionings.

How, though, can we represent this notion of security of functioning? It might be thought that the way to do this is to graft a notion of 'expected functioning' on to the model of 'expected utility'; i.e. multiply functioning by probability of sustaining it. Now one problem is that in most cases we do not have precise figures for probabilities. Moreover, even if such figures were available, dealing with the question in this fashion is not satisfactory. Combining the two dimensions – functioning level and probability – into a single figure loses important information. Consider two individuals, one with an insecure high income, the other with a more secure lower income. Saying that they both could have the same 'expected income' bleaches out the distinctive features of the two cases. Furthermore we would want to leave it an open question – at least at this stage of the analysis – as to whether there is a determinate answer to the question of whether either of them is better off than the other.

Rather than derive a single figure, then, it is better to retain the two dimensions of, first, a person's functioning level and, second, his or her prospect of sustaining it.[23] Schematically this is not difficult to represent by an amendment to the simple notion of a functioning map, introduced at the start of this chapter. Recall that the idea was that a snapshot of a person's functioning was to be represented as a bar chart. On the first version of this the heights of each bar represented the functioning level achieved, while the widths of each were not considered to be of any significance. Now, however, we can use the widths of the bars to represent 'security': the person's current power to sustain that level of functioning should they attempt to do so. So, if you face the average risk for your society for a particular functioning you will have a bar of average width; if the risk you face is higher than average, you will have a thinner bar, and so on. For example, considering employment, perhaps an employee in a medium-sized company will have an average width bar, a casual labourer a thin bar, and a tenured full professor an exceedingly wide bar. Of course, given that, as we have said, precise figures are rarely available, the width of the bar can only be determined very roughly in many cases, so this should be thought of as a schematic illustration rather than as a precise technical proposal. Furthermore in other respects the picture remains far from complete. We therefore turn now to discuss opportunities.

CHAPTER 4

Opportunity and Responsibility

4.1 Introduction

As explained in the previous chapters, Sen suggests that 'capabilities' are something like opportunities for functionings, also referred to as 'freedoms' to achieve functionings.[1] In this chapter we argue that the idea of 'capability' is unfortunately too vague, and thus we replace it with the idea of 'genuine opportunities' for secure functioning. After analysing this concept we explore the conditions under which it is right to say that someone has a genuine opportunity.

Sen motivates capability theory, we noted, by reflection on cases of people who choose to enjoy a lower level of functioning, in some respect, than they are otherwise capable of. And, we acknowledged, this produces the problem, at least at the level of theory, of an individual's responsibility for his or her own functioning. Further, reflection on other cases, such as self-inflicted poor health and voluntary unemployment, show that there is a serious practical and political issue here too. One way of putting the general issue is the following: some people (and many politicians, let us admit) believe that there are people who despite the fact that they are functioning at a particular level should, for political purposes, be evaluated and treated as if they had achieved a different level. Usually the case is of people who are functioning at a lower level as a result either of poor choices in the past or of the refusal to embark on particular courses of action now. In theory, however, the converse case, which we have not discussed so far should be of equal interest: where someone has achieved more than he or she could reasonably be expected to (say, with meagre resources). It is, though, the case of the person who achieves less than we would expect that has attracted most attention in the egalitarian literature.

4.2 Opportunity and Responsibility

We have already noted the apparent attraction of the capability approach. To expand, one advantage is often thought to be that it creates a space between government and its citizens in which a citizen is given freedom to choose between different options in life and hence is able to exercise a significant degree of responsibility for his or her own fate. Accordingly, on such a view, if a government provides for its citizens the proper capabilities to function, citizens have no complaint if, as a result of their own choices or actions, they do not achieve appropriate functionings. And correspondingly no one else has a complaint if an individual manages, through his or her own efforts, a higher level of functioning.

Whether or not this sounds appealing,[2] the contrast between the idea of a government supplying functionings on the one hand, and capabilities or opportunities on the other, is less clear than is often assumed. For, in general, it is impossible for a government to guarantee the functioning level of its citizens without extreme coercion. The old adage that 'you can take a horse to water but you can't make it drink' applies. Short of force-feeding you cannot guarantee nutrition levels, and short of incarceration you cannot guarantee shelter. Nothing can guarantee proper education because even when education is compulsory, and parents who do not send their children to school or who fail to teach them at home are put on trial and might be punished, still some children emerge from school functionally illiterate. And so, in practice and in normal circumstances, most goods – or at least most of the goods a government can legitimately offer – are opportunities.[3]

Yet this also points to the vagueness of the capability approach. If we think of capabilities as opportunities for functionings, then this typically means that the enjoyment of functionings will be conditional on performing some act – if only an act of speech – normally within the agent's power. Hence the central issue becomes the nature of the actions required of the individuals, or exceptionally others, to turn capabilities into functionings. Notice that egalitarian theorists have tended to talk in terms of choices but it is rarely as simple as this. Choices generally require other actions, and actions typically have costs, or at least risks. Consequently any capability theorist – and more broadly any theorist who wishes to give opportunity and responsibility a central place – has to consider which actions, and which costs and risks, should be required of individuals in order for them to enjoy a particular level of functioning.

To illustrate the problem consider the issue of the capability or opportunity to acquire private property in land. One way in which citizens in a particular society could be given such an opportunity is simply by registering at the central distribution agency to be allocated their parcel. If they neglect to register then they have squandered their opportunity. Another society could offer its citizens the chance to go through a lengthy and exhausting Lockean process of acquisition through labour mixing. Here exercising the opportunity is highly burdensome. A third society might operate a market mechanism where land, though scarce and very expensive, is available for purchase. Those who have labour to sell can eventually acquire land by getting a job and saving up, provided they are prepared to make other sacrifices.[4] In all these societies people have, in some sense, an opportunity or capability to acquire land, yet it would seem odd to say that political philosophy should never have anything to say about which arrangement is to be preferred. We seem to need some grounds to distinguish between different institutional arrangements. A simple appeal to 'capability' or 'opportunity' will not suffice. It is not acknowledged as often as it should be that capability theory, or any opportunity theory of distributive justice, is under-specified until it is settled what exactly is required for people to exercise their opportunities.[5]

It seems, then, the government, like Greek gods, has to decide which tests have to be passed and hurdles jumped before people can enjoy the goods they seek. The important issue for social policy is to be able to distinguish between cases in which in the politically relevant sense an individual *lacks an opportunity* and cases in which the individual *has the opportunity but fails to make use of it*. Therefore we need to know what it is to have an opportunity in the relevant sense.

Within the egalitarian literature this issue has been discussed most explicitly within the rather exotic context of 'expensive tastes'; that is, whether there are circumstances in which government should provide subsidies for people with expensive tastes; or, on the contrary, whether individuals should always be required to bear the consequences of their expensive tastes themselves. A standard example is of someone who is only satisfied with expensive champagne when others are happy with beer. Dworkin, of course, introduced examples of this type to cast doubt on theories of equality of welfare which appear to have the consequence – which Dworkin finds unacceptable – that an egalitarian society should subsidize champagne tastes.[6]

Cohen[7] and Arneson[8] have argued, in reply, that everything depends on the origin of such tastes. Those born with expensive tastes are in a quite different situation from those who set out deliberately to cultivate such tastes. The latter have the opportunity to attain a particular level of satisfaction by drinking beer, but by their choice to develop expensive tastes squander this opportunity. On a simple interpretation of such a 'choice' view of responsibility and opportunity, those who are born with expensive tastes have a case for subsidy, while those who deliberately develop such tastes do not. One bears responsibility for one's choices. If one chooses to develop expensive tastes one has simply failed to exercise one's opportunities for satisfaction in less expensive form. Alternatively, if one had no choice, one has no opportunity to avoid having expensive tastes, and no responsibility for bearing the costs.

Dworkin rejects the idea of relating opportunity to choice in this way. Although the nature of his own position is a matter of some dispute[9] the essential element in his approach appears to be that of whether people identify with their tastes, regarding them as part of their character or personality, rather than as a misfortune. On such an alternative 'identification' view of opportunity and responsibility – whether or not it is authentically Dworkin's – causal history is irrelevant. People are responsible for the consequences of their tastes when they identify with them. State subsidy is appropriate only when people fail to identify with their tastes, as, for example, in the case of unwelcome addictions or 'cravings'. It is Dworkin's view that a person deserves subsidy only in such cases.

Unfortunately neither the choice nor the identification view appears adequate in helping to develop a theory of responsibility and disadvantage that can be used in real social policy. For one reason, both involve a 'metaphysical swamp'. Resting the question of whether an individual should bear the consequences of their action on the question of moral responsibility, which in turn rests on whether or not genuine choice or identification has taken place, leads to questions which may be indeterminate.[10] These problems are already well known and need be stated only briefly, by means of an example. Imagine a person who is well nourished, but due to some ideology chooses to go on a strict diet (say, he eats only lentils) and ends up very ill and is hospitalized. Should the state cover the cost of his treatment at the hospital?

The issue becomes very complex and the information we need to ground our decision is never-ending. What if this person only restricts his diet to lentils because of his religion, yet he decided to join this religion because of a trauma which he suffered when he was a child? Should he still be held responsible? Does it matter if the trauma happened at a state school or at home due to his father beating him? And if the latter, does it matter if his father treated him violently because he was unemployed due to the state's policies, or because he had suffered psychologically in the war while he was serving? These questions go on and on, and it is hard to know how to approach them. But if we want to make the question of whether the state should pay for treatment turn on the question of choice or individual responsibility, we need answers.

Quite independently of the swamp argument, another criticism is that while the choice and identification views may seem plausible candidates for a theory of opportunity and responsibility in ideal circumstances of equality, when we step outside such circumstances they are highly implausible, being either too harsh or too soft in their consequences. That is, in the circumstances of the real world, where people are choosing against the background of inequality, choice and identification theories are very unappealing. We address this criticism particularly to the 'choice' view, as this appears to be the more plausible version, yet we also make some comments to show how it can be modified to apply to the identification view. The argument is best introduced by means of an example of someone who is suffering effects of inequality and so is in the bottom half of the distribution according to whatever theory is in play.

Consider, then, the example of an unemployed single mother who has no savings and turns down a menial, low-paid, full-time job some distance from her home, in order to be able to see her young children to school and look after them in the holidays.[11] She has *chosen* to reject full-time salaried work, and let us add that she *identifies* with her role as an active mother who personally cares for her children. Should she be eligible to receive state support (above, perhaps, a bare minimum for her children)?[12]

A first application of the choice view would seem to lead to the conclusion that she should not receive support for herself. She has made a choice, and she had the opportunity to make a different choice, and so must bear the consequences. However, many will think that this is too harsh, particularly given her difficult circumstances and relative poverty.[13] How, then, may the choice view be amended to avoid this unwelcome consequence?

One response to this case is that, contrary to our assertions, it does not at all show a problem with choice-based accounts of responsibility.[14] For this single mother is poor, and consequently has less opportunity for secure functioning (or preference satisfaction, or resources) than others. Allowing her state support even when she turns down a job will bring her closer to equal opportunity, and so a choice-based theory of responsibility, when combined with a theory of equality, would accept that this single mother, as a victim of inequality, should not be held responsible for her choices made under conditions of inequality.

The difficulty with this response is that it seems to presuppose that a person is responsible for the consequences of their choices if and only if that person has opportunities at least as high as the average for their society. Although both sides of the biconditional are problematic,[15] let us concentrate on the 'only if' claim, which entails that one is not responsible for the consequences of one's choices if one has below average opportunities relative to one's society. This we might call the 'exoneration view'. This, we believe, can be too soft. While it is right that one's material position, including one's relative material position, should be taken into account in evaluating responsibility, the exoneration view goes too far. Sometimes you should be responsible for at least part of the cost of your choices and actions even when you are, unfairly, the very worst off in society. Consider, for example, a case where you fail to take a very cheap and easy precaution, yet your failure to do this has enormous costs for others. Perhaps you suspected that you had left a candle burning on your kitchen table, and you knew it to be near a pile of newspapers, and you were aware of the danger this presents, but on your way out of the house you could not be bothered to put your head round the door to check whether you had put out the candle. As it turns out, the candle causes a fire which burns down several homes, including your own. Yet it seems bizarre, and extremely patronizing, to say that just because you have less opportunity for secure functioning than others you are not in any way blameworthy and responsible for this. Furthermore, taken literally, the exoneration view would seem to have the consequence that those towards the bottom of the distribution would escape criminal liability too.

The dilemma is that it seems wrong to say that people are always responsible for their choices and wrong to say that under conditions of inequality the poorly off are never responsible for their choices. One possibility would be to generate a limited version of the exoneration view in which you escape responsibility only if the fact that you are badly off is causally related in the right way to your actions;[16] that is, the fact that you are badly off in some way led you to make the choice you did. Some version of such a theory could, perhaps, excuse the single mother, while not excusing the person who fails to check whether the candle is still alight. Now, though attractive in theory, this places us squarely in the metaphysical swamp: could someone, for example, claim that all their bad decisions are a consequence of the depression and lack of concentration caused by their relative poverty? How could we tell whether this is true? Would there even be a fact of the matter?

Our conclusion is that if we have policy in mind it is preferable by far to avoid the choice and identification views if there is an alternative. The best way forward appears to be to disconnect, in part at least, the question of what people are morally responsible for from the question of what burdens it is reasonable to hold people to. This is not to say that questions of moral responsibility are irrelevant, but rather that they do not determine the question of burden, which at the end of the day is the relevant one when policy is at stake.

In our view instead of asking whether a choice has been made, or whether an individual identifies with the choice, it seems more promising to ask *whether it is reasonable to expect someone to act one way rather than another.* Whether it is reasonable will, in turn, depend on the potential impact of so acting on other aspects of that person's functionings, including their security. If exercising an opportunity will involve undue cost or risk to other functionings – which we described as inverse cross-category risk – then it is not, in our sense, a genuine opportunity.

In the case of the single mother if she were to take the job it would put several of her functionings – and to complicate things further, those of her children – at risk. These include emotional well-being, her ability to care for others, and possibly her health and control over the environment.[17] For as long as this is true there is a strong case that the government should support her, provided at least that in doing so this does not force others into even more extreme risks to their functionings.[18]

In judging whether someone should be held responsible for the consequences of their actions we should take all the impacts – costs and benefits – of potential action and non-action into account. On the view developed here, someone has a genuine opportunity to do x only if doing x is reasonable for them, in the sense that the costs of doing so are reasonable for them to bear. The relevant costs are the impacts on other functionings, and what is reasonable depends on the context. Under circumstances in which it is reasonable to hold someone to account for the consequences of their actions and decisions we say that they have a *genuine opportunity.* This view supposes that someone has a genuine opportunity for achieving a functioning – and hence a capability – when it is reasonable to expect him or her to take steps to achieve that functioning. In the above example, it is true that this woman could get a job to pay for rent and food if state support was cut off, and so in some sense she does have an opportunity for achieving the functionings of shelter and nutrition. Yet on the theory presented here the cost of exercising that opportunity is unreasonable, and so the opportunity does not exist in the relevant sense. For ease of expression we can adopt the distinction between '*formal opportunity*' and '*genuine opportunity*' to capture this holistic sense of responsibility.

How, then, can we cash out this view of responsibility in detail? This is equivalent to the question of what makes an 'undue' cost (the idea is that if exercising an opportunity will involve undue cost or risk to other functionings, it is not a genuine opportunity). The basic guidelines, which will have to be clarified in practice through a democratic political process, will include a number of parameters. Naturally, the first will be the cost to the agent's other secure functionings: if the cost is 'too high' then it is not reasonable to expect the agent to bear it, and so exercising an option which has a serious risk of high cost to another functioning is not a genuine opportunity. However, this will often depend on a second parameter: namely, the agent's secure functioning level, both relative to that of others and in itself. For example, if an agent is doing very well, then what might be a prohibitive risk for others may not always be for this person. A further parameter is the cost to others of the agent failing to act in that way. If failing to act will cause high costs to others, then an agent may be required to act even if acting this way involves some cost or risk. The same is true if the agent has some general or special moral or social obligations to act one way rather than another. Finally, sometimes special excusing factors may apply to the agent.[19] All of these will help determine whether a cost or risk is 'undue', and conversely whether or not an opportunity is genuine.

Note that in deciding whether an individual should pay all, part, or none of the costs of their actions, moral responsibility is one factor among many, and that in many cases it will be an irrelevant or minor consideration, especially where it is uncertain. Putting these factors together should help us to make decisions about whether the costs of an individual's actions should fall on the individual, on society as a whole, or some mix. However, although this is a highly contextual question, which requires consideration on a case-by-case basis, it would seem highly problematic to attempt to resolve each case on its individual merits. For this could easily lead to partiality, inconsistency, a sense of intrusion, and resentment, and hence threaten legitimacy. Rather, then, we need to come to general social policies about the circumstances in which people should bear the consequences of their actions. This will at least set a background of legitimate expectation.[20]

There is nothing to rule out the possibility that policies may properly vary from society to society, depending on a variety of contextual factors. But we admit that in any society there will be cases where there will be reason for evaluating someone's functioning level as if he or she had achieved more and hence may be required to bear all or some of the costs of their choices or actions. For this reason we accept that it is not appropriate to restrict evaluation of well-being to an individual's achieved functionings.

Earlier we mentioned that on Sen's view a capability set is in effect the set of sets of alternative functionings (i.e. the set of functioning maps) that a person could achieve. This still remains important. Some people can change their functionings across a wider range of alternatives and/or with greater ease than others. In effect they have wider opportunities even if they presently achieve the same functionings. In response it might be argued that the factors likely to bring about such flexibility – wealth, education, intelligence – are themselves functionings and so will already be included in the representation. Hence it is incoherent to suppose that two individuals could have the same achieved functionings but different opportunities. However this is not correct. What is true is that if the social structure offers two people a different range of possible paths, then there must be something about those people that allows these different possibilities. However, it does not follow that the difference must be a difference in functioning. It could be, for example, membership of different religions, which could lead to a huge difference in opportunities, even between two people with the same achieved functionings. Consequently for some purposes it will be necessary to come to an understanding of not only what a person has achieved, but also what else is, or was, possible, and once again at what cost.

4.3 High Performers

Finally we should briefly address the case in which an individual has achieved a functioning level higher than could be reasonably expected. Perhaps by working at two jobs, when others have one, or by spending leisure time on home improvements, an individual may be able to achieve a higher level of functioning, at least in several respects, than others who do not put in this extra effort. Now, we noted that there are cases where people should be treated, politically, as if they are functioning at a higher level than in fact they are (Sen's affluent faster is an example). The mirror image of this would be that some individuals should be treated as if they are functioning at a lower level than in fact they are; in effect as if they are disadvantaged, when their achieved functioning level is on a par with people who are not disadvantaged. But can we accept this?

To clarify, we are not interested here in broader questions of justice and desert, but rather in cases that affect our conception of disadvantage. So, what would it mean in any case? Consider two people of equal circumstances and talents, who are impoverished and receive support in securing the relevant functioning to bring them closer to the average for their society. One puts in immense effort and sacrifice, and becomes able to earn a larger income, and so no longer qualifies for income support. The other remains benefiting from this support with no reasonable prospect of bettering his circumstances. Although we can recognize that the wealthier person is now functioning at a higher level than it is reasonable to expect, it would nevertheless rarely occur to anyone to say that we should treat this person as if she were still poor, and continue to provide income support. Indeed it may even seem absurd.

It is worth pausing to consider this asymmetry. Any opportunity or capability view should attend to people on the basis of their opportunities, and not it seems on the basis of what people make of those opportunities. If two people have the same opportunities and one does well and the other does not, opportunity theory would nevertheless seem to suggest that they should both receive the same level of income support in view of their poor opportunities. Yet if one is doing rather well and the other is still stuck, then it seems very strange to suppose they are entitled to exactly the same state help. The obvious and natural explanation is simply that only one of them needs support. Strictly, on an opportunity view, this may be unfair, yet such a claim may seem to carry little if any weight. Interestingly, in the light of the fact that she is not in need, that resources are scarce and that they must be gathered from others, it would seem unreasonable to insist on receiving one's 'fair due', based on one's opportunities rather than actual functioning.

Consider another case, perhaps more familiar in kind. Two neighbours live in poorly insulated, and hence energy inefficient, houses. One goes to the expense and trouble of insulating his house while the other spends comparable time and money enjoying cable television. The following year the government announces a programme of generous grants to pay for home insulation, which allows the television watcher to install insulation without cost or personal effort. But should the grant also go to the person who has already insulated his house? Some people would argue that fairness would seem to dictate that it should, although for a host of reasons this would be unlikely to become government policy, even if the application of some retrospective subsidy would surely not be unfair. Thus, even in this case it seems not unreasonable to attend to actual functioning levels rather than opportunities for functioning. This will leave one person ruing his bad luck and poor timing (although, perhaps, he could also be proud for doing it by himself), while perhaps at the same time accepting that the government has made the right decision.

It seems, then, that while in some cases the state will assess an individual's functioning as if they had achieved a higher level, because it would have been reasonable for them to have done so, it will be much rarer that the state will take into account the fact, when it is a fact, that it would have been reasonable for them to have achieved a lower set. Consequently, it appears that government support, when provided to individuals, should be provided on the basis of achieved (secure) functioning, rather than opportunity for functioning, except where an individual has unreasonably declined to make use of genuine opportunities.

4.4 Conclusion to Part 1

To review the argument of Part 1, in Chapter 1 we motivated the idea of a pluralist theory of advantage and disadvantage by arguing that monist theories, which put all forms of advantage and disadvantage on a single scale, must accept that the loss of something on that scale can, in principle, be 'made up for' or 'compensated for' by enough of other things on that scale. Given that money will be something that appears on the scale, and everything else is exchangeable against money, it appears to follow that on a monist view there can be no objection in principle to cash compensation as an all-purpose remedy. However, we think there are good reasons for rejecting cash compensation as an all-purpose remedy, and therefore we believe that there are good reasons for rejecting monist views of advantage and disadvantage.

The particular form that the resulting pluralist view should take can be developed by considering when substitute goods are, and are not, acceptable to remedy a loss or shortfall. Some substitutions are likely to be better than others and this should allow us to cluster different goods into groups or dimensions of advantage and disadvantage. However, rather than trying to reinvent the wheel, we take as our point of departure in Chapter 2 the capability theory developed by Sen and Nussbaum. In particular we build on Nussbaum's list of ten essential 'functional capabilities', adding a further four of our own, developed through theoretical reflection and empirical research, including our own interviews which provided an important perspective on the list of functionings.

Chapter 3 explored the issue of risk, allowing us to introduce the concept of 'secure functionings' which seem to us – or at least so we want to suggest – a natural development of the capability approach. In Chapter 4, however, we argue that the idea of 'capability' is unfortunately too vague, and thus we replace it with the idea of 'genuine opportunities', exploring the conditions under which it is right to say that someone has a genuine opportunity, and when they should be held responsible for failing to make use of their opportunities. This, then, puts in place the main outlines of our *'genuine opportunity for secure functionings'* view of advantage and disadvantage. The next challenge, which is the task of Part 2 of this book, is to work out how all this might be brought into contact with reality.

PART 2

Applying Theory to Practice

Introduction to Part Two

So far we have argued for the 'genuine opportunity for secure functionings' view of disadvantage. The emphasis on functionings emerges from considerations about the pluralism of advantage and disadvantage, while the idea of 'secure functionings' is a response to the recognition of the vulnerability of the disadvantaged, who are often involuntarily forced to take risks that render their functionings insecure and vulnerable. Finally, the idea of 'genuine opportunities' is a reaction to the inadequacies of the choice theory of opportunities and responsibility.

Now, it is all very well to present an account of advantage and disadvantage, but such a theory has no practical application until we have an answer to the question of when the government, or some other agent, should act to address disadvantage. As we argued in the Introduction, within egalitarian theory there is a broad consensus that special attention should be given to the least advantaged. How strong such priority should be remains to be discussed later in this book, but however it is settled it is necessary to understand what it is to be among the least advantaged. This, indeed, is the indexing problem, introduced in Chapter 1.

Yet as we have pointed out in the Introduction, while the idea of the 'least advantaged' makes perfect sense on 'monist' theories of disadvantage, such as a preference satisfaction theory in which the least advantaged are the least satisfied, or a resource based theory in which income and wealth are the measures, in a pluralist theory, with many measures of advantage, the task of picking out the least advantaged is obscure. For any egalitarian theorist this is quite a challenge, in more than one way. Beyond the technical difficulties, many might feel that the very task of identifying a group of the least advantaged is rather distasteful, given the stigmatizing pitying and patronizing overtones of such an idea. However, this need not be the case. As we have already shown, such a theory can be constructed with the participation of the disadvantaged, and on the basis of dynamic public reflective equilibrium. This will help both with the technical question of identifying the least advantaged (which we address in the next three chapters) and pave the way for our solution to the question of stigma, which among other things we discuss in Part 3. But to return to this Introduction to the contents of Part 2: Chapter 5 begins with the argument that one obvious and appealing proposal for avoiding the indexing problem is not satisfactory, and moves on to our own proposal for indexing; how, in other words, to compare 'functioning maps' for different individuals. Chapter 6 then explores the question of how to measure functionings, in order to derive functioning maps for representative individuals. In Chapter 7 we then analyse a phenomenon which we call the clustering of disadvantages, which on the one hand allows the identification of the very least advantaged, and on the other offers a way forward towards rectifying disadvantage.

CHAPTER 5

The Indexing Problem

5.1 Introduction

The spectre of the indexing problem – how to identify who the least advantaged on a pluralist view – has hovered above the discussion of Part One. But perhaps it can be avoided. In this chapter we begin by exploring the proposal that if disadvantage is plural, then perhaps pluralism is not the problem but rather the solution. Perhaps the state should aim to isolate each functioning and challenge each area of disadvantage separately. The first question we discuss in this chapter is whether such an approach can be sustained. Our conclusion is that while this is an immensely appealing proposal, it cannot avoid the indexing problem in a satisfactory fashion. So an overall index of disadvantage seems inescapable. In the remainder of the chapter we clarify why such an index is needed, and show how it can be provided. In doing this we take for granted that it is possible to measure the functioning level of each representative individual for each functioning. This, of course, is a major assumption and in the next chapter we to explore how such measurement can and should be done. In this chapter, though, such concerns are put to one side in order to focus on the indexing problem.

5.2 Justice Sector by Sector and its Problems

We start with the question of whether perhaps the pluralism of our approach itself provides a way out of the indexing trap. While identifying the least advantaged overall may be fraught with difficulty, it may be possible to pick out the least advantaged with respect to each category – certainly with respect to each category of secure functioning.[1] But if so, might it not be that we have all we need? That is, it may be that all our practical purposes can be served without coming to an overall assessment of advantage and disadvantage. If this were so, we would not need to solve the problem of constructing an overall index. Education can be left to the department of education, employment issues to the employment regulators, while those lacking bodily health and thus in need of medical services should receive treatment, irrespective of how they fare in other functionings, and so on.[2]

The idea that each policy maker should look only to the area under his or her immediate view is what can be called the 'local justice' approach, to use a term coined by Elster[3] and adopted since by Rawls and others. It should be noted that the local justice view is not automatically one which asserts that the least advantaged in each area should be given priority. For example, many would argue that in education considerable resources should be devoted to those with the highest potential. However our purpose here, initially at least, is simply to consider how to combine pluralism with the view that governments should help the least advantaged, and the local justice approach is one such way. We should say, however, that we find the term 'local justice' slightly unfortunate in that it conjures up images of parish councils and boundary disputes between neighbours. Accordingly we will generally use the term '*sectoral justice*' to capture this idea: justice sector by sector.

There is no doubt that this is an appealing view, and it seems likely that any complete account of governmental responsibility would have to make space for a significant area of sectoral justice (as we will show later). However we cannot settle matters so neatly and easily.

A first problem is that there is often leakage between areas of decision making. This can happen in at least two ways. First, trying to address one concern may have unplanned or unforeseen effects elsewhere. So, for example, attempts to prioritize the claims of the least advantaged in terms of health might inadvertently have effects for the same people's opportunities for work and leisure, for example from an inflexible system of hospital appointments. But there may be less easily avoided effects: for example, addressing disadvantage in education[4] or employment law may have broader economic and social consequences which cannot be avoided. Elster notices a version of this problem himself and claims that 'it is more than marginal but less than pervasive'.[5]

But just as importantly, someone may suffer in one area as a result of a problem elsewhere.[6] In one of the interviews we conducted, an activist who works with people on workfare plans claimed that single mothers who were forced to work could not afford to put their infants in proper (and therefore rather expensive) child care, and had to compromise by leaving the child with illegal caretakers, each of whom would often be looking after as many as ten children. As a result these women's children suffered from insufficient attention and stimulation, and may well later be far less well prepared for education. Low educational achievement might then lead to unemployment, even homelessness, and in general unemployed and homeless people typically suffer greater health problems. Quite possibly the only sustainable way of overcoming such health problems would be to address their homelessness and joblessness, but this in turn might mean tackling low educational achievement. So a priori it is hard to accept the claim that such leakages are 'less than pervasive', and it seems that these various 'leakage' phenomena render sectoral justice insufficient, in the sense of being inefficient, perhaps even to the point of counter-productivity.

Indeed we can press this point further by reflecting on the little-discussed point that political philosophy has tended to take an interest only in a very narrow range of public decision making; essentially those decisions taken explicitly for redistributive purposes. Note that this is not the point, discussed in the Introduction, that there is more to equality than the distribution of material goods.[7] Rather, it is that even within the sphere of material goods governmental action can have important indirect effects. There are vast areas of governmental action which, while not redistributive in their intent, are at least potentially redistributive in their effects. This can include, for example, some actions taken to facilitate growth. Consider the decision about where to locate a new airport, or whether to extend a motorway system, or build a new science park. These will impose costs on some while generating benefits for others. Indeed, the same is true even of the economic management decision to maintain a particular interest rate, or aim at a particular unemployment or inflation target. For example, it has been noted that a period of high inflation is good for people with cash debts, such as those with mortgages on their houses, and bad for people with cash savings.[8] Although rarely thought of in these terms, many central economic decisions have latent redistributive effects and so should come within the scope of distributive justice. To put this another way, potentially any implemented decision may well redraw what we have called the 'functioning maps' of many people. However, because these effects are not within the purview of any redistributive agency, and further, these decisions often create multi-dimensional effects, they simply cannot be approached within a sectoral justice perspective.

What, however, is the force of these objections? The suggestion we are considering is that we do not need to find an overall index of disadvantage. The sectoral justice argument is that we can match disadvantage against agency and leave each agency to attend to the least advantaged in its own sphere. The considerations of leakage and redistribution appear to show that this is over-simplistic. However, they do not show that we need an overall index of advantage; rather they may show only that we need inter-agency communication, co-operation, and co-ordination: joined-up government, as it is sometimes called. The feasibility of this is a further question, but it is at least a theoretical possibility. These problems require a response from sectoral justice theorists, but are not devastating.

However, a deeper, if rather obvious, problem is more threatening. Sectoral justice lacks a general perspective, and therefore cannot tell us how much of a total budget to allocate to particular functionings. Should government spend more on bodily health? On use of imagination? On securing bodily integrity? How can we decide? Now, perhaps this may not seem a real difficulty. What we should do is to aim to bring everyone to a decent level of sufficiency in all functionings, and we should set budgets according to this criteria, rather than raise a general budget for public spending and then engage in an unseemly squabble about how much of it goes where, as we see in contemporary politics. Is such 'multiple threshold' approach to priority setting an appropriate response?

Attractive though this may sound, there remain severe difficulties with this view.[9] First, any threshold view faces the problem of setting a non-arbitrary threshold. The first difficulty is whether there are salient thresholds for all functionings or even for any. Even if it is possible to define what counts as, say, unacceptable bodily health or use of imagination, it might be much harder to define non-arbitrary thresholds for control over the environment, although of course it is always possible to set a standard by some means or other, if only by a democratic procedure or a poll. In that sense the threshold will not be entirely arbitrary. Still, the real difficulties come to the surface when we have to decide how to allocate resources under conditions of scarcity when we cannot meet every threshold for every individual. Under such circumstances the only obvious guidance such a theory appears to give is to maximize the total number of thresholds met in society.

The difficulty of this is easily brought out. Suppose that a certain amount of resources might be required to bring an individual from just below a threshold to just above. Call this '*crossing a threshold*'. On a 'strong threshold' view crossing a threshold is more important than anything else one might do with the same amount of resources, whether it is bringing someone well below the threshold to just below it, or someone above the threshold to well above it, or any combination or iteration of these possibilities for many different people. But exactly for this reason, the strong threshold view seems implausible. Even if there are some examples where it may seem justified to give such weight to threshold crossing, they are surely the exception. The particularly difficult cases will be those where it is possible but extremely expensive to make the last bit of progress from just below the threshold to the threshold itself, whereas with the same resources a great deal of good could be done for people who are even worse off, yet as things stand no thresholds would be crossed. The 'strong threshold' view therefore seems to fetishize a particular level of functioning, leading both to the possibility of inefficiency and to the neglect of the worst off.

Perhaps, then, we should prefer a 'weak threshold' view in which bringing people towards the threshold also has value, even if the threshold is not crossed, and in some cases this value could outweigh crossing the threshold. Thresholds remain relevant, however, as on this view we should never prefer to use the resources on those already above a threshold, however much good we can do.[10] Unfortunately, though, with this modification the view loses much of the theoretical advantage of a threshold view. For, in the presence of inevitable scarcity, it reintroduces the need to weigh and balance differing factors, yet avoiding this was, at least in this context, the prime motivating force behind the multiple threshold view. With the weak threshold view we are back where we started with respect to the indexing problem; indeed, we are worse off. Not only do we need relative weighting principles, we also need to define thresholds.

We can now see a further difficulty. The attempt to avoid weighting leads to an implicit assumption that all categories – or at least all threshold points on all categories – are of equal importance; an entirely arbitrary principle smuggled in without justification. Its motivation is unclear. Should, for example, we really be as concerned with hitting the threshold for '*other species*' (being able to live with concern for and in relation to animals, plants, and the world of nature) as we are with hitting the threshold of the rich categories of '*bodily health*' or '*control over the environment*', for example? Indeed putting this point together with the last shows the difficulty of this view: it assumes first that for every category there is a salient threshold where one is disadvantaged with respect to that category if and only if one falls below it; and second, meeting this salient threshold has equal importance to meeting the salient threshold for every other capability. It would seem remarkable if each functioning had a threshold of this nature.

In sum, we conclude that despite its attractions, the threshold view is insufficient to avoid the indexing problem in any plausible way. The strong threshold view is incomplete, failing to offer any guidance in some cases, while offering implausible guidance in others. The weak threshold view does not avoid the indexing problem. It may well have some role to play, like setting minimum desirable standards, but this is not sufficient in itself to settle questions of budget allocation. An overall index of disadvantage seems prima facie unavoidable if the government is to allocate its budget in any systematic fashion. The question we want to discuss now is whether facing it in practice is actually a manageable task.

5.3 The Problem of Complexity

Our conclusion from the previous section is that, much as states or governments would like to avoid it, they have no alternative to facing up to the problem of trying to solve the indexing problem at least to the extent of identifying those in society who are least advantaged. But before we can square up to that task, we need to return to the question of what it is, exactly, we need to index.

If we are to make a judgement as to whether one person is better off than another we have to be able to come to an understanding of how well each individual is doing with regard to various functionings. The theory of disadvantage adopted here pays attention not just to achieved functionings, but also to the *risk of losing functionings*, together with alternative possible functionings an individual might achieve. We have explained how this might be represented by means of sets of two-dimensional functioning maps. However, it is very hard to see how such sets of maps could be an input into any practical decision procedure. This is what we call the *problem of complexity*.

One tempting way of approaching the complexity problem is to try to attempt to construct a single, cut-down version of the theory of disadvantage – disadvantage-lite, we might call it – for use for practical purposes, of both index and application. However, it is not sensible to start on that task without being clearer, first of all, what we wish to do with a theory of disadvantage. After all, we want a practical theory of disadvantage, which is no more or less complex than required by the task for which we need to use it.

When this is kept clearly in mind the task appears not so daunting after all. The picture we want to put forward is that at no stage does any authority or official need a full account of any individual's state of advantage or disadvantage. Different authorities – depending on their rank in the hierarchy of authorities – will need information of varying complexity. Some will need very general, broad-brush information over the entire range of relevant functionings, while others need very detailed information, but only over a very narrow range.

To explain, let us start by thinking of addressing disadvantage with regard to functionings such as health, bodily integrity, affiliation, use of imagination, and so on. At the front line are doctors, nurses, physiotherapists, social workers, teachers, housing workers, and other professionals. What information do they need in order to take care of their patients and clients, as well as to decide who the least advantaged among them are? It seems absurd to suppose that these people can function only with simplified information. Rather, we think, much of the time they need the most detailed and complex information they can find about the people in front of them. So, for example, a doctor, a nurse, or even a clerk in an emergency room may have to decide which patient should be seen next, and will need sufficient details to deal with such questions fairly and efficiently. By contrast, hospital managers do not need such detail about each patient; indeed it would be distracting. They need to abstract from certain things, but still need fairly detailed information so they can, say, know what to order for the medical stores so they never run out of drugs or let them go out of date. Further up the chain of command, as more strategic decisions are made, a wider range of less detailed information is needed to address questions such as what the hospital should spend its budget on. Different information again is needed for a research council to decide which types of research it should sponsor. In general, there is a hierarchy of abstraction, and the further removed the decision is from the action, less and less detail is needed, but over a wider and wider scope of activities. (And what is true for health is, of course, true for all other functionings, not to mention those who deal with several functionings simultaneously.) At each of these levels some general, perhaps rather vague principles may apply, and the decision makers will need to know only the information that allows them to apply their principles; and this will vary considerably. So eventually, only in areas where one has more than one functioning under one's authority is the index problem relevant.

Therefore, at the highest levels of decision making some sort of overall assessment of disadvantage is needed. Essentially, we accept that while much could be left to sectoral justice, supplemented by joined-up government, the one thing that could not is budget allocation or priority setting. There is no place within the sectoral justice perspective to help. Hence what is needed of an overall theory of disadvantage is merely enough for governments to make decisions about budget allocations, which in practice will almost always be decisions about *raising and lowering existing allocations*. This in turn will require the central agency to know about disadvantage in each sector, but not the facts about the lives of each disadvantaged person.

This inter-sectoral perspective is complex: each ministry or minister should compile statistics and other data about levels of functionings within their sector. Then the treasury (or the government as a unified body) needs a way of deciding how to weigh disadvantages in different sectors, assuming that the budget is never large enough fully to solve all the problems. It is at this stage that an index is necessary. The major question that remains is how the government is able to focus on the least advantaged overall, when presented with only this type of information. The government as a unified body does not need a full statement of each individual's functioning level in order to do its job.

To make one further remark of clarification, we are, in effect, proposing a division of labour between the government and its agencies. At its simplest the government's task is to allocate budgets, with the aim in mind of improving the lives of the least advantaged. The agency's task is to spend the budget according to its agreed rules. Although this picture will become more complicated in Part 3, the salient point for the moment is simply that each decision maker needs to know only the information relevant to the task.

5.4 Avoiding Philosophical Indulgence

The indexing problem, we have argued, cannot be avoided by 'sectoral justice' or a 'multiple threshold' view. Consequently, it seems we need to come to some sort of overall judgement of who is most disadvantaged among people who are disadvantaged in different ways. If we find a way to index disadvantages we could turn a non-reducible plurality into an overall assessment of people's advantage and disadvantage.

Let us, then, continue to postpone to the next chapter the question of how to measure a representative individual's performance on each secure functioning, and imagine that this has been done. We assume that we have, so to speak, representatives of the least advantaged in each category. Now we want to compare their disadvantages, in effect turning an array of functioning maps into a social ordering of relative advantage. Here it might be objected that, despite our reassurances in the last section that the informational requirements are not as daunting as it might seem, nevertheless this is an impossible task. Pluralism is simply the doctrine that different disadvantages are incommensurable. The issue is complex, however, for several reasons. First, as we argued in Chapter 1, different things can be meant by incommensurability. All we are committed to here is what we call 'substitution pluralism', or in other words a narrow sense of incommensurability according to which more of one functioning does not always rectify or make up for the disadvantage or lack of another (even if sometimes this is the best we can do, and is better than doing nothing). Second, although we have accepted the incommensurability of functionings in the sense explained, we have also pointed out that capabilities are conceived as providing alternative possibilities of achieving different functioning sets. So in this sense alternative functioning sets are comparable, at least for a given individual.

This latter point is further confirmed by the fact that particular individuals clearly make such decisions for themselves, being prepared to sacrifice some functionings, or rendering them insecure, for the sake of others. This is possible because some means – especially time and money – can be used to achieve alternative sets of functionings. However, these fragments of commensurability are unlikely to be much help. First, they appeal to individual preferences; and second they are unlikely to yield much of a structured ordering, as there remain limits to the flexibility of any set of genuine opportunities and the sets of functionings it can provide. Hence many people will conclude that we must accept a form of incommensurability which rules out the type of indexing disadvantage needed for the present project.

Sympathetic though we are to this argument, we are conscious that there is a sense in which insisting on incommensurability is a type of philosophical indulgence which is all very well in the seminar room, but very obstructive outside, given the practical problems governments face in designing social policies. Priority setting between budget heads is unavoidable, and if political theorists decline to set out a theoretical structure in which this can be approached, the field is left open to lobbyists and interest groups to pressurize the government to act in ways which may have little to do with the general interest or with ethical considerations. Of course, we would never suggest that lobbyists and interest groups do not have a key, legitimate role in a democracy; on the contrary. However, egalitarian theorists have their role, too. Part of this is to devise ways in which the broader public too should have a fair chance to influence the decision-making process, given that relatively few people have access to decision makers. Ideally this will amount to the provision of a general theoretical perspective, informed by public views, which can provide guidance when special interests collide. Therefore, if it is *only* lobbyism and pressure groups that play a role, then from an egalitarian point of view, this is a serious difficulty and an obstacle to equality.[11] Hence it is incumbent on political theorists (cooperating with the public, as we have described) to think through the task of suggesting ways of bypassing incommensurability and trying to identify the least advantaged.

5.5 *Towards an Ordering of Advantage*

Let us begin schematically. Suppose that at any given time each individual has a given value for each functioning, in terms of their percentile place within the overall population into which they fall, as introduced in Part 1. Note that this is purely an ordinal map. Aspects of cardinality – absolute values and intervals – will be considered in Part 3. As described earlier, a functioning map would be a bar chart with bars at different levels, for each functioning.[12] As we have said, certain policy decisions will in effect redraw people's maps or charts, as they impact on different individuals. The general question, then, is how to provide a way of deciding which impacts to seek.

However, figuring out what counts as being worst off in the comparison of bar charts requires us to translate the bar charts into a single score to determine a total ordering. If there is dominance (where person A ranks higher than person B overall if and only if A and B are comparable among all relevant dimensions and there is at least one in which A ranks higher than B and none where B ranks higher than A) then the matter is straightforward. However, in the presumed absence of dominance a weighting of the functionings is required. This might seem a vain hope and indeed it has often been thought very difficult to go beyond the partial ordering one can derive through a dominance principle. Nevertheless many solutions have been proposed, sometimes providing highly technical or abstract accounts, and sometimes with application to practical reality.[13]

Before moving further we should repeat that we are not, at this point, looking for a definition of the least advantaged in the sense of a philosophical analysis. Rather we want to offer a philosophically grounded mechanism which provides confidence in the judgement that a group is among the least advantaged, for it may seem obvious that there is no one 'true' answer. As children we may have asked: what is worse, being blind or being deaf? To such questions we do not expect that there is a metaphysically true answer. Despite this, many people are in no doubt about the correct answer. And it may be that there is something to be gained by comparing such answers, for it may turn out that there is some sort of broad consensus. Whether or not this consensus implies anything about the ultimate truth of that answer, it could help to initiate and legitimize policies. This, then, provides the clue to a way forward. Rather than attempt to legislate a single answer to the weighting problem – how to weight the different categories – we should explore and compare the answers given by different people. Only when we know the extent of actual (reasonable) disagreement will we know the depth of the indexing problem: how to identify the least advantaged.

At this point the reader may see the rationale behind the way we have suggested to move forward. If it is incumbent on philosophers to think through the task of suggesting a theory of the least advantaged, but there seems to be a problem of the sort we have analysed, why shouldn't we try to frame a democratic procedure rather than search for a truth where there is doubt that there is one? There are benefits here both in terms of the likely progress we will make with the project and the legitimacy with which the results might be received.

It is true, however, that individual valuations might be liable to distortion, false consciousness, or the result of limited experience and thus ignorance of the real nature of various alternatives. Therefore philosophical input is needed too: the philosopher cannot merely abdicate responsibility to democratic politics. This is consistent with our general method of dynamic public reflective equilibrium. Keeping both sides in play is sensitive to the fact that legitimacy in a democracy builds out of people's voices, while at the same time recognizing that not everyone has the interest, insight, or aptitude to speak, but that these people still need to be spoken for.[14] Hence the two approaches can act as a check on each other, providing a standpoint by which citizens can critically scrutinize other citizens' preferences and evaluations.

5.6 Weighting Sensitivity

To move to the details, the heart of the indexing problem is to turn a profile of assessments of apparently incommensurable elements into an overall score. This may seem daunting. However, we should not overestimate its difficulty. We are not unfamiliar with systems with similar aims. Decathlon scoring is a prime example.[15] In some sense sprinting is incommensurable with shot-putting. Yet this does not stop us determining who is best at the decathlon. And, of course, we generally assume that this tells us something else we want to know: who is, all things considered, the most talented all-round sportsman. Second, the task is made easier by the fact that in the case of the disadvantage index there is no need to try to derive anything close to a complete ordering. Rather, at first we need only to identify the *least* advantaged group (by means of a representative person), or perhaps a group of least advantaged groups of different types. Hence it will be better to think of wanting to identify those towards the bottom of the distribution. This is far short of a complete ordering.

Still, even assuming that in principle there is no general conceptual barrier to turning a bar chart into a single score, we are left with the question of how to determine the relative weightings of the different categories. In the decathlon perhaps some athletes believe that the current method of scoring is unfairly biased towards those who are particularly proficient in one event, say the 100 metres. Presumably any functioning weighting we derived would be vulnerable to the same criticism, unless we could find a strong justification for it. How then could we even think that we could derive a weighting that commands general assent?

Moreover, in the decathlon there is a sense in which incommensurability is bypassed. The scoring tells us nothing about the essence of sports, or about the value of the 100 metres versus the long jump. Instead, it reflects empirical achievements in the past.[16] To simplify, suppose 1 per cent of the population of the top 1,000 athletes has run the 100 metres in 10 seconds, while 2.4 per cent has managed 10.1 seconds, and 3.6 per cent 10.2 seconds, and so on, the points one would get for running 100 metres in 10 seconds, or 10.1 seconds, and so on would reflect these relative achievements. Correspondingly, the same points that were given to those who ran 100 metres in 10 seconds will be given to those who achieve the best 1 per cent results in the long jump, and so on. In other words, any metaphysical incommensurability is pushed aside, and instead a mechanism of comparing results is provided, based on statistics of achievements. The latter is commensurable.

This mechanism cannot fully apply to the case of comparing disadvantages because the question of the essence of each category – e.g. what it means to experience a disadvantage in, say, bodily health versus sense imagination and thought – cannot be pushed aside by reducing it to mere statistics. It is clear then, that comparing disadvantage is not like comparing achievement in sporting events where elaborate statistical records can be converted into the judgement that a result in one category is equivalent to a result in another.

Nevertheless the idea of the decathlon is introduced merely as an analogy to show how it can be possible to translate a series of assessments into a single overall ordering, and what can be gained by this, at what price. How is this translation to be done in the case of disadvantage? We already have our categories of functionings, from Chapter 2. Suppose we can rank each person under consideration in terms of their percentile score in each dimension. We assume that because there are a large number of functionings the dominance relation will yield very little. What do we do next? Let us return to the decathlon, conceived now as a way of trying to determine the order of the competitors as all-round sportsmen, rather than as a technical event in its own right. As we have seen, dominance may be of little help in determining an ordering. Consider one pairwise comparison. Suppose one person – Geoff – is an expert shot-putter, but the other – Daley – is far superior in the other nine events Now, it is perfectly possible that some will honestly believe that shot-putting somehow embodies the spirit of athleticism in a way in which no other event can approach, and so propose a method of weighting the events which gives shot-putting enormous influence. By some such measure Geoff may be ranked higher than Daley. We would not want to rule this out. However, this will surely be unusual. In a survey of athletes, past contestants, officials, knowledgeable spectators, and even members of the general public, very few – probably not even Geoff – will agree with a weighting system that puts Geoff ahead of Daley.

This approach yields two clues for developing an indexing methodology. First, rather than arguing about the ideal weighting system or principle, we can use many, different proposals. Second, these weighting systems or principles are not to be generated in any arbitrary fashion, but through democratic consultation. This does not exclude the possibility of using abstract theory – including our own – either as a supplement to other forms of consultation, or in its own right, but this should be just one input into the process. This procedure we call '*Complex Evaluation*'.

It may well be objected that Complex Evaluation is incoherent; using many weightings will lead to a chaotic profusion of inconsistent results. But we have already seen in the Geoff/Daley case that generally this need not be so, and it is easy to produce similar examples in the sphere of disadvantage. Consider a comparison between an unemployed person generally doing badly in most categories of functionings, and a high-flying city trader who does well in every respect except the functioning of play. Perhaps some weightings emerging from a process of consultation will give immense weight to play, and so put the trader below the unemployed person. But, we assume, this will be rare; the great majority will not put the trader, who cannot play, below the unemployed person, who is in poor health, whose shelter is insecure, who lacks social relations and whose sense of affiliation is weak, and so on. This should give us great confidence in the judgement that in terms of overall advantage the city trader does better. The ordering that puts such traders above the involuntarily unemployed will be *very robust*. It will survive the great majority of possible weightings. It will only be defeated in those cases where we afford extreme importance, and a very high weight, to play.

To try to make this idea somewhat more precise, let us use the idea of '*weighting sensitivity*'. A social ordering is weighting sensitive to the degree that it changes with different weighting assignments to the different categories. A social ordering, therefore, is weighting insensitive – *robust* – to the degree it does not change with different weighting assignments to the different categories. The limit case of weighting insensitivity is dominance, where no recalibration can change the ordering. In all other cases weighting sensitivity is a matter of degree.[17] In the Geoff/Daley case and the trader/unemployed person cases the rankings will be highly robust, though falling short of dominance.

Let us emphasize again that the policy task is made easier still by the fact that there is no need to try to derive anything close to a complete ordering. Rather, we need only to identify those groups towards the bottom of the social ordering.

Consider how this might be done. It goes without saying that 'social groups' are not natural kinds, and so any decision to split society into groups will be partly theory driven, partly socially relative, and partly political. Of course the government should always be open to the possibility that it has missed some salient groups, and so should always be prepared to add more, or perhaps merge some categories, or eliminate others. Nevertheless, suppose the division into salient groups has been done, and the government finds itself with, say, fifty groups, and thus fifty representative people (representing populations of different sizes), each assessed for how they perform on each functioning compared with the population as whole.

Clearly how such assessment – performance on each functioning – itself is to take place is another subtle and difficult question. Unlike in the case of the decathlon, the stopwatch and tape measure will not suffice as instruments. As noted, we will return to this vital question in Chapter 6. But let us continue to put it to one side for now. Let us assume that there are fifty functioning maps, and the task now is to determine which maps represent those who are (among the) worst off.

Imagine that through our consultation exercise, the government has arrived at twenty different schemes for weighting categories of functioning (just as there might be twenty different proposals for scoring the decathlon as a means of determining the best all-round athlete). The government's next task is to compute the social ranking for each separate weighting scheme. Hence it will have twenty social rankings of the fifty representatives. Finally, the twenty social rankings should be compared, paying particular attention to the bottom end of the scale.

Suppose it turns out that, on inspection of the social rankings, the same ten representative people almost always turn up in, say, the bottom 25 per cent. Then, first, the social ranking is reasonably robust at the lower end, at least relative to the input weighting functions. Second, as far as social policy is concerned the government can be pretty confident that these people should be at least the initial focus of its attention. This, we believe, would be a very significant result. It would mean that the government had identified a number of groups which could reasonably be called 'the least advantaged' without having to engage with the question of whether one sort of disadvantage is worse than another.

What would make a ranking robust? There are two possibilities. Either the great majority of weighting proposals must be very similar (i.e. there is normative and, in fact, political agreement about which functionings are most important), or disadvantage clusters in the sense that those who are disadvantaged in one respect (or functioning) are also disadvantaged in others. Obviously, a society in which disadvantages cluster appears highly inegalitarian.[18] In such a case, in whatever way these dimensions are weighted, the same people will do badly overall.

However, suppose that on the contrary it turns out – surprisingly enough – that disadvantages do not cluster, and that the social ranking is highly weighting sensitive. In other words, every time we adjust the weightings the orderings change because different people find themselves disadvantaged in different categories of functioning. Thus those at the top on one weighting are found near the bottom on another. If this turns out to be the case, then perhaps the world isn't such a bad place after all. To see why, compare it with the conclusion we would draw in the decathlon case if it turned out that every time we changed the weighting of the individual events, the ranking changed. We would probably conclude that, taking everything into account, these athletes are pretty evenly matched in all-round athletic ability. So in the social case we might conclude that the world is reasonably equal after all. This doesn't mean that there is nothing to be done, but it would mean that there is no clearly least advantaged group, at least in ordinal terms. Here we have our central ideas in solving the indexing problem. These ideas of weighting sensitivity and the clustering and non-clustering of disadvantage will be central to the analysis of the remainder of the book.

5.7 The Pragmatic Method

The method just described for indexing disadvantage shows, in principle, how to solve the problem set out in Chapter 1 of combining a realistic account of disadvantage with a way of indexing disadvantage. To carry out this project in detail would, no doubt, be very laborious and time consuming, although not beyond the resources of the state, and comparable in scale to forms of research routinely undertaken by governments and their agencies. Nevertheless, such an exercise is necessary to acquire a fully accurate picture of the most disadvantaged groups in society.

However, for practical purposes it is worth considering a different approach which while perhaps not as accurate as we ideally might hope, nevertheless may yield useful results with far less expenditure of time and resources. Recall that in particular we were hoping to identify those towards the bottom of the ordering of disadvantage, which is a matter of whether a robust social ordering would be generated at least in the lower reaches. In the last section we argued that a robust lower social ordering could be the consequence of only two possible factors: either there is a great consensus on weighting schemes or there is clustering of disadvantage in the sense that there is a group, or several groups, that suffer from a combination of disadvantages. To obtain this information in detail requires the lengthy process of Complex Evaluation summarized above and explained earlier.

However, there is a way of providing an approximation by means of a potentially very powerful shortcut. Rather than going through the process of generating a plurality of weighting schemes and evaluating the functioning levels of the representative people one by one to check if the ordering is robust, the government could directly investigate whether the factors that would make the ordering robust are present. That is, they can investigate first whether there is convergence on weighting schemes, and second whether there is clustering of disadvantage. If the answer to either of these is positive, this alone should be enough to tell the government whether there are groups of the least advantaged in society. Such an approach can be applied in a relatively economical fashion. This is especially important if the authority that operates this exercise is not the state with all its resources but rather a smaller authority, say a local municipality, that unfortunately does not have access to such resources. Furthermore, it has the consequence that an early start can be made, without having to wait years for the results of a major new research project. Either convergence on weighting or significant clustering should be sufficient to reveal what the authority wants; that is, to identify those towards the bottom of the social ordering.

Indeed, putting the two sides together, a new, even more economical possibility presents itself. Suppose it is found that there is general agreement that several categories of functionings were more important than the others, but that there was no agreement about how to rank these relative to each other. On its own, this cannot generate a group of the least advantaged. While it would allow the authority to identify those who do badly on each of the 'high weight' categories, it would not generate a ranking between someone who does badly on one category relative to someone who does badly on another. However, if in addition the authority can detect clustering of low performance on the high-weight categories of functionings, then once more it can reach agreement on who the least advantaged groups are. This combined approach has a tremendous advantage. Only a limited investigation of clustering becomes necessary, massively reducing the empirical work needed. We call this the pragmatic method.

We have to concede that this method is not perfect, as it will not pick out those who do very badly in a number of 'low weight' categories of functionings, who may well be towards the bottom if the process of Complex Evaluation were used. That is one reason why the present method is less satisfactory than the full method introduced in the last chapter. However, it may be the best method currently available.

Indeed our own investigations suggest that the pragmatic method is a most promising route. Within our interviews (see Appendix 1) we did not attempt to ask people to rank the categories of functioning, for in the absence of detailed scenarios we feel that such an exercise is not helpful. Instead, in the fourth phase of the interview we asked interviewees to list the three most important categories of the fourteen already presented to them on the showcard. Hence by this time they were aware of the categories in which we were interested. In early interviews we simply asked people to name the functionings they found most important, but this led to long lists. It was very easy for people to name four, five, or even more. It was only when we asked people to name just three that we became confident that people were thinking hard about the difficult decision involved.[19]

One problem in our interviews, however, was that some interviewees used terms which were not on the showcard as a functioning, such as housing, clothing, or education. Indeed, usually these terms are used to identify needs or goods. Therefore some interpretation was required to fit such responses into our schema. This interpretation was done usually on the spot while interviewing, by asking the interviewee for clarification and directing them to use the language of functioning. Still, even then interpretation was needed afterwards. A concern for housing, for example, seems to go beyond 'adequate shelter' included under the head of 'bodily health' but neither is it captured by the idea of 'private property' included under 'control over the environment'. Rather, for most interviewees, the salient idea was a 'home' rather than shelter or property. Arguably, this is best understood in terms of 'control over one's environment' and so that is where we will place such concern, although there are elements of 'affiliation'.

'Education' is another term that came up several times at this stage, but it did not always seem to be captured well by the idea of 'sense, imagination, and thought' which is where it is placed on Nussbaum's list. Within our interviews the role of education, especially among the disadvantaged, seemed far more instrumental, as a means towards employment and participation as a full citizen. Hence a concern for education could be seen as a concern for affiliation and control over the environment. 'Security' came up fairly often, too. Within our analysis, however, this is in part a matter of bodily integrity – freedom from arbitrary interference – and in part a matter of control over one's environment (especially when it implies security vis-à-vis foreign threats), but also – and this we find very interesting – partly to be understood in terms of the ability to sustain one's other functionings, rather than as an independent functioning in its own right.

It is interesting then that not everyone felt comfortable discussing categories of *functionings*, and that some interviewees settled more easily into 'basic need' talk. However, putting everything together, we believe that there is a broad consensus, within our sample, that the following categories are to be considered the most important:

- Life;
- Bodily health;
- Bodily integrity;
- Affiliation (more often described as 'belonging');
- Control over one's environment; and
- Sense, imagination, and thought.

We do not claim that 'more important' means 'lexically prior'. Taking risks to health and life in pursuit of other goals of lesser value is part of a normal human life, not to mention the extreme cases such as that of homeless people who put their lives at risk to care for their dogs. Rather the point is that we believe we have good reason to think that in any serious attempt to find relative weightings of the categories some would come out higher than any others, and that they are likely to include, perhaps even comprise, these six. That is not to say that we think that by interviewing a small number of people in the UK and Israel and asking them about the relative importance of our categories of functionings, we have demonstrated what 'the public' believes. However we do have a degree of confidence in our results as we have sought out the particular perspective of 'experts', whether their expertise is derived from being professionals who take care of the disadvantaged, or from experience of being disadvantaged. So what might appear as *subjective* knowledge is, in fact, *democratic* knowledge. Interviewees are not asked about their own preferences but rather about their experience and their intuitions and theories following this experience. Nevertheless, in the event that on a more extensive study a different set of categories emerged this could be accommodated – even welcomed – within our method of dynamic public reflective equilibrium. We do not think that matters can be settled once and for all, and the methodology allows for new data and information to replace that which is now outdated or seen to be inaccurate.

It is also interesting to note that several interviewees commented that while these categories are fundamental, their importance is not so much that they provide the key elements of a flourishing or meaningful life, but rather as preconditions for the achievement of the other functionings. As one interviewee rather cryptically put the point: these are more important, but not in a 'moral sense'.

Now, our study was not, in any case, sensitive enough to detect complete convergence in weighting, even if it does exist. All we can say is that we have identified a group of high-weight functionings. Consequently, as suggested above, this means that the government would need also to investigate clustering of disadvantage in order to identify a least advantaged group. However, as noted, the degree of convergence within the study means that this task will be far more tractable than it otherwise might have been, for once again in order to shorten the process it is only necessary to investigate clustering between the categories of functioning designated most important. In our case the interviews generated the six most important functionings. Several more, such as understanding the law, communication, and mastering the local language, were mentioned a number of times, but our study is too small to conclude anything on this basis. However, the point is that if any government accepts our approach it can easily conduct a wider exercise and interview many more people to get a more accurate picture. It would then need to examine clustering only among these most important functionings.

To conclude, the task of identifying those towards the bottom of the ordering now comes to this: the government needs to take the categories of functionings (now, for this purpose only, reduced to the six or so most important ones) and investigate clustering between them. That is to say, it has to investigate whether, within the general population, there are groups of people who appear towards the bottom in several important categories of disadvantage, whose functionings in these categories are at a low level or very insecure. They will be among the least advantaged. We will show how to make a start on this empirical investigation in Chapter 7. First we turn to the issue of how to derive 'functioning maps': that is, of measuring functioning levels.

CHAPTER 6

Measuring Functionings

6.1 Introduction

Chapter 5 showed how to derive a social ordering from an array of functioning maps. But we have not yet approached the difficult issue of deriving such maps: that is, measuring each functioning. So far we have assumed that each representative person can be assessed for their percentile achievement of the functioning, compared to the rest of the population. But the question remains of how to place people in such an ordering. (There is also the question of whether we need cardinal measurements as well as ordinal. We return to this in Part 3.)

A first problem, which we might call the *problem of fracture*, suggests that it may be very far from straightforward to think we can put people in an ordering with respect to any functioning. Consider again bodily health. The determinants of health may themselves be plural and thus give rise to exactly the same form of problem we have been considering; for example, how does heart disease compare to a digestive disorder? The obvious answer is to try to use the same multiple weighting mechanism, although this time higher hopes are necessary for the output: not just identifying the worst off, but producing an ordering with some structure. This, at least, can be attempted. However, the problem strikes again. After all there are many forms of digestive disorder; how are these to be compared? Here, then, lurks the annoying but intriguing possibility that the problem has a 'fractal' structure: there is pluralism at every level, or at least at every 'macro' level.

While this may create problems for some projects it does not necessarily do so for ours. Remember that our reason for rejecting the 'sectoral justice' approach is primarily that it could not answer questions of priority setting between budget heads. Consequently it may be that an index of overall disadvantage is needed only for this high-level project, and for this fine-grained information is not necessary. Of course health professionals may need very detailed information over a narrow range, but there seems to be no practical purpose that requires a complete statement of someone's advantage level with respect to health 'all the way down'.

Nevertheless, even broad appraisal is far from straightforward. As we said, while the decathlon measures performance with stopwatches and tape measures, no such instruments are at our disposal to measure disadvantage even within a single category of functioning. In some areas proxy measures may be possible, such as years of post-compulsory education, or square metres occupied per person (in housing), but for some functionings on our list, such as health or affiliation, this will be much more difficult. In addition, as previously mentioned, there may often be a clash between professional judgement and subjective experience. Again health is a likely case, but so is sense, imagination, and thought, and practical reason, or the sub-functioning of having shelter.

Consider an example from the European Social Survey of 2002, conducted in fourteen European countries, with regard to how being a member of a group suffering from discrimination affects one's sense of satisfaction with life. Naturally, we could assume that if one belonged to such a group, it would affect one's satisfaction with life *negatively*, and indeed this is generally the case. However, both in Israel and the UK, when it comes to people who define themselves first and foremost as 'members of a group discriminated against', such as ultra orthodox Jews in Israel and radical Muslims and orthodox Jews in the UK, then the more one has a feeling one belongs to such a group, the more one is satisfied with life.

Another example occurs with access to and use of the Internet. Typically we would assume that high use of the Internet would be a sign of affluence, of a good job, and would provide a source of enjoyment, and therefore frequent users would be more satisfied with their lives than people who did not use it so much. Indeed this is often the case. However, when we examine only immigrants or newcomers (those who arrived in the past five years), both in the UK and in Israel, we see that for them the more they use the Internet the less they are satisfied with their lives. Again, this makes sense. Perhaps it reveals the fact that they are not assimilated into society, they do not have friends, and so on, and therefore spend time on the Internet; or they are desperate for information and have no other source. The important point is that because a theorist's assumptions can go wrong we must keep in mind *subjective* measures of disadvantage as well. Yet as mentioned above there are many well-known reasons concerning misreporting, false expectations, and adaptive preferences, just to mention a few, which should make us suspicious of subjective measures, and push us back towards objective measures. Which measure is the most salient, then?

6.2 *The York Model*

There would, it seems, be every advantage in devising a method, that combines both subjective and objective measures, gaining the benefits of both, each providing a cross-check on the other. One very promising model comes from a recent study conducted by Jonathan Bradshaw and Naomi Finch, both from the Social Policy Research Unit at the University of York. For convenience we shall refer to it as *the York Model*. Bradshaw and Finch consider the measurement of poverty. Our interest is not so much with poverty, which in itself does not match up with any particular functioning although it is relevant to many, but rather with the approach these theorists take to measurement. This is worth emphasizing. We are interested in the York Model only for its methodological approach to measurement and not, or at least not directly, for what it measures.

On the face of it nothing should be simpler than measuring poverty: to be in poverty is to have very little money at your disposal. However, matters are more complex. Poverty can be measured in terms of low income, lack of basic necessities,[1] or the inability to afford what someone deeply wishes to do or be: lacking these is often referred to as being 'subjectively poor'.[2] The study suggests that there is an incomplete correspondence between different measures of poverty.[3] For poverty researchers there is an obvious question: which of these indicators provides the best measurement of poverty? Let us review this interesting research and then put forward a suggestion about how to apply it to the problem of assessment.

Bradshaw and Finch base their analysis on a study called *The Poverty and Social Exclusion Survey in Britain*.[4] First they note that in the report rather than using a single measure of poverty, the three mentioned above were used: being subjectively poor, having a relatively low income, and lacking socially perceived necessities. They then make the remarkable observation that while the proportion of poor by each dimension is fairly similar (between 17 per cent and 20 per cent), it can be seen that while 33 per cent are poor on at least one dimension, 16.1 per cent were poor on two dimensions and only 5.7 per cent are poor on all three measures simultaneously. In other words there is surprisingly little overlap between the three poverty indicators.

So, they ask, how can we use these dimensions to identify the poorest people in society? Two approaches are discussed: (i) taking a straight cumulative approach;[5] (ii) giving priority to one measure over another. The authors show why the 'cumulatively poor' is a better (more reliable) predictive tool (or a way of identifying the most poor (or the least advantaged)), and also a better way of distinguishing the poor from the non-poor.

Why do Bradshaw and Finch believe that giving priority to one measure is not a good way to approach the question? Couldn't we attach such priority to, say, subjectively feeling poor (because it indicates that one has all the psychological problems associated with poverty)? Or couldn't we say that current income poverty is not really an indication of poverty? Indeed, the group of those who are income poor but not poor on any of the other dimensions is the largest, which may suggest that income poverty is not a good indication of poverty.

Bradshaw and Finch show that those in overlapping poverty have different socio-economic characteristics to those identified as poor by one measure alone. For example, the proportion of labour market excluded (the unemployed, retired, and those not seeking work) among those who are poor on necessities is 18 per cent, among those who are poor on necessities and income is 54 per cent, but among those who are poor on all three dimensions – subjectively poor, lack necessities, and very low income – the proportion of labour market exclusion rises to 60 per cent. Another example is 'lacking any contact with family and friends'. The frequency of those who lack such contact among those poor on necessities is 8 per cent, among those feeling subjectively poor is 9 per cent, but among those poor on all three dimensions it rises to 13 per cent. In general, those who are cumulatively poor on all three of the dimensions are a group whose socio-economic characteristics are *more unlike* the non–poor than any of the single dimension groups. In other words, the more accumulatively poor one is, the more one's socio-economic characteristics differ from the non-poor. In addition, Bradshaw and Finch analysed how social exclusion was associated with each of the dimensions of poverty. Social exclusion implies exclusion from labour market, exclusion from services, and exclusion from social relations.[6] Again, the more accumulatively poor one is, the more one differs from the non-poor. For example, 4 per cent of the non-poor were service excluded. Among the subjectively poor 37 per cent were excluded, among the necessities poor 46 per cent were excluded, but among the poor on all three dimensions 60 per cent were excluded.

It is interesting to explore why there is so little overlap. Bradshaw and Finch offer six possible reasons, on which we add further comments:

- At least a small lack of overlap is inevitable given the different proportions identified as poor (or in our research as disadvantaged) by each measure used.
- There are cases of transition. For example, some people who have recently retired are poor in the sense of income, but (still) not in the sense of necessities. Or, in the context of our research, a person can become homeless but still be healthy and even still hold a job. Here,

though, issues of risk become highly relevant. Under such conditions these functionings will not be secure.

- 'False consciousness': in the subjective measure, people may claim to be in poverty when they are not by other dimensions, or vice versa, as people might be too shy or too ashamed to admit to poverty.
- 'Low aspirations' can occur in relation to the deprivation measure. People develop a sense of not wanting what they cannot afford.
- Technical, statistical explanations (for example, before or after housing costs).
- Perceptions of poverty vary according to how resources are distributed within the household. Men and women answer differently, in particular in cases where a female non-breadwinner respondent feels poor because her breadwinner partner does not share his income with her.

All these explanations suggest that we should also take very seriously the position of those who are in poverty (or in our case those who are disadvantaged) on at least two of the three measures. Consider the following examples. First, consider those of low income and in deprivation who do not subjectively feel poor. Surely, the best explanation of this is false consciousness, or adapted preferences, or failure to make psychological adjustments to their new situation. Now consider someone who feels poor but is also poor only on a single objective measure. Those on low income who feel poor and yet experience no deprivation must be highly dependent on others such as relatives, friends, neighbours, or charity organizations, or are using up savings or getting into debt, and are therefore highly vulnerable. Those who are materially deprived and feel poor, but have a decent income, could be people with a large number of dependents, or expensive needs such as health treatments, or are servicing accumulating debts. All of these people surely legitimately count as poor. That is to say that their better performance on the third measure could merely reflect some form of false consciousness or misapprehension, or could be a transitional or technical matter.

We conclude that this model suggests that using *two objective* and *one subjective* measures and looking for overlap between at least two measures is a very promising way of assessing disadvantage within each category of functioning. It would be wrong to rely on subjective reports alone because of false negatives and false positives (false consciousness and so on). To counter this, the government should look for either dissatisfaction plus one objective measure, or two objective measures. Hence the least the government can do is take three indicators, one subjective (most often being satisfied or dissatisfied) and two objective.

6.3 Echoes of the York Model

We were sufficiently impressed by the York Model to want to investigate whether it could be applied to measuring performance within our categories of functioning; that is, by means of the combination of two objective and one subjective measures for each category of functioning.[7] Accordingly we asked our interviewees what *three key questions* the government should ask in order to know who are the least advantaged *within* this interviewee's special area of expertise, and we did this referring to a problem with a particular functioning (health, affiliation, use of imagination and reason, and so on). If the interviewee was a recipient we thought of him/her as an 'expert' in the sense that s/he experienced this disadvantage. So we asked about people who had the same disadvantages (e.g. disability, homelessness, unemployment). If the interviewee was a professional expert (social worker, volunteer, doctor, nurse, etc.) we asked about the group of people s/he was serving. We deliberately did not ask them to distinguish between subjective and objective measures, but we were surprised how many of them did refer to this distinction, even though we asked them to do this 'on the spot' and intuitively.

For example, a social worker in Israel who works with teenagers in distress suggested that in order to know to what extent these girls' bodily integrity is insecure, the questions that need to be asked would be two objective and one subjective questions. The two objective questions are: what is their economic situation (the rationale was that the poorer they were, the more difficult they found it to get out of distress) and whether their case involved meeting violence, the rationale for the latter being that if it did, the harm was both physical and emotional and made it almost impossible for them to cure themselves. However, she then added a subjective question: whether they thought they were in distress. When we asked her why this was so, she explained that in most cases people who were in trouble were not aware of it, and since nobody would say they were in distress for no good reason, it implied that if people did answer positively to such a question, the government could assume that they were indeed in serious trouble, which implied that they were likely to be the least advantaged. However, she added, relying on subjective information alone would not be enough because most teenagers in distress wouldn't be aware of their situation, and therefore we could miss cases where there was a genuine problem.[8]

Another interviewee who was at the time unemployed, but who used to work with teenagers who were involved with petty crime and drugs, and who were usually out of school, mentioned three indicators for the extent to which the teenagers he took care of could be autonomous and feel affiliated to their society once again: bodily health, whether they are addicted to drugs, and whether they trust themselves, or believe they have the power to get out of their situation and lead a better life. (Notice also that he used another functioning – bodily health – as an indicator of the degree of disadvantage in the functionings he was referring to, namely autonomy and affiliation. We shall come back to functionings and disadvantages which make an impact on other functionings in Chapter 9.)

A lawyer who works for an Israeli NGO helping Palestinians in cases of human rights violations also suggested two objective and one subjective indicators to describe his clients' control of their environment. The two objective ones were the clients' economic ability (the rich can approach private lawyers and expect better service) and whether the case was attractive to lawyers (if it is, private lawyers will take the case for even a small fee).[9] Then he added a subjective measure, namely how the client viewed their case, which he called 'the degree of desperateness'. As an example he referred to two women who needed to enter to Gaza because their husbands were there, but were blocked by the military; one of these women was emotionally supported by her husband whereas the other was not, and therefore the latter viewed the case as much more difficult to cope with than the woman who was supported.

A blind student who was interviewed suggested three questions which need to be asked in order to know who are the least advantaged among the blind. The first is the degree to which they are autonomous. The second is their bodily and mental health. The rationale for this is that a significant number of blind people have an additional health problem which is related to the fact they are blind. For example, many find concentration very difficult, which obviously affects their studies. The third is a subjective measure: whether they feel they have reached 'self fulfilment' in any way.

We should add that sometimes our interviewees did not suggest subjective measures, but these were often cases when the clients were not capable of using autonomous reasoning. For example, a psychiatric nurse who works with drug addicts suggested three objective measures for sense, imagination, and thought: financial means, whether the person is completely immersed in the drug, and their health. On the other hand, an interviewee who works with the unemployed believes that the emphasis should be on the subjective and therefore suggested *two* subjective measures.

But in general, a significant proportion of interviewees suggested a combination of two objective and one subjective measures. Of course we do not want to suggest that this on its own settles anything, and in every area more detailed investigation are necessary. But we believe this to be a very promising approach to indexing performance *within* a single category or functioning. With regard to each functioning, the government should ask the experts (both by experience and by profession) for two objective and one subjective measures, and then come to a definition of the least advantaged within this category of functioning according to these measures.

This method of assessment is particularly appropriate given our understanding of disadvantage as incorporating the idea of risk to functionings. This is revealed in both these objective and subjective measures; but in particular insecurity typically leads to anxiety and lack of satisfaction, although not invariably so. As we have noted risk is not always accompanied by anxiety, but even where it is, people may not experience lower levels of functioning than others in objective terms. So even though the York Model does not encode all we need to know about risk, to a degree this measure of disadvantage is naturally more accommodating of ideas of risk and security than some purely objective measures.

A further advantage in incorporating the subject's own perception of their functioning level is best explained by means of an example of some fascinating data from the European Social Survey of 2002 concerning the way in which employed and unemployed people value strong social relationships. Typically the unemployed report a lower success rate in this, while at the same time giving it a higher importance, and for a good reason: unemployed people are often greatly in need of friends and family. How well one does on a functioning and how high one values that functioning are, of course, independent dimensions. However, putting the two together yields what we might call someone's 'intensity of dissatisfaction', how much they care about the fact that they do badly. This seems a vital piece of information. It is important to see that for unemployed people lack of social networks is a major problem, whereas for those in work it is probably rather less so. Even though the York Model does not directly measure this, it does make room for some recognition by incorporating self-assessment. In doing so it provides one way of allowing some place for intensity of dissatisfaction. It allows representative people to give extra weight to the dimensions they most care about, and fail to do well in, by allowing them to report their dissatisfaction as more intense. By contrast, those who are relatively indifferent to the same category may well report little dissatisfaction even if their performance on some objective measure is low.

6.4 Risk and Security

Before ending the discussion of measuring disadvantage we must turn to the question of risk and security. The reason this arises is that the task of the government on our view is to provide genuine opportunities for *secure* functionings, hence the government needs information about the security of functionings of its citizens – whether they are able to sustain their achieved functioning level – and the question arises of how it can acquire this.

Although, as we noted, the York Model allows some room for anxiety about the future to have an impact on the level of disadvantage, it does not automatically encode objective aspects of risk. The fact that I have a job today says nothing about whether it is a day's casual work or a sinecure for life. And the fact that I am healthy today does not imply that I will be in a year's time, if hazardous wastes are being transferred for burial near my house. However, taking a wider view and looking at the individual's social circumstances or context immediately provides more information.

Indeed, statistics will provide much of what we need. Imagine that among certain groups – perhaps the young, recent immigrants, or the low paid – there is a high degree of mobility in employment or housing, with those moving jobs or homes also experiencing periods of unemployment or homelessness. This, then, gives a prima facie reason to believe that these functionings are not achieved securely by people within these groups. The fact that fifty honey collectors are eaten by tigers every year in Sundarban is surely proof enough that honey collectors experience gross insecurity of life and health. In general, then, although individual functioning is not an indicator for the degree of security, statistics often can be.

Furthermore, owing to what we earlier called 'cross-category risk', one risk can spread to others. Consider someone under threat of being homeless. This would also make other functionings very insecure. Statistics show that for homeless people life expectancy is lower, that it will be harder to maintain health, to avoid attacks and beatings, and to remain within the law. Hence one disadvantage can be a 'risk factor' for others.

However, statistics cannot show *all* insecurity. First, there are some new threats where there will be no statistics yet. Second, the fact, say, that no one has died in the last ten years from an explosion at a nuclear power station is not sufficient to demonstrate that the risk of this happening can be discounted to zero. Past frequency does not equate to probability in such cases, and so statistics will inevitably be misleading. In addition, some apparent insecurity is welcomed as a part of lifestyle choice, especially among certain groups. Therefore statistical trends provide a reasonable but not complete picture of security and involuntary insecurity of functionings. Judgement, including normative judgement about the acceptability of risks, will also be necessary.

We need, nevertheless, to distinguish the type of investigation we are interested in from that which already pervades society. Every week a new risk is discovered, newspapers are full of the details, agencies are criticized for slow reactions, while politicians promise swift, firm action. A vast amount of effort and energy is spent in identifying, contesting, and reducing risks, and a huge academic literature now exists in response.[10]

Our own primary interest, at least from the point of view of this project, is much more limited. We are especially concerned with sub-populations who are involuntarily exposed to exceptional risks. Although vitally important in themselves, risks that spread throughout the whole of the population are the concern of distributive justice in a different way. Society needs to take a decision about whether to use its resources to mitigate a risk, and these resources must be drawn from somewhere. It may be that the burden falls unevenly, or especially on those who are already worst off, who may find other services withdrawn to pay for the new programme. Thus even risks that fall on everyone raise questions of distributive justice. However, for our purposes the government needs especially to know about exceptional risks; either those that are considerably out of line with the rest of society, or where a large group is living with a much higher degree of risk than they need to be, given the possibility of adjustments elsewhere, e.g. when a nuclear reactor is built near their homes, or when public hatred and intolerance targets one group, such as anti-Semitic or anti-Muslim attitudes in Europe. When and whether risks are genuine will often be a contested matter. But the general point remains. It will often be a task of government to take into account the fact that some groups of people are forced to take risks that others are not, and, on our view, they need to know this in order to construct an index by which they can determine which groups in society are least advantaged.

6.5 Conclusion

This, then, concludes our account of how to measure disadvantage and thereby derive functioning maps. We do not pretend to have given a complete method, still less a practical approach that could be used right away. Still we think that the York Model provides a sound approach which from the point of the view of the current project has many advantages. With this now in place, we can move to the next question:

whether there is reason to believe that disadvantage in the 'high-weight functionings' identified in Chapter 5 cluster together. This is the task of the next chapter, and it will provide an answer to the question of whether there are clearly identifiable groups of people in society who are among the least advantaged.

CHAPTER 7

Clustering of Disadvantage
and Empirical Research

7.1 Introduction

One of the main conclusions of Chapter 5 is that there is a reasonable consensus that the most important categories of functioning are life, bodily health, bodily integrity, affiliation, control over the environment, and sense, imagination, and thought. This is not to say that other categories are not important, or that everyone places these six categories above all others. Indeed we know this not to be the case. Rather, we believe, if our interviews are in any measure representative, the great majority of people will acknowledge the importance of these six categories, and that no other functioning receives such widespread acknowledgement. Any group doing badly on all of these – and here we include vulnerability to loss of functioning as well as low functioning – will be included uncontroversially amongst the least advantaged in society. But any group that fares badly in several of these categories will also be among the least advantaged according to our method. On the other hand if we find no clustering among these functionings then we would conclude that there is, all things considered, no least advantaged group in society.

To find whether there is a least advantaged group or set of groups in society, it is necessary to conduct empirical research, surveying the level of functioning of people in society on the six salient categories identified above. To explore this ideally we would conduct a wide and systematic survey using the York Model looking for three measures, two objective and one subjective, of each functioning. Unfortunately no such data exist, and to acquire them would be an enormous undertaking. In the absence of such data, however, it is possible to get useful, if less accurate, data by looking at other, existing studies. To be clear, it is beyond the scope of this book to attempt to carry through the systematic project of identifying the least advantaged group in any society. Rather our aim has been to provide, and philosophically justify, a method which is able to do this. Here we demonstrate how the approach will work, and by doing so we hope to identify some groups of which it can be said with a high degree of confidence that they are towards the bottom of the social ordering. If the method we put forward is accepted, it will then be possible for governments to carry out a similar exercise on a larger scale. Thus the following chapters should be read as a report of a *pilot* research project.

7.2 Objects of Empirical Research

When we come to explore empirical research which looks at performance on the six categories of functioning among different social groups, it is worth distinguishing three objects of empirical research, each having a different rationale.

(1) *Clustering and dynamic clustering.* The simplest project is to look at 'snapshot' figures that reveal correlations between different forms of disadvantage. This can help with the indexing problem as correlations among forms of disadvantage constitute the type of clustering, which, we have suggested, would indicate that a group or a number of groups are among the least advantaged.

While researchers look for clustering of disadvantages, they should pay special attention to how clustering of disadvantage may persist, and indeed accumulate, over time. We call this *'dynamic clustering'*, by which we mean both cases where a person 'accumulates' disadvantages over time, and the reproduction of disadvantage over generations. An example of dynamic clustering for a single individual would be a case where one is first unemployed, then becomes homeless, then loses one's friends, and then becomes very ill, and yet this does not all happen immediately but rather accumulates gradually over time. An example of cross-generation dynamic clustering would be a case where parents' disadvantage (e.g. drug addiction or teenage pregnancy) appears among their offspring.

Notice that at this stage and with this object of research, there is no need to investigate causal relations, but only to find clustering of disadvantages. Identifying clusterings is essential to the task of indexing disadvantages, according to our method.

The notion of dynamic clustering may seem particularly important in the analysis of this book, as it appears that it can help identify groups who are at particular risk, even if they do not as yet suffer problems. So if, for example, a social group has statistically a higher prospect of developing heart problems, this gives reason for considering preventative social policies for those who are not yet ill or with any apparent problems. Yet without knowledge of causation, quite what would count as a preventative policy is uncertain. If, for example, the cause of poor health is poor affiliation, then this should lead to different social policies than if the problem is poor diet. But in any case, in order to be sure that there is more than accidental correlation, we need to know more than bare statistics; we need to understand the causal patterns behind clustering. This brings us to the second object of research.

(2) *Corrosive disadvantage.* A second project, which clearly requires more sophisticated methods of study, would be to look at *causal relations* between disadvantages, to try to understand *why* patterns of disadvantage form and persist. Clustering on its own refers to 'joint frequency' of different disadvantages – poor or insecure functionings in different categories. To go beyond this and show causation we have, obviously enough, to look for reasons to believe that one disadvantage is the cause of another. We will call the sort of disadvantage that has negative effects on other functionings *'corrosive' disadvantage.*

Corrosive disadvantage can also be dynamic; it is often transgenerational too. Exposure to particular disadvantages, it has been argued, can cause harm to the offspring of the disadvantaged.[1] Conversely, advantage at home cause advantages for the children once they grow up. For example, better-educated parents tend to talk more to their children and use a wider vocabulary,[2] which in turn allows them to succeed at school and university, and thereby find better jobs. Those who lack a wide vocabulary find it frustrating to communicate, and are more likely to get angry and lose their temper and even become violent.[3] So this is an example of a corrosive disadvantage which takes effect over and through generations. It is far fetched to suggest that growing up with disadvantaged parents is *necessarily* a disadvantage in the sense that it implies that the child's functionings must develop less successfully. But it does imply that some of these functionings are at greater risk, and this in turn makes it likely that the child will have to invest more effort and time, and perhaps to risk other functionings, in order to secure these functionings.

(3) *Fertile functioning.* Our project in this book is not only to consider clustering of disadvantage, but also to try to investigate a further question: how is it to be overcome? Consequently, side by side with looking for corrosive disadvantages, empirical researchers should seek out functionings,

or perhaps the preconditions for functionings, which spread their good effects over several categories, either directly or by reducing risk to the other functionings. This we call a *'fertile functioning'*.

Understaning corrosive disadvantages and fertile functionings are vital for effective social policy, and we will discuss what is currently known about them in Chapter 8. Now, though, we will take up the question of whether it is possible to demonstrate that clustering takes place.

7.3 *Clustering of the 'High-weight' Functionings*

Although, as noted, to carry through our project in detail an extensive and elaborate new empirical research project is needed, we have said that we can at least illustrate the method by looking at examples of clustering presently available in the literature. However, at this point one might raise doubts about whether there will be much research of relevance. After all, the results of the last chapter mean that we are specifically interested in detecting clustering between six 'core' functionings: life, bodily health, bodily integrity, affiliation, control over the environment, and sense, imagination, and thought. Thus we have a very specific research agenda, and given that other available surveys and research are often based on categories such as resources (e.g. money, housing), preference satisfaction, or satisfaction with life, it may seem that we will struggle to find much. Within our list of categories neither resources nor preference satisfaction make a direct appearance. Rather resources are, by and large, implicitly considered as something that is desired mainly as a means of achieving some of the functionings, at least in predominat market societies, and preference satisfaction, again by and large, is treated as a consequence of doing acceptably well in a sufficient range of functionings. It may seem that this makes existing research unavailable to us.

However, in some surveys the categories of functionings might be latent, but can be drawn out of the data. For example, in the above mentioned ESS, people were asked about their social affiliation and relationships (e.g. whether they could trust others around them) and about their health, and it is interesting to note that there is a remarkable clustering of bad health along with feeling one does not have proper relationships.[4]

A second reply, though, is more important. Remarkably, a number of important recent studies do use the language of functionings, or something very close to it. For example, John Hills' significant work refers to some functionings such as having friends (affiliation), when he discusses social exclusion and its clustering with exclusion from production, consumption, and politics.[5] And in the widely cited research by Deepa Narayan et al.,[6] it is claimed that poverty has psychological dimensions such as powerlessness and voicelesness (lack of control over one's environment), dependency (lack of use of reason and being autonomous), and above all loss of affiliation (to which Narayan et al. add a loss of a sense of solidarity and respect). Narayan et al. claim that social solidarity is one of the most important assets for the disadvantaged or the poor. It is observed that the poor initiate what we termed '*Inverse cross-category risk*' (see Chapter 3) when they make considerable sacrifices to ensure that they maintain (or gain) a sense of affiliation and social solidarity.[7]

So what can we learn from existing research? Consider, for example, the notable and innovative works of Michael Marmot, Richard Wilkinson, and associates[8] on the social determinants of health. This research turns out to be enormously important for our project, showing a clustering in several core functionings. The functionings in questions are life, health, affiliation, sense, imagination, and thought, and control over the environment. Just as interestingly, these works emphasize the importance of one's relative place in a hierarchy as perhaps even more important than one's absolute position. This of course makes our particular version of the clustering method of measuring disadvantage particularly appropriate, as it too takes disadvantage to be relative. Marmot and Wilkinson together consider five of our categories of functionings. The sixth, bodily integrity, is also included in a smaller-scale study of the Chicago heat wave by Eric Kleinenberg,[9] which also brings in many of the other categories too. Hence these studies are especially interesting from the point of view of this book, so we shall consider them in more detail.

Michael Marmot's *Status Syndrome* argues that there is strong correlation between on the one hand control over one's environment and on the other one's health and longevity. The lower one is on the social hierarchy ladder, the fewer are one's opportunities for control over one's environment, and therefore, Marmot claims, the worse one's health and the shorter one's life expectancy. Marmot lists several disadvantages that cluster: the lower the prestige of one's job the worse the health of the job's possessor; if one lacks control over one's life and lacks love and social connectedness, one is more often ill;[10] the less one has the skill of use of sense, imagination, and thought, the earlier one is likely to die.[11] Marmot dismisses the suggestion that higher income is in itself the reason why hierarchies and relative position may be important for health: he claims that money matters much only with low levels of income and only because it increases one's capabilities.[12] On the other hand, he suggests that the functionings of social affiliation and status, and control over one's environment, explain why hierarchies impact on health.[13] He writes: 'All societies have rankings because individuals are unequal in a variety of ways; but not all societies have the same gradient in health. What matters is the degree to which inequalities in rankings lead to inequalities in capabilities. (...) The lower in the hierarchy you are, the less likely it is that you will have full control over your life and opportunities for full social participation. Autonomy and social participation are so important for health that their lack leads to deterioration in health.'[14]

The conclusion of the research is that lack of social affiliation and relationships, which can in turn result from racism, stigmatization, hostility, and unemployment, may lead to lower life expectancy. This social exclusion also prevents people from being properly educated, or experiencing control over their political environment (by participation), and is psychologically damaging and harmful to one's health. Social exclusion even increases the risk of disability,[15] further harming one's control over environment and bodily integrity.

Not being able to work also clusters with other disadvantages. According to Wilkinson and Marmot's report, 'evidence from a number of countries shows that, even after allowing for other factors, unemployed people and their families suffer a substantially increased risk of premature death.'[16] This, Wilkinson and Marmot stress, is true not only when people actually become unemployed, but also once they *sense that their job has become insecure*, which brings out once again why it is so important to include risks and vulnerability in the analysis of disadvantage. Those whose employment is insecure are 2.5 times more likely to suffer poor mental health, and 1.25 times more likely to be ill, than those whose employment is secure.[17]

Wilkinson and Marmot go on to show clustering of health with affiliation and social relations.[18] Age-adjusted mortality among white Americans with a low level of social integration is twice as high as the age-adjusted mortality rate among white Americans with a high level of social integration. In Sweden the figures are even more dramatic: four times as much. In addition, clustering occurs between bodily health, housing, and whether one uses hard drugs, which arguably can be seen as, or can lead to, lack of control over environment. Those with poor health, homelessness, and no access to work are nine times more likely to use drugs than those with no such disadvantages.[19]

An important study by Eric Klinenberg also points to the clustering of disadvantage. He argues that heat waves such as the one that took place in Chicago in 1995, in which 739 people died, are not merely a *natural* disaster.[20] In the terms employed in our book, heat waves exert their influence by combining natural phenomena with lack of social relationships (isolation), lack of control over one's environment, poor sense, imagination, and thought (not being able to understand the news), feeling insecure about bodily integrity, and poor health. Analysing their isolation, Klinenberg notes that more than a fifth of the Chicago victims died alone. He indicates that many elderly isolated people live in literally segregated areas that do not allow their inhabitants to establish social connections. Moreover, since these are areas notorious for their high levels of crime, many of the victims were too afraid to open a window or go out into the streets to escape the heat at home, and so died of heat-related causes. Their concern was not only about theft, but perhaps even more worryingly, personal assault and hence risk to bodily integrity. To protect themselves from risks of crime many people took risks with their health, which in a significant number of tragic cases led to death: an *inverse cross-category risk*, in our sense.

But isolation was not the only problem. These people were also disadvantaged in the sense that they never got to participate in the formation of the public agenda and therefore had no impact on what (and how) news would be broadcasted. Klinenberg claims that news reported about the forecasted heat wave focused on what interested those who were not going to be most adversely affected by the heat wave, ignoring these elderly isolated people who did not get the information and advice they needed. The officials interviewed on the radio and TV expressed their thoughts in terms of a coming 'natural disaster' ignoring the social problems that would concentrate its effects. The conclusion of Klinenberg's study, then, is that in the circumstances of this particular heat wave, lacking social relationships, poor use of imagin-ation and thought, as well as a high fear of crime, were risks to one's health and life.

Finally, the convergence of disadvantage in health and in use of sense, imagination, and thought was mentioned in one of our interviews as well. We asked one of the physicians to point to *the* key factor that might determine the chances of a seriously ill patient being cured. In reply she immediately pointed to the patient's intelligence. Uneducated and unin-telligent patients, she said, would become aware of the fact that some-thing is wrong with their health later than would intelligent people. According to this physician unintelligent patients will then be reluctant to seek advice, or will tend to seek the advice of non-professionals (thus they will turn to friends, religious leaders, or witchcraft, instead of their GPs), and when they do meet their doctors they will often fail to understand the diagnosis, and then fail to follow the prescriptions. Thus being educated and the use of imagination and thought, cluster with health.

7.4 Further Examples of Clustering

There are many examples of existing research that also points to clustering of various other disadvantages. Below is a brief review of just two
studies.

Living within the Law, Affiliation, and Control Over One's Environment
In his book *Why Social Justice Matters*, Brian Barry discusses a somewhat
neglected clustering of disadvantages among blacks in the USA; between
their inability to live within the law, their loss of a sense of affiliation and a
growing sense of alienation, and finally their loss of political rights, which
is part of the functioning of control over one's environment. Let us
explain.

In more than twenty US states there is a 'three strikes and you are
out' policy.[21] For example, in California 'any person convicted of a
serious felony who previously has been convicted of a serious felony in
this state or of any offense committed in another jurisdiction which
includes all of the elements of any serious felony, shall receive, in
addition to the sentence imposed by the court for the present offense,
a five-year enhancement for each such prior conviction on charges
brought and tried separately.'[22] In some states the actual implication
of this law is that those found guilty three consecutive times serve a life
sentence.

Now, according to Barry, since blacks in the USA are convicted of
more felonies than whites for various reasons[23] the percentage of blacks
who are sent to prison as 'third time strikers' is much higher than their
size in the general American population. In California, for example, the
ratio is 6:1.[24] One enormous problem in the USA, Barry rightly argues, is
that those convicted of drug offences suffer a lifetime ban on receiving
welfare benefits, and – we should add – find it immensely difficult to find
a job, in view of the fact that nobody wants to hire a convicted drug
offender. Therefore they are drawn into crime again. We see then a
clustering of disadvantage: these people cannot live within the law, they
lose control over their environment – even if they initiate a move towards
returning to work they are not likely to be hired – and they can't feed
themselves or their families. Furthermore, they lose their right to vote,
and therefore their affiliation to the political community. As Barry argues,
the impact of this on black people is massive.[25]

Sense, Imagination, and Thought, Health, and Nutrition
As we noted in Chapter 3, when a family spends less on food, their children
might fail to get the right balance of vitamins, minerals, and proteins; at the

same time they consume too much sugar and carbohydrate. But there is yet another disadvantage that enters this clustering, namely not being able to use sense, imagination, and thought properly. In Israel, when the economic situation deteriorated in the late 1990s and a significant portion of the population became poor to the extent that children went hungry, teachers reported time and again that these children could not concentrate at school and their educational achievement declined. Indeed, many researchers have found that children who are hungry cannot study properly and their results are much inferior to satisfied children.[26] In the USA the poorest 20 per cent spend about 60 per cent of what the middle twenty per cent spend on food,[27] and this must imply that these children do not have the same chances to flourish as the middle or the upper classes .

As we mentioned when discussing the idea of *inverse cross-category risk*, in order to secure the functionings of health and bodily security one often has to risk other functionings. If a patient has to stop working in order to be hospitalized, or if a person has to switch to organic food due to allergies, these might be very costly, and many poor people cannot afford them. Alternatively, they have to risk other functionings. Thus clustering is almost inevitable and is even initiated by the disadvantaged person herself. The situation is even harsher among ethnic minorities, e.g. Israeli Arabs, French Muslims, American blacks, and so on, who tend to be poorer. For example, while 42 per cent of the Jews in Israel reported that they neglected their dental health to secure other bodily health, 64 per cent of Israeli Arabs had to do so.[28] We do not know of figures for those who turned to crime, such as tax evasion and purchasing stolen goods, to meet their needs, but we can speculate that this must have happened too.

7.5 Conclusion

The main aim of this chapter has been to take first steps towards determining whether, on our method, any social group or groups can be identified as being among the least advantaged. In the light of the argument of previous chapters this reduces to the question of whether there is clustering between the categories of life, bodily health, bodily integrity, affiliation, control over the environment, and sense, imagination, and thought, which are the categories that emerged from our interviews as the most significant. In addition, we wanted to point out that elements of clustering could be detected very clearly. The above examples seem to supply strong enough evidence that clustering does take place.

It should, however, be noted that these studies are suggestive rather than provide a definitive answer. That is, they show convergence of various disadvantages, and suggest that there might be causal relations between disadvantages for particular groups of individuals, and that these causal relations are systematic, which will explain why clustering exists. However in themselves they are not comprehensive enough to identify the least advantaged in society, and that is not their aim. Still, they do provide evidence that there are some groups that are very likely to be among the least advantaged, and provide every reason to believe that when detailed studies are done, other groups – of which there may be many, partially overlapping – will clearly emerge. While there is room for further research and analysis of existing research, our aim here was to show that there is enough evidence that disadvantages cluster and that therefore there must be groups in societies which can uncontroversially be regarded among the least advantaged. Now we want to move forward and ask what societies should do about this.

PART 3

Public Policy

Introduction to Part Three

The consensual starting point of this study – that governments need to give special priority to the worst off – has now become the injunction to 'decluster disadvantage'. The least advantaged, on this view, are those who suffer from very low, or from insecure and vulnerable, functioning across a range of functionings. A society which successfully declusters disadvantage in effect gives priority to the worst off by making it unclear who the worst off are. Some will be less well off in one respect, others in a different way, but no one by multiple measures.

So far, however, we have said little about the social policies that may help achieve these aims. One thing we have said, however, is that governments have every reason to try to discover what we have called corrosive disadvantages (those which cause other disadvantages) and fertile functionings (those which benefit other functionings). This topic naturally follows from the last chapter. The search for correlations between disadvantages to demonstrate clustering can hardly avoid at least speculation about causal connection, and so we now try to deepen the analysis by exploring such causal connections and thereby try to identify fertile functionings and corrosive disadvantages. This is the task of Chapter 8.

Chapter 8, therefore, discusses what we could call the 'where' question: where should governments act? Two other questions of equal importance then arise: for whose benefit should they act, and how should governments do it? The 'who' question returns us to the issue of strength of priority to the least advantaged and combines philosophical issues about urgency of claims, with technical issues about the meaning of declustering and policy issues concerning the division of labour between government and its agencies. All of these are addressed in Chapter 9.

It is one thing to have identified groups of people to benefit, and to understand the general areas in which they need help. It is yet another to say what sorts of social policies will be appropriate to address a particular problem. This is a particular challenge within a pluralist view in which benefits in one area can create costs for the same people, or for others in other areas. Hence we need to be sensitive to the total impact of a particular policy. This generates the third question: *how* should governments intervene? Chapter 10, the last of the main chapters of this book, explores some of the complexities surrounding this issue.

CHAPTER 8

―――――

De-clustering Disadvantage

8.1 Introduction

As argued in the previous chapter, the causal pathways which bind forms of disadvantage together need investigation. Now, it is very plausible that such causal mechanisms exist. For example, in Chapter 3 (on risk) we introduced the concept of *inverse cross-category risk*, where an individual's attempt to achieve or secure one functioning led to risks for other functionings, such as the attempt to overcome a feeling of hunger and achieve satiation by consuming food laden with sugar and carbohydrates led to risks to health. In other cases there are more direct causal connections between functionings, where functioning at a low level in one area will lead to poor functioning in another. In these circumstances there will tend to be a variety of mechanisms clustering disadvantage. Chapter 7 introduced more subtle cases, such as poor social networks leading to risk of early death. In de-clustering disadvantage the authorities need to target these mechanisms to achieve the appropriate effect.

In this chapter we explore the issues of de-clustering disadvantage. Sections 8.2 to 8.4 look at some examples from social science, which may help theorists and governments identify corrosive disadvantages and fertile functionings. Sections 8.5 and 8.6 then explore some more technical questions: 8.5 looks at ordinal and cardinal measurements, and 8.6 at some undesirable forms of de-clustering.

8.2 Corrosive Disadvantages and Fertile Functionings

For clarity, we distinguished in Chapter 7 between two cases. First there are those where a disadvantage in one functioning leads to disadvantages in others. This we have called a '*corrosive disadvantage*'. In other cases, doing well in one functioning (or preconditions of a functioning) will lead to improvements in other functionings. This we have named a '*fertile function-ing*'. It may be tempting to assume that these are simply different ways of referring to the same thing – that one functioning can have good and bad effects elsewhere. However, it should not be assumed that this would always be the case. To see this, consider the example of lack of secure bodily integrity, such as living in constant fear of arbitrary assault. This will hamper an affected person's life in many ways. At the same time, it does not seem that it is always the case that full bodily integrity will lead to any further advantage. So absence of bodily integrity is corrosive, whereas its presence is not necessarily fertile. For a contrary example, consider a 'sense of humour'. A lack of a sense of humour may have relatively few other effects, but those with a sense of humour may find it helps them through life in a number of positive ways. Hence its absence is not corrosive, but its presence may well be fertile.

This last example may seem somewhat contrived, and one may say that a lack of a sense of humour might also be corrosive in some social contexts – for example in trying to make friends in the first year at university – but not in others. However the general point, that corrosive disadvantages and fertile functionings are not mirror images of each other, can be brought home merely by reflection on the point that what causes a problem for someone may not always provide a causal pathway out. If someone falls into drug addiction because of parental abuse, ending that abuse, even replacing it with parental love and affection, may not be sufficient to end that addiction: physiological intervention as well as psychological help may have become necessary to undo the damage. 'Causation in' is not always the same as 'causation out'. To use a well-known example, if someone is run over by a steam roller, then the cure is not to have the steam roller reverse back over them.

Conversely, even when a cure for some malady is discovered, it is important to be careful also not to reason from the cure to the cause. Think of getting rid of a headache by an aspirin. It is a quick, cheap way and is effective. However, this does not mean that lack of aspirin is the cause of the headache.

With this in mind it is worth reflecting on a very interesting argument provided by Susan Mayer, which provides what we believe to be another example of the distinction between corrosive disadvantages and fertile functionings. It is well-known that severe poverty leads to problems with being educated, maintaining one's health, and finding shelter. Yet the further benefits of income and wealth beyond a certain level are often contested. Mayer's book opens with a detailed and depressing description of how poor children have more than their share of problems:

[Poor children] usually weigh less than rich children at birth and are more likely to die in their first year of life. When they enter school, poor children score lower on standardized tests, and this remains true through high school. Poor children are also absent from school more often and have more behavior problems than affluent children. Poor teenagers are more likely than teenagers from affluent families to have a baby, drop out of high school, and get in trouble with the law. Young adults who were poor as children complete fewer years of schooling, work fewer hours, and earn lower wages than young adults, raised in affluent families. As a result, children raised in poverty are more likely to end up poor and in need of public assistance when they become adults.[1]

In other words, Mayer describes a case of clustering of disadvantages where not being able to earn a proper income correlates with a whole cluster of other disadvantages, and the evidence suggests that lack of money is a corrosive disadvantage. However, Mayer claims that the relationship between parental income and children's outcomes is more complicated than it might seem. She accepts that transferring more money to the poor's children to meet basic necessities would help. Basic nutrition, health, and comfort make a huge difference. But will money for goods and services beyond *some minimum* significantly increase a child's chances for success? Mayer's thesis is that once children's basic material needs are met, additional money on its own is only of marginal benefit. Characteristics of their parents become more important to how children turn out than anything additional money can buy.[2]

Mayer points to an interesting phenomenon, but what we should conclude from this is less clear. From her findings she reasons that the fact that poor people's children fare worse than rich children 'does not suffice to prove that lower parental income *per se* hurts children'.[3] We suggest that things are somewhat more complex: the data *are* consistent with the interpretation that lower income causes the harm. However, this is independent from the claim that a higher income is necessarily the cure. Not being able to earn a proper income is a corrosive disadvantage, because it often prevents one from having genuine opportunities to secure one's functionings; but – beyond some minimum – being able to earn more is not necessarily a fertile functioning. Aside from the fact that income is not a functioning (rather it is a facilitating precondition of many functionings), having more money is not always fertile, in the sense that it does not necessarily secure other functionings, or at least not as well as some other functionings can. (We return to this example below.)

There are many further important gains if the state is able to detect causal relations between different categories of advantage and disadvantage, namely by identifying corrosive disadvantages and fertile functionings. In brief summary, one gain is that observing such causal relations will provide evidence that clusters of disadvantage are in some sense systematic, rather than accidental or a coincidence. This will presumably raise legitimacy for a policy of de-clustering.

Another gain is that some disadvantages are very hard to address directly. Melancholy or chronic stress, for example, are unlikely to be susceptible to purely medical intervention, or at least not in a sustainable fashion; and so the causes of melancholy or chronic stress need to be investigated if robust methods of removing them are to be found. In addition it may turn out that there are many cases where direct strategies are not economically or politically feasible, if, for example, they involve massive intrusion and supervision in individual lives.

Finally, there is every reason to seek particularly effective means for improving people's lives, whereby supplying one functioning leads to beneficial effects elsewhere. A truly fertile functioning is a 'golden lever' of social policy, and so it becomes an important question to discover whether there are indeed any fertile functionings, which we explore in the next section.

8.3 Identifying Causation: The Difficulties

The pressing question, then, is whether we have any indication that there are fertile functionings and corrosive disadvantages. The obvious problem is that causation is not directly observable. Even if there is a well-established correlation, how do we know, say, whether people's longevity is relatively short because they did not graduate from high school, or whether there is a deeper cause of both? Furthermore, when a social policy is based on a presumed causal connection yet the policy fails and thereby appears to undermine the claimed causal pathway, there is an almost irresistible intellectual urge to suppose that the real cause of the problem is some particular other thing, whether or not there is good evidence for this. Consider, for instance, the following famous remarks from Ronald Reagan:

In 1964 the famous War on Poverty was declared and a funny thing happened. Poverty, as measured by dependency, stopped shrinking and then actually began to grow worse. I guess you could say, poverty won the war. Poverty won in part because instead of helping the poor, government programs ruptured the bonds holding poor families together.[4]

Enormous amounts of money were spent to try to help improve the position of the disadvantaged. By some measures, so it is claimed, it made things worse. Reagan, or at least his advisers and speech writers, claim to know why, in part at least: government policies ruptured family bonds. They may be right, yet their causal claims seem speculative, to say the least.

Another problem is that often various correlations between disadvantages appear within theoretical frameworks and so the authorities must always guard against the possibility that an apparent causal connection is merely an artefact of the conceptual framework within which the problem is approached. Taking the example of causal influences on childhood development, there are numerous theories.[5] Economic deprivation theories place heavy weight on economic circumstances such as family income in which a child is nurtured to explain child attainment. Psychological theories of socialization, emphasizing role models, claim that influences during early childhood determine a young adult's achievements.[6] 'Coping strategies' theories pay attention to the effects of parental expectation and attitudes, the parents' ability to cope with changing circumstances, or their being stressed interfering with competent parenting. Some theories refer to the effect of parental status on children's attainments, and some examine school policies, comparing different educational reforms, and so on. It would not be surprising at all if in some cases the background theoretical framework has an influence on what a study determines to be the most salient causal connections.

Perhaps related to this is that while ideally research conducted by sociologists, policy analysts, and political scientists would offer clear evidence to identify the most corrosive disadvantages, in practice this is not always the case. Scholars often come to different, sometimes even contradictory, conclusions concerning the same issues. For example, while Robert Haveman and Barbara Wolfe survey many studies and come to the conclusion that 'growing up in a family in which the mother works seems to have a slightly adverse effect on educational attainment',[7] Susan Mayer suggests that research shows that it is better for children's attainment if their mother works, even if this means less time spent with the child;[8] and while Haveman and Wolfe refer to the poor's stress as having an impact, Mayer argues that the model of stress's impact is at odds with culture theories, according to which the long-term poor develop values and attitudes which allow them to reduce their stress.[9] (It might, therefore, be the case that middle class parents who are eager to have more, and who compete to 'keep up with the Jones's', would be under more stress than poor parents.) Thus Mayer's approach implies that at least we should disconnect stress from income. However, as Marmot and Wilkinson both suggest (see Chapter 7), it may be important to distinguish the chronic stress typically suffered by those who feel a lack of control over their lives (in Marx's phrase, they are playthings of alien forces) and the type of stress that accompanies a single, high importance event or decision. The former, it seems, is much worse for health and well-being than the latter.

8.4 *Corrosive Disadvantages and Fertile Functionings: What Do We Know?*

Despite these difficulties, it remains highly important to try and find corrosive disadvantages and fertile functionings in order to de-cluster disadvantage. A corrosive disadvantage, we said, is something whose absence or insecurity will lead to problems with other functionings. A fertile functioning is something the secure presence of which will lead to positive effects elsewhere. Our question now concerns the extent to which existing social science gives us reason to believe that there are corrosive disadvantages or fertile functionings of particular importance.

Here we should note that although for the purposes of measuring disadvantage, in Chapter 5 we identified six 'high-weight functionings', there is no reason to restrict our attention just to these six when looking for corrosive disadvantages and fertile functionings. Rather we need to find variables which exert their effects on the high-weight functionings, perhaps among others. These variables could be high-weight functionings, minor functionings, or preconditions of functionings. It is also worth noting that although identifying high-weight functionings is, for us, a matter of empirical survey of judgements of importance, and hence largely subjective, discovering corrosive disadvantages and fertile functionings requires a quite different type of empirical work. Here quantitative work, including sophisticated longitudinal studies, will be central, although qualitative work and fieldwork observation also have their places.

In what follows we focus on a number examples where it has been claimed in the social science literature that there are causal connections between functionings. In each case these involve sub-categories within our high-weight functionings of 'affiliation', 'sense, imagination, and thought', and 'control over the environment'. In discussing these examples our aim is not to reach final conclusions about these functionings, but rather to set out examples of the type of work necessary to turn our investigation into a comprehensive and systematic set of policy recommendations.[10]

Affiliation

It is very difficult to avoid the conclusion that there is strong correlation between being very poor and lacking many functionings on the one hand,

and lack of social interaction and affiliation on the other.[11] Some scholars claim that it is still an open question whether it is poverty that causes lack of affiliation or vice versa. Further analysis is needed, they say, to settle the question.[12] Amartya Sen is less cautious, and believes that there are diverse ways in which social exclusion can cause deprivation, poverty, and harm to many other functionings.[13] Taking Adam Smith as his authority, Sen argues that 'a good deal of the *Wealth of Nations* is concerned with the instrumental importance of exclusion and involves analysis of the effects of particular types of exclusion. (...) [Adam Smith] investigated the characteristics of social exclusion within a broader concept of deprivation, in the form of inability to do things that one has reason to want to do.'[14] Sen goes on to claim that not to be able to mix with others may directly impoverish a person's life and, additionally, reduce economic opportunities that often come from social contact.

In the opinion of our interviewees, affiliation is probably among the most fertile functionings. It serves, they claim, as a sort of immunization in the sense that people who experience a high sense of affiliation are better equipped to cope with threats and risks to their functionings. According to our interviewees, those who experience affiliation tend to be more optimistic about their life chances and possible positive change in their lives.[15] One reason for this is that those who feel they 'belong' to a wider group or community feel much more self-assured about their ability to handle negotiations with the authorities. Some of the interviewees thought that affiliation was related to feeling self-esteem. But most interviewees did not point to a particular direct relation; instead they suggested that affiliation is just something that cheers people up. In particular, the disadvantaged who still feel affiliated take heart from feeling they are needed, respected, wanted, and from belonging itself.

Similar claims for the latter were made in an interview with two women who volunteer to work with people in 'weak' neighbourhoods in Jerusalem, where the average unemployment rate is high and average income is very low. It seems that there is a great difference between one neighbourhood where there is a sense of community and affiliation and another neighbourhood where people do not feel the same.[16] In the former people are more positive about their chances to escape poverty, and feel control over their environment. These women asserted that 'affiliation was the best means to achieve empowerment'.

Several interviewees stressed that while affiliation was not a replacement for the loss of other functionings (thereby supporting our arguments for a form of pluralism), it could help people to avoid losing these functionings completely. A woman who works in an advice centre in one of the poorest neighbourhoods in the UK told us that a strong community life – in church, clubs, even bingo halls – is actually a lifeline for this neighbourhood and its inhabitants. The importance of the meetings at the church or club, to her mind, is that they give people something to do; they supply opportunities to chat with people who share the same experience; they supply a place to go to – even to escape boredom. An unemployed woman in Israel, who lives in a remote small town where unemployment rates are the highest in the country, reinforced this view when she told us about her experience, which was the opposite. In her town 'there was nothing to do' and therefore, she said, people never felt at home, which was according to her the most important obstacle to securing other functionings.

The cumulative evidence from our interviews and analysis of similar claims from people with wide and diverse experience, is impressive. An impressive systematic study of cases of breakdown of social infrastructure, undertaken by Liz Richardson and Katherine Mumford, is clear. Based on their studies in Manchester and Newcastle, they claim that the loss of a sense of community causes a high risk to a sense of shelter, even if only because people try to leave the community, or are afraid that others will.[17] One of our interviewees, a formerly homeless person in the UK, affirmed this view. He told us that he grew up in what he called slums in London in the late 1940s. While his family was very poor they did feel that they were supported by the neighbourhood's community, and had a sense of belonging. People helped each other. However, when he was a child, the government decided to demolish the slums and offer this neighbourhood's residents new housing. Alas, this was a blow to community life; the social fabric collapsed, and as a result his family became homeless and unemployed.

Richardson and Mumford take this further and claim that the loss of community also causes a breakdown in informal social networks. This, in turn, undermines informal social institutions, and anti-social behaviour escalates, drug dealers move in, and 'problems worsen alarmingly rapidly'.[18] Richardson and Mumford argue that where there is a sense of community there are 'shared rules of behaviour that are commonly accepted', and they describe what we would term as people having control over their environment. But the problem is that once there is a loss of a sense of community, respect for these rules drains away, and they become increasingly difficult to enforce. Consequently people lose control over their environment.

There seems good reason to believe that affiliation is both a corrosive disadvantage and a fertile functioning. This impression is reinforced when particular groups of disadvantaged people are examined. A person who volunteers with disabled people told us that to her mind, the least advantaged among them were those who did not feel affiliation and had no friends. This was not only an emotional problem, she said, but also a practical one. Disabled people who lacked affiliation could not find people to take care of them when they needed to, or to help them when they faced a physical obstacle.

A social worker who works with elderly people told us that belonging and a sense of affiliation was the most important functioning for elderly people because it could help them cope with everything else. A study conducted among elderly people in Israel sustains this view in a dramatic way: affiliation supports the functioning of life. This research followed people who were Seventy years old in 1990, and examined how many of them were still alive in 2002. It then analysed the correlation between death and a variety of parameters such as suffering from high blood pressure, being diagnosed as having mental problems, and also feeling lonely. The latter is significant: among those who did not feel lonely in 1990 29 per cent died before 2002, whereas among those who did feel lonely 61 per cent died.[19]

Further support for the conclusion that affiliation is a fertile functioning comes from Klinenberg's study of the Chicago heat wave, discussed above.[20] We used this study to illustrate the point that those who believed that their bodily integrity was at risk, through fear of crime, tended to stay indoors with their windows shut, and so were at greater risk of death during the heat wave. Yet living in company with others, or having regular visits from friends and families, kept people alive in other equally impoverished neighbourhoods. Equally important was having safe places to go during the day, such as air-conditioned cafes and stores.[21] These are all aspects of affiliation, which helped secure the life and health of even the materially very poor. Such effects are also observed in Michael Marmot's and Richard Wilkinson's studies of the social determinants of health, in which strong social networks keep people alive longer and in better health.[22]

Finally, further strong support for the thesis that affiliation is fertile is found in a study conducted very recently, but not yet published.[23] In the months prior to Israel's pullout from the Gaza strip (August 2005) hundreds of Kassam missiles were launched at a few towns and kibbutzim by the border. This has, in fact, continued even after the withdrawal. While these missiles rarely cause casualties, they inflict tremendous damage to houses, and the inhabitants of these towns and kibbutzim had to cope with constant fear. Children and the elderly were those who suffered most. Orit Nuttman-Shwartz and Rachel Dekel, two lecturers in social work, noticed that while some people reacted by becoming clinically depressed others actually developed a more powerful self-image and personality during and after these traumatic events. These people realized that if they could manage and cope with this threat to their lives and tranquillity, this meant that they were 'strong', 'balanced', and so on. Nuttman-Shwartz and Dekel interviewed about 180 people in both a kibbutz and a town that suffered from these attacks, asking themselves whether they could find a single variable that would be able to predict who got depressed and who, on the contrary, built up their personality. They discovered that there was no such variable, not even whether somebody was from the kibbutz or the town, apart from one: affiliation. Those who had felt affiliated to their community managed to cope more easily and did not get disheartened. Moreover, these people even defined their affiliation and their attachment to the place in stronger terms following the traumatic experience.

So altogether it seems that there is strong evidence that affiliation is a very fertile functioning. If so, then measures taken towards sustaining affiliation could be very helpful in addressing other forms of disadvantage. Such measures could take many forms, such as building clubs for these people to meet, improving town planning, including the provision of local shops and community centres, and so on. We say more about this in Chapter 10. This is a very welcome result for those interested in social equality.

Sense, imagination, and thought: being educated
It is an article of faith among many – especially those who make their living through teaching – that providing better education is the key to addressing other forms of disadvantage, which is to claim that being educated is therefore an important fertile functioning. To translate this into our terms, these people believe that particular aspects of having control over one's environment, and being able to make good use of one's imagination and thought, are fertile functionings.

Research on education does show, for example, that being properly educated and taught during a child's first two to three years is highly fertile.[24] However, systematic evidence about the benefits of education is not that easy to come by. Some would go even further and challenge the position that being educated is a fertile functioning. For example, according to the European Social Survey, the correlation between education and how satisfied people are with their lives is not statistically significant. That is to say that it is not the case that the more people are educated, the more they are satisfied with their lives. However, in our terms, improving reported satisfaction of life is not the sole goal of social policy. Moreover, it is easy to speculate that better educated people have wider horizons and aspirations, and would be less easy to satisfy for this reason, as well as being more critical of society, their friends, and themselves, and there-fore not necessarily more 'satisfied with life'. And when we look else-where we see strong indications that being educated turns out to be a fertile functioning when correlation to others is examined (although the statistics do not prove causation). The highest correlation is between being educated and health.[25] What we can learn, though, is that while it is difficult to prove that being educated is a fertile functioning, there is strong evidence that lacking education is a corrosive disadvan-tage, especially when it comes to chances of securing employment. As Table 1 shows, the less educated, the more likely one is to be unemployed.[26]

At the same time we cannot generalize that education guarantees work and a high salary. To see why, imagine that everybody had a college education. Presumably, there would still be noteworthy income differ-ences, and some would not be able to find a job. Other mechanisms would sort people into jobs. The explanation for this is that education is, at least in part, a 'positional' good, in that at least some of its instrumental benefits depend on how many other people have it.[27] Fifty years ago an undergraduate degree in the UK was a passport to interesting and well-paid employment, but as the participation rate rises towards 50 per cent this can no longer be the case, and other 'filters' will be used to assign people to the most attractive forms of work. However, the value of education is not purely positional. Aside from the fact that it is usually valuable in itself, even the instrumental benefits of education are not purely positional. In the realm of employment, education provides people with skills to equip them for the workplace, and obviously if no one had such skills then there is much that simply couldn't be done, and the world would be an almost unimaginably poorer place for everyone.

Table 1   Level of education and unemployment in Israel, 2002

Years of education	Rate of unemployment
0–4	14.3
5–8	13.1
9–12	11.5
13–15	6.9
16+	4.5

Source: Ben-David, Ran (2003), 'Employment in Israel: International Perspectives', *Israel Economic Review* 50.

Furthermore in other contexts, such as providing people with the skills to access and assess information beneficial to health, education is not a positional good. This complicates the picture, and is consistent with the suggestion made earlier that in some cases, the question whether a functioning is corrosive or fertile can be context-dependent. However, we can conclude that lacking education is always a very corrosive disadvantage, particularly with respect to vulnerability of functioning, whereas its fertility appears to be much more context-dependent; both in terms of which other functionings we are concerned with, and how many other people in society are educated to the same level.

The situation of differential employment prospects for those of different education levels described above is not unique to Israel, of course. In 2000 the USA and the UK had among the lowest levels of unemployment in the OECD. However, access to employment was distributed unevenly between the educated and the poorly educated, and among the educated those with higher education had an advantage over those without it. Moreover, when these figures are analysed, we can see that the impact of the rise in overall employment rate and the drop in unemployment rate on those with university education were much higher than on those with the lowest level of education. The less educated were far less able to take advantage of a growing economy.[28]

In general, the less one is educated, the worse one's chances of finding employment. In other words the risk to the functionings connected with employment (such as affiliation, control over one's environment, and practical reason), which as we know from our interviews are functionings likely to be damaged if one does not work, is higher the less educated one is. This is even more so when it comes to having a satisfying and interesting job. Thus lack of education seems to be a corrosive disadvantage.

Control over one's environment: soft skills

Social policy theorists have introduced the concept of 'soft skills', and some have argued that the experience of social workers shows such skills to be increasingly important.[29] In essence, soft skills are the skills that allow people to 'work the system': to get their children into better schools; to get medical attention when they need it; to get cheap short-term loans in emergencies; to manage their savings and investments; and so on. In other words, having soft skills is a precondition for reaching a sense of autonomy and control over the environment. In addition, such soft skills are yet another manifestation of use of imagination and reasoning: they combine knowledge, bargaining power, and raw cunning, with perhaps other traits such as personal charm. In our interviews, many social workers and people who work with asylum seekers defined the least advantaged among their clients as – among other things (recall that we asked them to mention three such parameters) – those who lacked soft skills. One of them said that among the unemployed those who did not know the art of job interviews suffered most and became the least advantaged; others mentioned basic communication skills, which would enable people at least to convey to others their situation and their particular needs.

To bring home the importance of soft skills, one needs only to think of those – especially recent immigrants, even those who are highly intelligent – who find themselves powerless in the face of a Kafkaesque bureaucracy, shunted from office to office, and back again, not knowing when is the right time to make a scene, or a joke, or when to ignore instructions, or which paperwork is vital and which irrelevant. A local guide is invaluable, and not only in a jungle.

Soft skills cannot always be fertile. If the system's rules are strict and rigid then one's skills are less likely to make a difference. Is this a good thing? Should we try to improve soft skills for all, or instead try to devise social structures where soft skills are impotent or unnecessary? Ideally speaking, in a truly egalitarian society, soft skills would not be needed, but we have to assume that at least in the foreseeable future those who can use soft skills will benefit. Moreover, while better general provision of knowledge may help level the playing field, it is hard to see how to make all methods of allocation resistant to those able to spot a short-cut or loop-hole. The best hope is simply to try to ensure that a lack of soft skills does not leave people far behind, and here there are important roles for social workers and advice workers in helping people navigate through ever more complex systems. What would this imply in practice? It would require institutions to double-check their services to see that those lacking soft skills do not suffer discrimination. For example, it is often said that when one goes to the clinic or when one, unfortunately, is hospitalized, it is good to know the 'better' physician. Perhaps this is unavoidable. We cannot expect patients not to look for better medical treatment. But an egalitarian medical institution, whether a clinic or a hospital, should see that if there are more experienced or more successful doctors, surgeons, and the like, access to them is distributed as arbitrarily as possible, or according to urgency, and not according to patients' skills in knowing how to get what they want.

More important, perhaps, are cases where soft skills are non-rival, namely when lacking soft skills is a disadvantage, but one person's having them does not lessen the ability of another person to use them effectively. One example is the soft skill of being a parent, which unfortunately is not taught at school; we might wonder why not. Another example is the soft skill of managing one's bank account, which has only recently become part of the curriculum in a rather minor way in the UK, and is ignored entirely in other countries. Youngsters nowadays are given credit and debit cards but they are not taught enough about how to manage their accounts, which could be easily done and save much agony.

Control over one's environment: autonomy in the workplace and worker control
One interesting aspect of control over one's environment is autonomy in one's working environment. The kibbutz experience, and the existence of co-operative forms of work, is now well documented[30] and, in general, successful experiments have shown that worker autonomy in this form can increase the joy of working, and perhaps self-respect, and hence can have positive effects on other functionings. More recently, however, the claim has been made that worker control can have health benefits for the workers involved. This is part of an argument recently made by Richard Wilkinson.[31] Wilkinson's *The Impact of Inequality: How to Make Sick Societies Healthier*, is a powerful and convincing exposition of the thesis of the social determinants of health, discussed in Chapter 7, drawing on Wilkinson's own research and that of others, which suggest that particular social conditions can have detrimental effects on health and life expectancy. Earlier, then, in discussing the work of Marmot and Wilkinson, we provided examples of corrosive disadvantage. Wilkinson wants to go further, however, and suggest ways out of the malaise.

Wilkinson is particularly concerned by the effects of low social status, having few friends, and painful early childhood experience,[32] all of which, he argues, are corrosive disadvantages. Yet despite the positive message of the subtitle of the book, Wilkinson devotes only a few pages explicitly to the question of what actual policies governments can pursue to improve things in societies as they currently exist. Some passing comments are made concerning advertising codes to make people less status conscious, and to measures that will increase public access to health, education, and transport,[33] but the only proposal discussed at any length is to increase employee ownership of businesses to above 50 per cent so that employees can exert significant control over the workplace.[34] This is an important suggestion, drawing on earlier socialist and co-operative traditions of thought, and at the level of pure theory we would be very sympathetic. Yet it is also very radical, with perhaps far-reaching presuppositions and consequences for the economy and society as a whole, which are not pursued by Wilkinson. What would be the effects on productivity, inflation, the interest rate, capital flight, and a host of other economic factors? And what would be the further consequences of these effects for individual functioning? Evidence that significant worker control on any large scale is either possible or would have positive health effects is very sketchy at best.[35] Wilkinson provides a wealth of evidence concerning the causes of ill health but nothing comparable about how to cure it. This suggests that while academics, governments, and the public in general may know a significant amount about corrosive disadvantages, especially in the area of health, they currently know very little about fertile functionings.

Losing control over one's environment: poverty as a corrosive disadvantage
While a large area of social policy concentrates on the provision of collective goods, such as hospitals, public transport, and so on, nevertheless public discussion of disadvantage and inequality is still generally presented in terms of poverty, understood as low income, and a great deal of social policy is conducted by means of tax and transfer. There is a good and obvious reason for this: money can buy people many of the things they want or need, in the particular form they want or need them. Consequently certain readers may feel a particular frustration with the discussion so far. Isn't it obvious, they may say, that the root of so many other disadvantages is poverty in the very concrete sense of low income? If the incomes of the poor increased, wouldn't this make many of their other problems disappear?

Sen's argument, which we have adopted and followed here, is that when it comes to one's well-being, what primarily matters is not how much money or resources one has, but what one is able to do and be. We find this argument intuitive and attractive, and yet this does not imply that no disadvantage has anything to do with money. The fact that money is not everything does not mean that it is nothing. There are many obvious examples of the effect on poverty on people's lives and choices, some which are somewhat less obvious. Consider the example of work. Some people have fulfilling jobs and others have rather boring jobs. Some people can afford to have a fulfilling job even if it does not carry with it a substantial income because they have other sources of income, such as inherited capital or a partner's income. Clearly, then, there is a difference between those who do, and those who do not, have what we could call the advantage of not having to worry constantly about increasing one's income. Is it possible to show that lacking this advantage is a corrosive disadvantage (although having it is not a functioning)?

While answering this, some people accept the argument of the Beatles' song 'Money Can't Buy Me Love', denying that money can bring the things most worth having in life. Robert E. Lane presents evidence that the main sources of well-being in advanced economies are friendships and a good family life, and that, once one is beyond the poverty level, a larger income contributes almost nothing to happiness. Indeed, he advances the thesis that, as prosperity increases, aspects of non-material well-being decline.[36] Important though these findings are, in this book we are not so much interested in the impact of money on being happy, as in its impact on many functionings and disadvantages discussed above. In addition, our interest is not only in actually having income and money, but also in the disadvantage of being constantly worried about income and money. Our question, then, is whether reducing people's worries about money will help them gain genuine opportunities for secure functioning.

A good example of the relation between anxieties over money and other disadvantages is disability. Usually we think of disability as the cause of other disadvantages. And indeed, it is no surprise, for example, to find that disability will lead to difficulties in finding a job, being able to visit friends, and other associated problems. However, detailed analysis, by following a cohort over several years, has been able to show that the causation also goes in the other direction. That is, as Tania Burchardt writes: 'There are strong associations between being poor, being out of work, having low educational qualifications and the risk of developing a long-term health problem or impairment.'[37]

Burchardt suggests that something about being poor leads people to develop a disability. On reflection this is not at all implausible. The poor are likely to take greater risks with their health, including more dangerous jobs, as well as not being able to find a sound medical alternative if they are let down by a national health system. They also face effects of chronic stress. Here we see the real possibility of mutually enforcing mechanisms, which create powerful clustering effects, as discussed throughout this book. In the present context the lesson appears to be that severe money worries lead people to take risks with other functionings, which in our theory is both a disadvantage in itself and likely to lead to other problems.

Of course, this is quite distinct from the question of whether income gaps are intrinsically unfair and unjust, which although important is not our topic. Our primary concern here is whether or not being poor is a corrosive disadvantage through the inability to purchase what one needs to secure one's functionings. What seems interesting here is that although lack of money can cause obvious problems, the steps taken to increase income can make things worse through exposure to risk. It seems fair to conclude that when one is continually worried about one's income and the need to increase it, this is a corrosive disadvantage, whereas being very affluent is not necessarily a fertile functioning, and adding money is not always the way to rectify the corrosive disadvantage of lacking it.

Susan Mayer's research, discussed above in this chapter, supports this position. Having presented compelling evidence – which is not in dispute – that children of poor families are less well educated than wealthy children, Susan Mayer considers whether boosting income would be of significant benefit. She concludes:

[On particular assumptions] we can calculate that doubling low-income families' income [from an average of $10,000 to $20,000 in 1992 dollars, affecting the poorest 20%] would reduce the overall high school dropout rate from 17.3 to 16.1 percent, and increase the mean years of education from 12.80 to 12.83. Male idleness would increase, and the percentage of young women who became single mothers would hardly change.[38]

This does not look very promising. The reason behind it, she feels, is that increasing the incomes of the poor will generally lead them to purchase more expensive consumer goods, which will do nothing to improve the education of their children. One of our interviewees offered an interesting explanation for this. People invest for the long run and save for the future, he claimed, when they have had a positive experience of progress. In other words, people whose lives can be described as a process of progress, interpret time in a positive and optimistic way, and therefore they have a sense of the future being better than the present. However, the very poor have not experienced life this way. For them there was no progress, and therefore there is no sign that the future should be better than the present. If anything, their fear is that what they have in the present, they might lose in the future. Thus we can often see poor people doing what appears to be wasting money on such present and short-term goals as expensive hairdressing, or spending a fortune on celebrating their children's wedding, whereas those who have more usually invest, save, and so on. Whether or not this is the right explanation for Mayer's findings, it seems that lack of money and being constantly worried about it is a corrosive disadvantage, whereas the simple solution of giving the disadvantaged more money may not solve the problem.

8.5 Ordinal and Cardinal Comparisons

Before moving on we need to consider a potential technical difficulty with the idea of de-clustering. Recall that in attempting to represent a person's functioning level we introduced the idea of a 'functioning map'. Thus we imagined them in purely ordinal terms, defined relative to how others are doing for each functioning. In sum, each person is given a percentile ranking within a population for each category. Given this, the task of identifying and assisting the least advantaged may seem very curious: whatever the government does, isn't it true that there will remain a group in the bottom percentile? Doesn't it therefore follow that the government needs cardinal measurements, so that it can judge whether the least advantaged in situation 1 are better or worse off than the least advantaged in situation 2?

Strictly, however, the scheme adopted here does not require cardinal measurements. As we have said, our approach allows the policy goal not so much of making the worst off as well off as possible, but equalizing in such a way that it makes it impossible to come to any generally agreed view about who the worst off are (remember the version of the decathlon where it was impossible to say which was the athlete with best all-round ability). This is what it is to *de-cluster disadvantage*. We believe that a society where it is impossible to say who the least advantaged are is in at least one important sense moving in the direction of a society of equals. For this task it is not necessary to adopt anything more than percentile rankings within each category.

However, even though the project of addressing special concern to the least advantaged does not force us to adopt more than the purely relative measurements of percentile ordering, we accept that it is essential to consider doing so for several reasons. First, the size of the gaps between percentile points can be significant. Consider two situations regarding, say, proper nutrition as a precondition for bodily health. In the first situation, although the citizens can be ranked in order of the quality of their bodily health, from top to bottom, the difference is not huge, perhaps between those being able to choose among only seasonal vegetables to those who can allow themselves to have any sort of vegetable any time of the year and so obtain the mild health advantage of better vitamin intake. In the second situation the gaps run from malnutrition, and consequently a serious problem of lack of many essential nutrients, to sophisticated food in plentiful supply. A purely relative ordering cannot distinguish between the two situations, but no one would deny that the situation of the worst off in the second situation presents a more urgent case for social action.

This, then, seems to be a reason for incorporating not only intervals, but also absolute positions into the scale. We could try to avoid this by saying that poor nutrition is only a desperately bad problem because it leads to other problems, and these will show up elsewhere on the functioning map, leading to clustering of disadvantage. Where there is no clustering, it might be argued, absolute position and intervals are of little importance. And where there is clustering, again, absolute levels do not add any extra information.

It is important to consider how far this answer deals with the objection which is, in essence, whether clustering provides all the necessary information about disadvantage. If this is so, we can rest content with relative orderings. One concern, however, is that finding clustering might be deceptive by revealing apparent disadvantages which are not significant. Here we need to consider whether there could be clustering which while systematic, is fairly insignificant in nature. If so, then two societies could look identical with respect to clusterings and relative orderings, yet one has a serious and urgent social problem but the other does not. To return to the earlier example, perhaps the group that consumes a slightly smaller variety of vegetables has also slightly worse health, on average, as well as lower life expectancy, and so on. And we could imagine a causal mechanism. Perhaps having fewer and a smaller variety of vegetables will lead to some minor health problems, maybe even to lower educational achievement because of tiredness caused by a less than optimal diet. Yet even if clustering reveals a problem, it may not reveal its degree of urgency.

A second reason for looking for more than the purely relative measurements of percentile ordering, is that some disadvantages might not be revealed by clustering. The salient case – which may or may not be a practical possibility – would be where a person does very badly indeed in one category, but without this having significant effects on their functioning elsewhere. Here there would be disadvantage without clustering, and so the clustering method would not reveal this. Information about absolute levels seems necessary to address this.

A third reason for going beyond merely relative comparisons is simply that the government would want to be able to judge what would make things better or worse within a single category of functioning. So it will want to know about the absolute fortunes of at least the worst off. More content than mere placement on a percentile scale is needed for this.

Fourth, in the literature a related question is whether priority fades as absolute position rises.[39] This is a question we feel can be postponed for practical purposes, on the assumption that in the developed societies with which we are most familiar there exist significant numbers of people who fare very badly in absolute terms, and so it would be something of a luxury to have to face this issue. However, to make this judgement it is clear that we rely on absolute measurements. A further, similar question is whether priority decreases when the number of people who are disadvantaged rises.[40] This challenge is serious because prima facie sometimes poor or insecure functionings are not so damaging when many people find it difficult to secure the functioning. Therefore it could be argued that Sen's example of appearing in public without shame is not so important if one lived in a society where many others suffered in a similar way. However whether or not it is true that if one is in a similar situation to many others the importance of this difficulty fades somewhat, it seems less plausible that it disappears altogether. Yet, once more, to make these judgements we need to rely on absolute levels of functionings.

Finally, there are undesirable ways of de-clustering disadvantage, such as a massive programme of destroying the advantages of the better off, but without giving any tangible benefit to others. Hence the government would want a cardinal 'audit' of de-clustering measures to ensure that positive steps in terms of de-clustering were not significant steps back in absolute terms. While it could be accepted that in some cases the right step may be to destroy forms of privilege, it is at least necessary to know whether and when this is taking place, if it is. (We look at some similar problems in the next section.)

Where, then, can this richer content come from? In fact it will automatically be generated by the form of assessment we have recommended: the York Model. People will, in general, be assessed on objective as well as subjective criteria, as a preliminary to placement in rank order. That information can be retained and used when necessary. There are, of course, limits to how much this information can tell us. For example, we can assess whether or not someone living in a cold climate has reliable, affordable heating. But this will not tell us how bad it is not to have heating. How can we find that out?

Part of our approach to this question is to say that, really, there are two criteria for determining how bad anything is: first, how it impacts other aspects of life (and this often will be a matter of how much people sacrifice in order to secure this functioning, i.e. inverse cross-category risk); and second, what in general people think (the democratic/consultative procedure on weighting). But these are already part of the process we have outlined. Hence to the extent that the government needs non-relative information, the process of complex evaluation, as explained in Chapter 6, will generate sufficient information to meet all the tasks set. The pragmatic method, explained in Chapter 7, will also do so, provided it builds on studies using assessments that are non-relative at least in significant part.

8.6 *Problems with De-clustering*

The main thrust of the argument of this chapter is that in order to de-cluster disadvantage governments ought to attend to corrosive disadvantages and fertile functionings. It might be objected that providing disadvantaged people with fertile functionings will not de-cluster disadvantage, but, on the contrary, will raise the targeted individuals in many respects, thus simply replacing one less advantaged person or group with another. This objection is most telling if disadvantage is defined in *purely* relative terms, whereas on our theory absolute position is also taken into account in judging whether a change has led to an improvement. However, even in relative terms the position is not so straightforward. First, the most disadvantaged people are disadvantaged in a number of respects, and it is unlikely that any set of measures will improve them in all, and certainly not all to the same degree. Second, it is important to remember that usually, when a government targets a certain fertile functioning, it does so *universally*, and therefore not only the very least advantaged benefit, but others as well by making them less likely to become disadvantaged. If, for example, a government removes a radioactive threat, not only the least advantaged who live right next to it benefit. We concede, however, that if de-clustering disadvantage were the only policy goal then, perversely, it appears that the way to do this would be to target one non-fertile functioning for one group, a distinct non-fertile functioning for another group, and so on, so that the social ranking becomes increasingly weighting sensitive. But of course we do not advocate this. De-clustering disadvantage is not the only thing that matters. Absolute position matters too, as does efficiency. Due to scarcity, governments need to spend their resources efficiently, and attending to fertile functionings is an important means to improving the absolute position of the least advantaged.

Before moving on, however, we need to consider a further potential objection to our proposals and introduce a qualification. We have argued that the means of achieving a society of equals is to de-cluster disadvantage, and this is likely also to require the de-clustering of advantages. If, for example, one does well on a fertile functioning, this is very likely to lead to a clustering of several functionings. Being educated, perhaps, will lead to a sense of fulfilment. But it would seem bizarre, even inhumane, to want to de-cluster these two advantages. It might be viewed as a particularly vindictive form of 'levelling down'. Conversely, if one disadvantage leads to another, there is a good reason to want to de-cluster this.

It seems, then, that we need to draw a distinction. Some cases of clustering are merely *institutional* in that they are the arbitrary consequence of certain social arrangements. Quite possibly the world could be arranged in such a way that education had no bearing on income. In that sense these cases of clustering are morally arbitrary. On the other hand, other cases of clustering are *constitutive* in a metaphysical sense. So just as Plato points out that part of the nature of being a shepherd is to care for sheep, many people agree that part of the nature of being educated is to become creative and perhaps satisfied with one's life, or to fulfil oneself. Hence if there is clustering between being educated and being creative or fulfilling oneself, then this is constitutive of the process of education and of the 'educated person'. While it would not undercut the 'meaning' of education, or undermine the integrity of the educated person, if education did not lead to higher pay (even if this may undercut the motivations of some to seek education), there seems a good case that fulfilment is different; it is part of what it is to be an educated person. A world in which education had no bearing on fulfilment would seem perhaps not a human world at all. Therefore while there is a good case that governments should try to de-cluster institutional couplings of advantage, they should not attempt to de-cluster constitutive couplings of advantage. To do so would be to strip out part of what is valuable in human life.

8.7 *Conclusion*

De-clustering disadvantage, then, is the policy goal we recommend for governments, subject to constraints which require them to take some account of absolute position, of efficiency, and of cases where de-clustering advantage would appear inhumane or simply immoral. The main means of de-clustering will be to attend to corrosive disadvantages and fertile functionings; there are steps governments can and must take to find out which disadvantages are corrosive and which functionings are fertile. While people often have intuitions about certain functionings being fertile, it could be very damaging to build social policies on hunches or mere observations of correlations.

Furthermore, those examining this will have to take into account that which functionings are fertile and which disadvantages corrosive might be influenced by context or culture. Thus, our research shows some differences between Israel and the UK.[41] Moreover, presumably even within these two countries differents cultural groups will have their own typical fertile functionings and corrosive disadvantages. But it is quite clear that it is easier to establish which are the corrosive disadvantages than to verify beyond doubt fertile functionings.

CHAPTER 9

———

Priority to the Least Advantaged

9.1 Introduction

Even if it were possible to pick out, with confidence, corrosive disadvantages and fertile functionings, we still have the question of where governments should focus their attention. A general idea of 'priority to the worst off' – about which, we claimed, there is prima facie wide agreement – is not enough to settle this question once we come to discuss actual policy. Here, then, we need to look at the various possible disagreements, and to clarify our own position.[1]

There are in fact two main areas where further discussion is needed. First, there is the question of the strength of any priority to the least advantaged and especially how this compares to the claims of others who are not among the worst off. Are we suggesting that *only* the claims of the worst off have weight? Second, so far we have argued that the least advantaged are those who experience a clustering of disadvantages in the sense that they find it extremely difficult to secure several of the six high-weight functionings. But does this imply that the authorities should pay attention only to the claims of the least advantaged *overall*, or should attention also be given to those who are least advantaged with respect to a particular functioning, even where this does not bring them into a group which does particularly badly overall?. These are the questions we shall now address.

9.2 Strength of Priority

Our question now is how to understand the injunction to give priority to the worst off. What does this mean? It could mean that if it is at all possible to improve the position of the worst off, then this should silence all other claims. Although there may be something to be said for this from the point of view of fairness, in practice it would seem to be a hard policy to live by. To see this, let us make a comparison with the 'triage' question, referring to a military practice in which in circumstances of war wounded soldiers are placed in three categories, two of which were not treated medically: those so badly wounded that only with a huge amount of time and medical equipment was there any chance that they would survive; and those who, even if left without treatment, could recover. All medical resources were allocated to members of the third group, those who were likely to be able to join the forces if, but only if, they were treated medically. By contrast, prioritarianism (i.e. priority to the worst off) prima facie demands that the most badly wounded be treated first, which in its extreme form requires all resources to go to these patients if there is any prospect at all of benefiting them.

The story of the triage itself can be treated for what it stands – the actual dilemma that the military doctors faced – or as a metaphor for cases where there is competition over scarce resources. This discussion is important and interesting, but to pursue it in detail is not necessary for present purposes.[2]

The triage brings out the point that in some sorts of situations it can be incredibly expensive to help people, and the good that can be done may be marginal. This means that it can be hugely inefficient to give absolute priority to the worst off, and hence we can call this the 'inefficiency argument'. To illustrate in the context of social policy, it is sometimes argued that people with extremely severe disabilities might require huge expenditure of medical resources, special transport facilities, and much effort by others, including twenty-four-hour nursing, to achieve even a minimal improvement in functioning. As one of the doctors we interviewed remarked, she was very happy she did not have to decide about such policies, but indeed there was a need to decide because doctors would always face such decisions, at least when it comes to allocating time and attention, if not budgets. A similar story might be told for those with severe educational difficulties. Presumably the thought is not that such people should be utterly abandoned, but that we have to be 'realistic' in our use of resources. The duty of humanity requires that people should not be left in extreme distress or pain, but economic constraints make it too demanding to do more. Once a very basic level has been achieved 'enough has been done', and it is time to turn resources elsewhere rather than to aim for improvements that are likely to be marginal, if achieved at all. Other cases where the chances of success are small and the cost is extremely high might include addiction services. It can, for example, be attempted to cure the addiction of a homeless drug addict, and if the cure were successful this would lead to a major improvement in the life of the former addict. However, if recovery rates are very low, and within a few weeks the 'cure' normally proves ineffective for those worst affected, it could be argued that resources are better spent on those who have less severe problems and are more likely to recover. For this reason many have become convinced that it makes sense in such cases to modify prioritarianism and introduce '*weighted priority*' in which a more sophisticated consideration takes place, involving the number of people who will be affected by the policy and the degree to which they will benefit, as well as what else might be done with those resources. Moreover, some will add, within a democracy a government may be keen to spread its resources in such a way that the largest possible group receives a benefit they consider to be significant.

Nevertheless political expediency should not be allowed to overturn considerations of justice. It is important to assess whether the inefficiency argument is, morally speaking, a good one. If it is, then there is at least one argument that could yield the conclusion that aiding the worst off in such cases is not a requirement of justice.[3] In response, we should first note that there may be fewer examples of this sort – of gross inefficiency – than may be commonly thought. When in support of the inefficiency argument, it is claimed that there are cases where on current circumstances little can be done, or chances of recovery are vanishingly small, it is important not to take such descriptions at face value, as if they reveal some sort of eternal truth. One problem lies in the perspective one takes. Sometimes, as Thomas Pogge argues, people tend to examine only the grand picture, ignoring the individuals who are its components. Thus they believe that very little if anything can be done because they think of the grand picture, rather than about bettering the life of a particular person. Justifying his demand that Western societies help the world poor more than they currently do, Pogge writes:

World poverty appears as one overwhelming task to which we, as individuals, cannot meaningfully contribute. One makes a disaster relief contribution after an earthquake and finds that, two years later, the damaged city has been largely rebuilt, with our help. One makes a contribution to poverty relief and finds that, two years later, the number of people living and dying in extreme poverty is still unimaginable large. The former contribution seems meaningful because we think of the task as limited to one disaster – rather than including the effects of all natural disasters, say. The latter contribution appears pointless. But such appearances arise from our conventional sorting categories. Seeing the global poor as one vast homogeneous mass, we overlook that saving ten children from a painful death by hunger does make a real difference, all the difference for these children, and that this difference is quite significant even, when many other children remain hungry.[4]

Although discussion of the global poor is outside the range of this study the general point and rationale applies. As Pogge argues, one problem is that people only see the grand picture and fail to see how they could solve individual cases. But we want to point out that in addition, interestingly, at other times the problem of perspective is inverse. Because people personally are in a situation where they as individuals cannot help, say, a homeless person, or solve a huge problem, they tend to ignore the grand picture and fail to acknowledge that what a state can do is very different from what an individual can, or for that matter from what an aggregation of individuals can. So people mistakenly conclude that 'there is very little that can be done', whereas this is not the case.

Second, the fact that an attempted remedy is expensive and generally ineffective proves nothing about what might be done with more imagination and a different approach. Those who have worked intensively with children with severe difficulties sometimes report amazing success as a result of new therapies, not all of which need be expensive. If we had already decided that helping such children was not cost-effective then those strategies may not have been developed and attempted. The same can be said for attempting to develop new ways of breaking addiction and homelessness. One of our interviews was with a social worker who has had great success with young people addicted to 'hard' drugs. He told us that the reason he had done so well was that he ignored conventional knowledge and standard therapies, all of which were very pessimistic. These, he said, were based on the practice of talking to the drug addicts, whereas the drug addicts were not interested in talking; as a matter of fact, in many cases they could not talk because they were constantly in crisis and in need of the drug. These conventional therapies, he argued, were designed to suit the therapist rather than the patients' needs. For the therapist the way to cure people is by talking to them, and since the drug addicts could not talk, the standard therapy had little chance of success. Therefore the social worker explored different forms of therapy that did not involve talking with the drug addicts, until he found a few which were very successful and not expensive at all. Hence it is important to recognize that research and the learning process is also part of the social justice agenda, and hence one way of giving priority to the worst off is to spend money on research and pilot schemes, so that society may learn how to operate in a cost-effective way. In a sense, then, a great deal of the government-funded medical research budget – many billions of dollars world wide – is spent in the hope of improving the lives of the least advantaged (from the point of view of health, if not overall).

Some problems are indeed expensive to address in proportion to the results they achieve, and in some sense the money or time or energy could be better spent elsewhere. We cannot pretend to have dealt with all such cases. However in many other examples asserting that it is too expensive to help is too hasty. We live in a dynamic world, and we can spend money in the hope of accelerating the pace of change. Moreover, even in the most extreme cases, for as long as we are concerned to create a society of equals it is important not to abandon any social group. As we have seen, affiliation and a sense of belonging is a core functioning, and leaving these people outside society, not doing anything to help them because this money can be spent elsewhere more 'efficiently', is in many cases only a self fulfilling prophecy: it keeps them outside society, and it renders other functionings insecure, causing them further disadvantage, to the extent that then it is even 'more evident' that 'there is very little we can do to help these people'. For as long as government is spending significant amounts of money to research cost-effective means of helping those who at the moment are the least advantaged but cannot be helped except in a very ineffective and expensive way, government has gone beyond the 'triage' mentality, and has not abandoned its least advantaged, even if currently it can offer such people little actual help.[5]

In a society of equals it is legitimate for people and governments to consider questions of efficiency, but only after they consider the moral reasons in support of the claims made by or on behalf of the least advantaged. And if the claim is found sound, it should take a very extreme case of inefficiency to override it. Moreover, in a society of equals people do not become indifferent to others' misery. But a society that does not direct its attention and its budgets to its very least advantaged because it is inefficient adopts an attitude of indifference. It tends to accept as 'given' the existence of homeless people, drug addicts, and so on, until it characterizes this situation as an 'inevitable part of modern society'. As we mentioned in the Introduction, some still remember how shocked they were when they first saw homeless people and realized that these people literally had nowhere to sleep or eat. Today many among the younger generations grow up in a situation where homeless people are part of city life, and therefore have lost their sensitivity to this phenomenon. It is not quite clear whether these people are indifferent towards this sort of misery because they think that solving the problem (e.g. of homeless people) is too expensive, or that they claim it's too expensive because they are indifferent. Thus in order to get rid of this attitude of indifference it is important to accept priority to the least advantaged.

Aside from the question of inefficiency, which we believe has some force but less than is often thought, a second objection to strong priority to the worst off is based on what we can call 'equity'. According to this claim, being serious about absolute priority would imply that the state should spend nothing on items that benefit, say, the middle classes for as long as there were others worse off than them. Yet, the argument goes, bearing in mind that the state runs its programmes out of tax revenues, and these revenues are collected from all, it may seem inequitable that those paying receive nothing back. The argument is not that everyone should get 'value for money' for it is unlikely that higher tax payers can ever get back the cash value of their taxes.[6] But nevertheless, it could be argued, some notion of 'something for everyone' seems not unreasonable.

We should make clear that we do not accept this 'equity' argument on its own terms, for it is premised on a theory of justice that is in conflict with the general approach adopted here. However, we do have some sympathy for two arguments suggesting that, for the sake of the worst off, the better off should receive some benefits from the state. The first is a pragmatic argument, namely that if the system is to receive support from its citizens, it may be important to show them that they too benefit from their taxes.[7] Hence, it is sometimes said, state support for such things as the opera is an excellent way of helping the very wealthy to become more sympathetic to the general idea of government spending, for which they after all are paying a significant share. This is a recognition of the fact that a distributive scheme can survive in a democracy only if it has the support of the people, and we do not assume that everyone can be persuaded by the moral force of arguments alone.

However, we can also appeal to a second argument of greater moral importance: if one group pays without receiving, whereas another receives without paying, this will be stigmatizing and humiliating for the recipient group, and mutually alienating for both groups. Hence, the argument goes, for reasons of social unity and solidarity it seems important that priority to the least advantaged – conceived in narrow terms – is limited by other principles that distribute benefits more widely.[8] By way of example, giving food vouchers to the poor to may be humiliating when they come to spend them. But if every member of society is given some quantity of food vouchers, but the poor are given more, then the stigma may be removed. Hence giving the middle classes food vouchers is in one way good for the poor, and therefore advances priority to the worst off, understood in broad terms.

To this degree, then, the objection that priority to the worst off requires governments to spend only on the worst off answers itself. Priority to the worst off, when understood in the broad sense of this book, requires that many groups in society, perhaps all, receive some services and goods from the state, so that their functionings are secured, and this should work to break down a stigmatizing and alienating distinction between 'providers' and 'receivers'. All will make some contribution to the 'social pot' (if only through forms of purchase tax) and virtually all, if not all, will receive, although the proportions will vary greatly and construed in material terms the rich will receive very little compared with their contribution. But such a system is needed in order to give priority to the worst off, not necessarily in purely material terms, but in terms of boosting their affiliation.[9]

In conclusion, neither the inefficiency argument nor the equity argument in its two versions leads us to conclude that we should ever abandon the worst off. The force of the inefficiency argument is often over-stated, and this can be seen from the fact that society spends huge sums of money in the search for cost-effective ways of helping the worst off; researching new strategies to overcome disadvantage can be one way of giving priority to the worst off. Finally, although we do not accept the equity argument we do believe that there can be good reasons for distributing some goods and services to all; reasons which are consistent with priority to the worst off. This becomes clearer once it is recognized that services and social goods are diverse in their nature and, for example, giving material goods to one group can boost the functioning of affiliation of another. Conversely, a 'more efficient' tax and transfer scheme which splits society into two groups will make the worst off even worse off in at least one respect. Despite this we do not deny that there are times when absolute priority will need to be over-ridden at least temporarily.

9.3 Priority and Sectoral Justice

A different and independent concern is whether priority to the least advantaged should focus on the least advantaged overall, or whether a sector-by-sector or perhaps functioning-by-functioning approach is more defensible. Our view appears to endorse the 'overall' approach yet earlier we expressed some sympathy for the 'sector-by-sector' approach, while at the same time arguing that it had inadequate resources to solve problems of overall budget allocation. Here it is worth explaining how an important role for sectoral justice fits our general theoretical framework, by means of a division of labour between government and its agencies.

For a stark example of where there may be a conflict between a 'sector by sector' approach and the 'overall approach', imagine a hospital that has to decide which of two patients should receive a heart transplant when only one suitable heart is available. The sectoral approach suggests that the doctors should decide purely according to the norms of medicine, perhaps which patient will benefit more in terms of successful health outcomes, quality of life, and life expectancy. By contrast it appears that our 'overall disadvantage' approach requires the doctors to investigate issues such as the level of each patient's education, affiliation, social networks, and control over the environment as well, and that a deficit in some of these areas would provide a reason for reversing clinical judgement about who should receive treatment.

This may seem objectionable. First, putting this type of decision making in the hands of doctors is problematic. It is intrusive and time-consuming for doctors to make such judgements, and they would need further training to be able to do so. Furthermore it may seem inappropriate to allow doctors access to such a range of personal information. Second, we have insisted that functionings are incommensurable at least in the sense that a deficit in one cannot always be fully made up for by a boost to a different functioning. Yet it appears that the tendency of our theory now reverses this, and that we are suggesting that one reason for giving someone better health is that they lack other functionings.

To respond to these important objections we need first to make clear that our theory does not require doctors to make such troublesome judgements. Our theory proposes a division of labour between the government and its various sectoral agencies. The government's goal is to improve the position of the least advantaged overall. Its means of doing this is to assign resources to various agencies. Those agencies will follow their own rules and priorities for spending those resources, which although able to be modified by government instructions by means of targeting, penalties, and incentives, will nevertheless be based on clear and accountable principles. These principles are very likely to include priority to the worst off in that sector. However, the amount of resource any sector receives, and the special instructions it is given about how to spend the resources, should on our theory be determined at least in part by a theory about the benefit this will bring to the least advantaged overall. Hence it is likely that a government will need to identify corrosive disadvantages and fertile functionings, and provide a higher level of resources in areas where providing the least advantaged with extra attention will spread beneficial effects.

In this way our theory gives priority to the least advantaged overall in the formulation of government policy, and it is very likely also to give a high degree of priority to the least advantaged in each sector as part of the means of implementing that policy. Different approaches to priority are taken at different points in the decision chain. Hence in the health case, it is likely that doctors will be able to exercise their clinical judgement about which patient receives the heart, although this can be modified by other distributive principles.[10] However, whether a hospital is even given the resources which will allow it to perform heart transplants will be informed, at least in part, by the question of whether this is part of an efficient package of measures which will have the tendency of improving the position of the least advantaged overall. But this decision will be made at a much higher point in the decision hierarchy than within a particular hospital.[11] This division of labour allows us to say that priority, in one sense, is given to the least advantaged overall, and in another sense most probably to the least advantaged in each sector.

To answer the concern about whether this view is in tension with our earlier points about the incommensurability of functionings, we continue to uphold and defend the philosophical thesis that in many cases where someone lacks a functioning, only the provision of that functioning, or means to it, can 'discharge' the claim. Nevertheless, under conditions of scarce resources it is entirely appropriate, we believe, to look at the total condition of people's lives to determine general social policy. From what we have said it is possible that our theory would demand that the government sets up institutions so that people who do badly in several areas may receive more help in one of them (if, for example, this is found to be a fertile functioning) than others who do worse in that area but much better overall. This is not conceived of as compensation but as a way of formulating policies to improve the lives of those who are worst off overall by de-clustering disadvantage in the most efficient way. In other words this policy is appropriate when the particular functioning is a fertile (or the disadvantage a corrosive) one.

9.4 Egalitarian Criticisms

At this point another objection might be raised, from a more egalitarian position. According to this objection, our theory plays into the hands of the economic right-wing, which is interested in avoiding complete equality and would be ready to pay the price of giving some special attention to the least advantaged. Our argument that the least advantaged should be of special concern might thereby seem to serve as a fig leaf to right-wing politics. We would like to dismiss this objection by arguing that in fact our theory is quite radical, politically speaking, in its implications, in three ways:

Shifting the burden of proof. First, our theory is radical because it shifts the burden of proof from the least advantaged to the state. Imagine that a government allows a mobile phone company to build an antenna next to Smith's house. Suppose we know that living in a radius of less than fifty metres from such an antenna can cause leukaemia. However, according to the current system, Smith is not considered disadvantaged (apart from the aesthetic matters involved, assuming that living next to such an antenna is not pleasing) until he becomes ill, and as long as he does not become ill, he is not disadvantaged. Moreover, if and when he becomes ill, he has to prove that his illness was caused by the antenna, which is unfortunately rather tricky, legally speaking. In contrast, according to our theory, since one aspect of disadvantage is for one's functioning to become insecure, the fact that the government allows this antenna to be built next to Smith's house, and knowing the statistics about correlation between such antennas and leukaemia, is enough for us to declare that Smith has been disadvantaged. Smith does not have to prove that he is ill. The very fact that his functionings become insecure and that he is involuntarily exposed to risks that others are not exposed to, is sufficient for us to claim that he is disadvantaged.

Reverse chain connection. Second, our theory is radical in the sense that it looks at the effects of the treatment of the least advantaged within the context of an image of society as a community of people who should develop relationships of care and not of indifference. It is plausible that not caring for the least advantaged would serve as a boomerang to the less disadvantaged. Once people become used to seeing misery around them, to homeless people, to drug addicts, to the growing number of mentally ill, and to poor people not receiving medical treatment, they will become more and more indifferent and develop a thick skin. These least advantaged people will become marginalized and excluded from society. But once this happens, the not so disadvantaged will be the least advantaged among those who are 'included' in society. Citizens, though, having developed a thick skin, will grow indifferent to their suffering as well – indifference will spread upwards – and will not lift a finger to help them. This reverse chain connection would, if correct, explain why in many Western countries and cities we see a growing number of unemployed, why there is a growing percentage of the population that lives below the poverty line, and so on.

Against generalized rising material expectations. The third way in which our theory is radical is that it does not promise everyone a rose garden – we do not claim that redistribution makes everyone better off in economic terms. We do, however, suggest that it will help build a society of equals. In what way do we not promise a rose garden? Well, other theories offered in the name of priority to the worst off often envision rising material expectations for all while trying to ensure that the worst off rise more quickly than others. Such policies improve the lot of the least advantaged without threatening the position of the better off. However, the policies recommended here make it likely that in selfish and material terms the world will become significantly less comfortable for some among the better off. Traditional policies of 'priority' to the worst off are compatible with retaining conventional structures of class and privilege. This is important. Even if 'a rising tide raises all boats' it may do nothing to stop the gap in size between the boats rising, or to strain the metaphor even further, stop those with bigger boats looking down on the smaller boats. On our approach ideally some advantages will be blurred or even eliminated by the rising tide. Many of those who are used to doing relatively well over a whole range of areas may find themselves overtaken by others in some. In selfish terms, then, this is less comfortable and more demanding for many people than other ways of pursuing priority to the least advantaged. Nevertheless, it will help achieve the goals of social equality, in which patterns of dominance are undermined, and with it relations of superiority and servility, inclusion and exclusion.[12] But we do not leave things here, because the theory offered is intended to move us closer to a society of equals not in a sense of strict material possessions, but rather in the way people live together. In that sense, evaluation of the better off's life after their advantages are blurred or eliminated should be measured over a whole range of functionings, including doing good to others, belonging and friendship, and so on.

9.5 Conclusion

To conclude this chapter, we have argued that when absolute priority to the worst off is extremely expensive and only marginally effective, this should encourage governments not to abandon the least advantaged but look for more cost-effective forms of support. And, we claim, this is what they in fact do by funding medical and social research. Further, priority to the worst off can encourage, rather than preclude, distribution of some services and goods to those who are not the worst off in society, both for pragmatic, political reasons and in order to boost the affiliation of the worst off. However we accept that in rare, extreme cases priority can be overridden. This does not mean, however, that such people are to be abandoned, but rather that some limits, in rare cases, are to be applied to how much of society's scarce resources should be devoted to finding ways of improving the lives of the least advantaged. We have also explained how, on our view, there is room for priority both to the worst off overall and to the worst off with respect to each functioning (where this is an appropriate goal within a sector). And we have also emphasized some ways in which our theory is more radical than it may at first sight seem. Having, we hope, settled the 'who' question – who the government should help – it is time to turn to ask our 'how' question: how should governments act? In other words, suggesting, that the government should de-cluster disadvantage by securing fertile function- ings and diminishing corrosive disadvantages, still leaves a potential problem. Might, for example, the government harm one functioning by securing another? To such matters we turn in Chapter 10.

CHAPTER 10

Addressing Disadvantage While Respecting People

10.1 Introduction

The very general lines of our approach, then, are in place. However, we want now to look in more detail at the strategies agencies have available to them to help disadvantaged people, and to consider reasons for favouring one strategy over another in particular circumstances. Recall that in the Introduction to Part 3 we distinguished between the question of *where* governments should act (which functionings), *who* they should be devoting their attention to, and *how* they should act.[1] We made some suggestions concerning the 'where' question in Chapter 8, and explored the 'who' question in the last chapter. Here we look in more detail at the 'how' question. Our task here is not so much to provide a systematic answer to the question of how governments should act in every detail, but rather to pinpoint some problems that might arise from what we have suggested so far, and consider possible approaches to these problems, illustrated with some practical examples of good and bad practice.

By way of introduction to this issue we can return to a debate mentioned in the Introduction, which has recently come to prominence in the egalitarian literature. On the one side are those who believe that the key to creating a society of equals is to find a good that should be distributed equally among citizens. These theorists try to answer the 'equality of what' question by determining the 'currency' of egalitarian justice. Their concerns are essentially distributive. On the other side are those who think equality concerns creating relations of a certain kind among people. Such relational egalitarians see the goal of equality as avoiding oppression, exploitation, domination, servility, snobbery, and other hierarchical evils.[2]

As explained, we find ourselves sympathetic to both sides. There must be more to equality than the distribution of material goods. On the other hand, if relational equality is not good for people, then it is hard to see its point. Hence, we feel, the answer to this dilemma is that a broad range of goods must come into play. The 'genuine opportunity for secure functionings' view allows us to do this. The goods sought by relational egalitarians are rarely stated in positive terms, but according to our analysis affiliation and emotional well-being are likely to be central, as is control over the environment. The negative relations just listed which are inimical to relational equality undermine an individual's sense of belonging and hence their affiliation. Servility, exploitation, domination, and so forth may also effect how individuals see themselves and thereby damage their self-esteem and hence emotional well-being in addition to their other detrimental effects, especially lack of autonomy and control over their lives. But the key point is that the relational equality critique points not to the idea of giving up distributional equality, but to its expansion, as we suggested in the Introduction. Our task now is to consider the question of how such *expanded equality* can be achieved. As we shall see shortly, the danger is that the attempt to fix one problem can create fresh problems of its own; in our terms, attempts to address disadvantage and to secure functionings can themselves have negative effects or externalities such as rendering other functionings insecure.

To illustrate the difficulties, let us consider again two examples discussed earlier in this book. The first, uncovered in our interviews, is of a policy of 'slum clearance' and relocation of people into newly-built tower blocks, where it became common to lose social networks and a sense of community. The example we discussed is of a person who subsequently became homeless. This is surely a rare case, but it was much more common for people in a similar position to suffer social dislocation and isolation, with further effects on health.

Some may be tempted to draw libertarian conclusions from this. Milton Friedman, for example, suggested that all government action has negative externalities[3] and one may assume that the appropriate lesson is to keep government out of people's lives as much as possible. Yet the story of Leah, from the Introduction, reminds us that this may be too hasty. Leah's attempts to improve her situation for herself, by seeking advice from mystics when her life was going in the wrong direction, in each case made things worse. When her first marriage collapsed, rather than taking this as an opportunity to complete her education or to gain other skills, she rushed into a second marriage. The combination of a patriarchal social system, enforced by her father and the community, with the compliance of her equally oppressed mother, and a lack of understanding of what was problematic about her life and how to deal with it, led her to compound problems for herself. The right conclusions to draw from the two cases together, we believe, is not that governments should withdraw from the task of trying to help people, but that they should act with a clearer sense of their goals and the impacts they will have. The remainder of this chapter explores some of the issues involved.

10.2 *Addressing Disadvantages: The Road to Hell is Paved with Good Intentions*

There are many ways in which government policies can go wrong. Sometimes they can be counter-productive in their own terms. Such claims have been made, or at least have become a matter of folklore, concerning several British pre-Thatcherite welfare policies. High income tax reduced the total tax take (at least by comparison with some alternative possibilities) by stifling innovation and encouraging capital flight.[4] A law which gave employees very secure employment rights after six months in post led to widespread casualization and very short-term contracts. A law which gave private tenants of unfurnished accommodation an automatic right to the renewal of their lease led to the end of the unfurnished rental market. In these latter cases the employers and landlords did what they thought necessary to ensure that their employees and tenants did not acquire the newly created rights against them.[5]

All this is not new. Counter-productivity can have many explanations, such as a faulty causal analysis or a lack of imagination about how the existence of a new rule or law changes people's incentives.

However, our particular interest is not primarily when a policy is counter-productive in its own terms, but when government action to help people has hidden costs in some other respect for those people, or for other disadvantaged people. Specifically attempts to help improve or secure a functioning can lead to lower, or less secure, functioning in some other respect. The slum clearance example is a clear case of this. Unsanitary and overcrowded housing is a threat to bodily health. Improving this, and thereby reducing health risks, led to grave damage to a sense of belonging and hence affiliation. For Leah, the attempt to secure affiliation was itself the problem. Observing local stereotypes – marrying young and having children – led to damage to her sense, imagination, and thought (poor education) and no doubt her autonomy, part of her control over her environment.

In the context of the present project, what interests us most are problems which can be expressed in terms of a potential conflict between distributional and social equality, and in particular when attempts to improve people's lives in material terms have costs with respect to their affiliation and emotional well-being. Ways of making people materially better off can lead to them feeling alienated from society. The further importance of this is that lack of affiliation is likely to be a corrosive disadvantage, whereas affiliation is a fertile functioning, as discussed in Chapter 8, and so the consequences of such policies could be profound.

One route into this issue is to return to the discussion of Chapter 1, where we considered the example of using cash compensation as an all-purpose means of addressing disadvantage. Let us return to this, as a way of understanding how government policy can undercut affiliation.

Earlier we gave two types of argument against the proposal that cash compensation is an appropriate remedy in every case of disadvantage. First, sometimes cash simply does not solve the problem. There is, we could say, a 'mismatch' between the problem and the attempt to solve it: people can suffer from disadvantages that cannot be solved by more money. Second, people sometimes find cash compensation humiliating, and it would compound that humiliation, rather than rectify it, by adding further cash to compensate for the harm to their self-respect, which as we have pointed out is to harm their functionings of affiliation and emotional well-being. The objections of mismatch and humiliation are importantly distinct, yet they often both apply simultaneously.[6] They are, for example, combined – perhaps even run together – in Elizabeth Anderson's well-known example of the State Equality Agency. She imagines the State Equality Agency sending letters to the 'ugly and socially awkward' in the following terms:

How sad that you are so repulsive to people around you that no one wants to be your friend or lifetime companion. We won't make it up to you by being your friend or your marriage partner – we have our own freedom of association to exercise – but you can console yourself in your miserable loneliness by consuming these material goods which we, the beautiful and charming ones, will provide. And who knows? Maybe you won't be such a loser once potential dates see how rich you are.[7]

One problem here is that of 'mismatch'. Giving people who are ugly or socially awkward more money is unlikely to be a route which will lead to friendship or companionship, or at least not in forms worth having. Yet beyond that, even when a policy is well-designed to meet a particular functioning at risk, and so does not suffer from mismatch, it can still be humiliating. Consider food vouchers and free school meals. These, on the surface, seem an excellent way of addressing poor nutrition or hunger.

Nevertheless, they can be stigmatizing if administered in such a way as to make it obvious that some people need to rely on state support. Other policies which involve means-testing require the poor and unfortunate to go through types of intrusive inspection that others do not have to face, thereby harming their dignity and self-esteem, and once more their functionings of affiliation and emotional well-being. In sum, attempts to implement equalizing measures can themselves be experienced as oppressive.[8] Indeed the point goes deeper. Even having to identify oneself as qualifying for assistance can require one to admit that one lacks functionings, talents that others have. Admitting this even to oneself can undermine self-respect.[9] Thus the mere making of a claim can be humiliating, independently of the question of how society responds to it.

This could undermine attempts to create the type of relations between individuals which are thought to characterize a society of equals. As we have said, equality means something beyond comparing what access to material goods people have. It is also a matter of how people respect each other[10] and how they relate to each other. Means-testing, we argued, can in the worst cases split society into those tested and those not, with the first stigmatized and the second treating them as lesser beings. This is bad not only for the person demeaned, but for all. We have noted that attempts to redress disadvantage can have powerful negative consequences, and these examples should be of particular concern to those sympathetic to equality. More promisingly, however, consequences – or externalities – of a positive form are possible too, as we may see shortly.

We can now see positive and negative externalities of action as 'leakage' phenomena, as discussed in Chapter 5 in relation to 'local' or 'sectoral' justice. The attempt to provide goods in one area can have good and bad effects elsewhere, both for the people acted upon and for others. As we have said, the aim we seek is not merely that of addressing individual disadvantage, but also of creating a society of equals, where this has consequences for all members of society. The failure, then, of humiliating forms of rectification of disadvantage is twofold. First, in addressing one disadvantage – poor nutrition, say – at least one other functioning, and possibly more – affiliation, emotional well-being – is undermined. Second, such policies create a division that undermines social solidarity.[11] The division may or may not be publicly acknowledged, but the mere fact that there is a division between those helped and those helping can itself have unwelcome effects. It may be thought that this last effect will always be a consequence of any redistributive scheme, and the right answer to it is to help people see that independence is a myth and everyone is dependent on many others at every stage of their lives, and hence this is nothing to be ashamed of. We are, of course, highly sympathetic to this point. Furthermore, on our view, such a policy of attitude change is part of the project of addressing disadvantage. Yet rather than propose schemes that today people find stigmatizing while trying to re-educate them not to feel stigmatized, we prefer the approach of looking for non-stigmatizing forms of action.

10.3 Forms of Remedy of Disadvantage

The types of policies which seem most likely to undercut affiliation are those which divide society into two groups by identifying, and thereby stigmatizing, those who need help. This is one reason for the popularity of universal benefits, such as the theory of 'unconditional basic income',[12] in which everyone receives a grant from the state, regardless of need. A practical example of this is child benefit in the UK where all mothers, rich and poor, receive an allowance for dependent children. By not distinguishing between cases, such policies avoid stigma, and they yield one clue about how to think about sensitive social policies. However, by providing financial benefits even to those who do not need them, universal allocations of money can be extremely inefficient, and are a very expensive way of avoiding stigma. Part of the problem of existing proposals may well be that they remain locked in the 'tax and transfer' mentality of what in Chapter 1 we called the 'compensation paradigm', where we raised the question of what alternatives there may be to cash compensation as a model for addressing disadvantage. We need to look at alternative forms of remedy to see if there are other ways of addressing disadvantage which avoid stigma. In this section we propose an analytic framework in which different forms of strategies, and their likely effects, can be understood and their presuppositions brought out.[13]

One way of approaching this is to ask what it is that determines an individual's genuine opportunities for secure functionings. Two sorts of factors come together: what the person has (or has access to); and what they can do with it. In considering what a person has, we can divide this into two types of factor: first, internal resources such as talents and skills; and second, external resources including wealth and income, but also less tangible matters such as family and community support. However it is not possible to 'read off' an individual's opportunities from their resources alone. It is also necessary to know how they can use those resources, and hence to know facts about the structures operating within that society: laws and customs, the influence of tradition, informal and formal power relations, religion, language, culture and other social norms, as well as the configuration of the material and natural environment.[14] We shall refer to all of this as 'social and material structure' (sometimes 'social structure' for short).

Thus the overall formula comes to this: the interaction of your internal resources and your external resources with the social and material structure within which you find yourself, determines your genuine opportunities for secure functionings, creating for you paths of varying cost and difficulty. In short, your resources are what you have to play with; the structure provides the rules of the game.[15] Understood this way, aspects of the social structure are just as important in determining your genuine opportunities for secure functionings as your internal and external resources.

Accordingly, we can see that if someone is thought to be lacking in opportunities, then in principle there are at least three dimensions in which we might try to address this: internal resources; external resources; and social structures. An attempt to tackle disadvantage in the 'space' of internal resources means, in effect, acting on the person (which of course is something agents may do for themselves). This would include education and training (including 'soft skills' as discussed in Chapter 8) as well as psychological, medical, and surgical intervention. This, for obvious reasons, we call personal enhancement.

Action in the space of external resources can take at least two main forms. One is cash compensation, in which individuals are given money to spend as they like. Yet governments also sometimes provide individuals with resources in either cash or concrete form with strings attached. For example, some students with learning disabilities are given cash to spend only on computers, or are given a computer. But this is not intended as a grant of a piece of private property, with all the rights normally associated, but rather the use of an object for a particular purpose and not for others. For example, such a student would not normally be permitted to sell his or her computer to get money for beer or even for rent. There are many similar examples, including the provision of a carer who is employed to perform some services but not others, and so for example cannot be hired out to the highest bidder. Food vouchers, still less education vouchers, are not considered saleable assets, but are intended only to be used for specified purposes. Granting people resources with use restricted in such ways we call 'targeted resource enhancement'.

Last, but certainly not least, there are ways of improving an individual's opportunities without changing his or her internal or external resources. We can, in effect, change the rules of the game so that people can do better with the resources they already have. This could be the result of a change in law or social attitudes, or a change in the configuration of the material environment, such as improved accessibility to buildings. In the case of Leah discussed above, promoting gender equality and changing social norms would have prevented her from seeking to marry and give birth so early, and would presumably have prevented the tragedy that followed. To be honest, it is not clear how much Leah could benefit *now* from changing norms, and perhaps it is fair to say that such a move would prevent future similar cases rather than help her. We elaborate below. We call this a *status enhancement*: a way of improving people's opportunities by, in some sense, changing the rules to improve their standing. The idea of status enhancement will play an important role in the arguments below.

So there are three different dimensions in which states or any other authority might address disadvantage, and there are at least four distinct *strategies* for doing so: personal enhancement; cash compensation; targeted resource enhancement; and status enhancement.

In some cases it will be obvious that some strategies are not available or cannot be pursued within existing resource constraints. In other cases more than one strategy may be possible. For some physical disabilities those who are disabled could be provided with surgery (a personal enhancement) or we could attempt to change the material environment so they can function more easily without changing themselves (a status enhancement).[16] How, then, should the choice of strategy be made? In attempting to meet their aims of addressing individual disadvantage and moving closer to a society of equals, governments must also consider a possible constraint: are there private areas into which the government should not pry? It is often alleged that government intrusion into certain spheres of life can be demeaning or undermine self-respect. If so, then there could be disadvantages that the government should not attempt to address. We need to explore this issue.

10.4 *Status Enhancement, Loneliness, and the Public/Private Distinction*

Having, in Section 10.2, introduced Anderson's example of the 'ugly and socially awkward' to illustrate ways in which addressing disadvantage can go wrong, it seems incumbent upon us to show how our own approach can illuminate these issues. This will also be a useful way of developing some of the elements of our argument in more detail, before returning to further discussion of the examples of slum clearance and the story of Leah, introduced previously. It is, of course, clear that we and Anderson agree that cash compensation should not be the manner in which the government tries to address the problems suffered by the people who are ugly and socially awkward. Yet reading a policy proposal simply from the letter quoted above also seems problematic. The alternative suggested appears to be for each individual in society to accept the social duty of befriending socially awkward and ugly people. To this suggestion, the rejoinder in the letter that it would interfere with other people's freedom of association is not absurd, even if it is rather unkind. However it leaves us in something of a policy vacuum.

One common thought is that such a vacuum is just as well for there are areas of life or certain disadvantages with respect to which it would be wrong for government to act. If this were so it would follow that society is supposed to accept the risk of leaving some disadvantages unaddressed (assuming that it might be the case that no other body addresses them). Within the liberal tradition it is common to draw a distinction between the public and the private, and to argue that there is a private realm for each individual where the government has no business interfering. Historically important examples – some of which have been challenged – concern freedom of thought and conscience, relations within the family, sexual conduct, and other issues of an intensely personal nature. In the current context it could be argued that even if people are disadvantaged in various ways in the private sphere, the government nevertheless has no business to interfere. Being socially awkward or ugly might be thought to be prime examples of disadvantages in the private sphere.

The doctrine of public and private, while appearing to capture an important truth, is hard to formulate in a way which yields policies of which liberals approve. Freedom of thought is rarely considered contravened by public health awareness campaigns. The privacy of the family does not seem to rule out criminalizing various forms of abuse within it. Equally, governments feel obliged to issue advice on sexual behaviour when health is also at stake, or to offer relationship counselling as part of social services.

Our view is that whether or not there is a legitimate distinction to be drawn between the public and private, the key issue is not so much whether there are *areas* of life from which the government should be excluded but rather whether there are *ways* of intervening which the government should not take. If there is a line, it concerns forms, rather than areas, of action. Often people's intuition that the state should not intervene has nothing to do with the liberal question of the boundaries of liberty. Instead it is because they are afraid that whatever the government does, it will act in an ineffective or inhumane way. The latter could result in harm to people's self-respect, even if the original action was motivated by respect for the individual affected. Nevertheless, the fact that government action can be intrusive, clumsy, and counter-productive does not mean that it should be prevented from taking sensitive and appropriate steps in particular areas.

To see this, consider the example of someone who, being in Anderson's terms somewhat socially awkward and never comfortable with strangers, suddenly loses their spouse, and now finds themselves suffering from desperate loneliness.[17] One possible argument that this should not be the concern of government runs:

- If loneliness is a concern of governments, then the lonely should be compensated by tax and transfer schemes, taxing those who are not lonely;
- Such a compensation scheme is absurd.

Therefore

- Loneliness should not be a concern of governments.

The second premise can be agreed, but the first premise is fallacious, as should now be obvious. It overlooks the fact that there are other ways of addressing loneliness than compensating the lonely with cash. As we explained in Chapter 1, cash compensation does not address the actual claim made by lonely people, and this is one reason such a compensation system would be absurd. So what else should be proposed? An example of a targeted resource enhancement would be free or subsidized membership of clubs, or free evening classes, for those who report to the local authority and undergo a test which proves that they are indeed lonely. Such people then have a chance to make new friends and rebuild social relations. While this solves the problem of mismatch by being focused in the right area, it still seems grossly insensitive, and potentially stigmatizing for those people who make use of their new opportunities and claim free membership. Having to identify as lonely in order to benefit can be a huge barrier.

In this case, though, the way to overcome stigma as well as mismatch is rather obvious: offer a modest status enhancement. Governments should provide a subsidy for social clubs and evening classes, to stimulate their growth in order, among other reasons, to provide means by which lonely people can establish social connections. This proposal is not that the lonely must register to obtain subsidized membership but that the clubs and classes should be subsidized generally, for the benefit of all. This universal approach may be more expensive than the conditional scheme considered and rejected above, but its further benefits are considerable. It is essentially a preventative measure, rather than a policy to rectify disadvantage. However if people do become lonely they will have a means of attempting to address this.

Under such a scheme, no one need identify as 'lonely' even to themselves to benefit, as there are many reasons for joining clubs or going to evening classes. This, then, is one non-stigmatizing way of addressing loneliness, or at least as non-stigmatizing as we can presently imagine. The suggestion is not so much that government sets up clubs but rather that the government subsidizes the voluntary or semi-voluntary associations of civil society, through tax breaks, reduced charges for use of public facilities, and so on.[18] This will help people in various categories as well as keep valuable voluntary associations relatively insulated from both the state and the market. It is a status enhancement because it increases people's opportunities without providing them with individual resources.[19] Such a status enhancement is, it is true, in some sense inefficient in that money is spent on some who have no entitlement to subsidy, and so will get an unjustified windfall benefit from the state. Yet taken as a whole it is an effective way of genuinely addressing disadvantage without humiliating people. Efficiency within the context of politics is a social term, rather than only an economic one, and social efficiency should include solidarity, emotional well-being, and the like.

This argument can be used as a model for the way in which disadvantage can be addressed. Increasing genuine opportunities in this way is an example of a status enhancement; a change to the social or material environment. It changes a person's genuine opportunities without changing the person or providing them with a larger bundle of individualized resources.

Status enhancement, therefore, avoids stigma and humiliation; it opens up opportunities to all and by this secures a sense of affiliation for everyone in society, not only those who directly benefit. Furthermore, it also reduces risk. To see this consider again the example of the recently bereaved person, but this time imagine them a year before their spouse died. If such a person lives in a society full of clubs, societies, evening classes, and other opportunities for social interaction, this is a benefit for such a person *even if he or she currently makes no use of such opportunities or has any interest in them*. The benefit may appear to be a purely hypothetical one: that if his or her spouse were to die then the opportunities to overcome loneliness would be appreciably better than in a society which lacked such associations. Yet in our terms *hypothetical* benefits are *real* benefits in that they are ways of reducing risk and thereby *securing functionings*. Societies full of clubs reduce the risk of loneliness and thereby make everyone better off in that respect. In sum, status enhancements are non-stigmatizing, boost affiliation for all, and reduce risk. They address individual disadvantage and help move society towards equality.[20]

10.5 Further Applications: Slum Clearance, Leah

Status enhancement, despite its attractions, is not unfortunately a solution to all problems. It works best in those cases where lack of opportunity is analogous to discrimination, and so changing the world can improve the opportunities of a group of people who suffer from social, cultural, or material barriers. It is also suitable where access to a collective resource can benefit people, as we have seen. However, many problems are not tractable in these terms. Consider again the slum clearance example. Here people within a whole street or neighbourhood were felt to be suffering from risks to their health through poor housing. Probably the houses lacked hot water, internal sanitation, and safe electricity. They would have been damp, with rotten timbers and inadequate windows, and quite possibly facing structural problems as well. The solution provided at the time was to rehouse these people in hygienic flats in a tower block. This addressed their immediate health risks, but created a new problem of social isolation and breakdown in social networks which had many further costs.

What should have been done instead? These people faced a particular threat that needed to be removed. Unfortunately in this case the people were transplanted to what was thought to be a safer environment that created new problems. At a minimum it might be thought that a policy of moving people from the same street en bloc into a tower block would have at least maintained social networks, rather than breaking up communities as was often done. However, the benefits of such a policy would be unclear. Informal social networks can depend on such things as the configuration of the street and the possibility of a chance encounter on the way home from the shops. When you pass other people's front doors only in a high-speed lift, everything changes.

Upgrading existing housing would have been another possibility, even if, unit for unit, it would have been more expensive in the short-term. But imaginatively handled there are further benefits, and avoidances of harms, that could have been achieved if done the right way. Our interviews suggest that empowerment of the community, especially in cases where community is already quite strong, can empower the local inhabitants. Although in cases such as that of housing policy it is unrealistic to think that it is possible to manage without experts, this does not mean that residents should be passive recipients of policy. Involving the residents in decision making about how their neighbourhood is to be improved would boost their control over their environment in the most literal sense, whether or not it leads to better decisions. But there is every reason to think that it will lead to better decisions.[21] Furthermore allowing the residents, if they wish, physically to take part in the rebuilding of their houses as commissioners of services or even paid employees would help them to build skills, and so provide a greater sense of connection and affiliation. In the terms introduced earlier in this chapter, this would amount to a targeted resource enhancement, but with room for flexibility and the exercise of some autonomy in the form it takes. As a further side-effect it may lead to personal enhancement in terms of skills development.

Of course in practice there may be many obstacles which would make this quite inappropriate. Nevertheless it is the sort of approach that should be considered if governments wish to consider the total impact of their policies and thereby use their resources in the most cost effective manner, all things considered.

Leah's problem is very different. As we noted, at the root of her difficulty is her perceived need to conform to local stereotypes, and thereby achieve affiliation, at grave cost to her personal development and hence to many of her other functionings, including sense, imagination, and thought, practical reason, and control over her environment. What can be done? If it could wave a magic wand, the government should break the cultural stereotypes which force her into such a confined, oppressed existence: a status enhancement. In the absence of such structural changes (and even if this is done, it may be too late for Leah herself) anything Leah herself attempts to improve her situation is very risky. Any personal rebellion risks damaging the one thing she does have, the love and support of her family. However, even if the government does embark on a process of encouraging and facilitating cultural change, any effects are likely to be slow and uncertain. Still, for the sake of future Leahs, such change should be brought about. If all goes well, future Leahs will look back to the current situation barely comprehending how people could have treated each other in these ways or failed to take advantage of the opportunities life has to offer. As a start, possible financial incentives for women to complete their education and gain employable skills would help. This would benefit women, create role models for the future, and begin to show men and religious leaders that they have nothing to fear and much to gain from emancipation. It may be, of course, that some other approach would be better – this is likely to be a highly contextual question – but by some means it is necessary to break structures which force women to choose between affiliation and personal development.

For Leah herself, although it may not be easy to see how governments can act with the confidence that they would be likely to make things better, not worse, there are nevertheless real possibilities. Governments can help create a range of opportunities, for education and interesting work, backed up with affordable, quality child care. This, coupled with the provision of advice centres, to replace mystics, and a wider range of subsidized social and leisure opportunities, could contribute to an atmosphere in which it would be possible for Leah to lead a richer, more fulfilling life without putting her affiliation at risk. Nothing, of course, can guarantee that this will be achieved. It could be that Leah is so oppressed that she is unable to see that these new opportunities are available to her. Still, there is a lot that governments can do, by means of a series of small status enhancements, which can greatly improve the probability that Leah sooner or later can take steps to improve her life for herself.

11.5 Conclusion

Throughout this chapter our concern has been to explore ways in which governments can act so as both to address individual disadvantage and to help secure relations of social equality. We have been particularly concerned to explore the externalities – both positive and negative – of government action. On our view there is reason to be optimistic that it is possible to intervene in ways which are not oppressive and do not undermine relations of equality: status enhancement and forms of targeted resource enhancement which have a strong place for individual autonomy are the models we have discussed and recommended. No doubt they will work better in some cases than others, and empirical research is needed to inform future practice. We doubt that general principles can cover every case, and we have conceded that sometimes governments will find it hard to act. However, we hope to have illustrated the types of considerations to which policy makers need to be sensitive. In particular, governments must recognize that the choice of how to go about implementing social policies itself has effects for the goods people in society enjoy. Good methods spread goods widely; bad methods can make everyone worse off in some respects. Our pluralist view allows us to understand how this can be so, but also to make some assessments of different policies.

Conclusion

Our explicit goal in this book has been to consider what needs to be done if societies are to move in the direction of equality. Some readers, no doubt, will have been disappointed that we have not engaged in detail in some of the debates that presently dominate the philosophical debate on equality. These include the questions of the definition of the essence of equality; how to extend egalitarian theories so that they apply to more than the 'basic structure';[1] and whether the 'cut' between cases in which the state should interfere and cases in which it shouldn't depends to what extent disadvantaged people are responsible for their own situation. Although throughout the book we express views which bear on these debates, our purpose has not been to criticize other people's arguments, but instead to shift the focus of the debate on inequality to new ground. Instead of debating how responsible a disadvantaged person is for their situation we think it is important first to understand more clearly what it is to be disadvantaged; and second, to be able to index disadvantages, so that governments have a clear notion of who the least advantaged are. Indeed, these are two of the three main theoretical contributions of our book: first, that the essence of disadvantage concerns not only low functioning but also must take into account the exceptional risks some people face, and the further impact this risk might have on their functionings; and second that even though disadvantage is plural, indexing disadvantages is possible, despite various theoretical and practical problems, which we explore. Our third major theoretical contribution, namely that since disadvantages cluster, governments should de-cluster them by securing fertile functionings and eliminating corrosive disadvantages, is, we hope, a modest contribution to the (real-life) political debate about inequality. We believe that we offer a way forward towards reducing social and economic gaps and diminishing disadvantage in contemporary liberal-democratic societies.

From the start we have indicated that our project has been to try to understand what a society of greater equality may be, and to consider what steps could bring society closer to that ideal. However, it will also be apparent that we have, in some respects, run the project backwards. That is to say, we have tried to pay close attention to what goes wrong in current societies; how this may be improved; and how such a process of improvement may eventually lead to a form of society which deserves to be called a society of greater equality. That would be, in our terms, a society which has successfully de-clustered disadvantage by securing fertile functionings and reducing corrosive disadvantages.

In arriving at this result we have drawn on abstract philosophical theory as well as empirical research, and to a lesser extent social policy. We hope that in doing so we have shown how all can benefit from this encounter. Political theory, we hope, can now better comprehend the ways in which individuals can be, or become, disadvantaged and consequently political theory now has available a more realistic conception of disadvantage, as well as reasonable proposals for improving the lives of disadvantaged people. Empirical researchers can conceptualize their work as part of a grander, systematic project of identifying disadvantage, and the means to address the problems of the least advantaged, and this can help determine priorities between possible projects for research. More important still, it should help determine priority-setting in social policy. Together, then, our theory should provide a resource for those who design and implement social policies, in that it can help them select between possible strategies for creating a society of greater equality and ending disadvantage.

***

All in all, the argument of this book contributes to our understanding of equality in a number of significant ways.

(i) *Redefining advantage and disadvantage.* First, we redefine advantage and disadvantage, building on but modifying the well-known theory of functionings, advanced by Sen, Nussbaum, and others. We consider disadvantage as lack of genuine opportunities for secure functionings. In that sense our theory offers a new understanding of what it is to be disadvantaged. While the idea that disadvantage is plural is not novel, the notion of disadvantage as involving insecurity of functionings and lacking genuine opportunities for secure functionings is, we believe, a step forward towards developing policies that could work towards eliminating disadvantage.

(ii) *Tracking the least advantaged.* Second, we meet a challenge that every authority faces: to find out who the least advantaged are. The concept of the 'least advantaged' is heavily used in the egalitarian theory literature on justice and equality. However, it seems fair to say that very little has been said about who these least advantaged are, and even Rawls conceded that 'it seems impossible to avoid a certain arbitrariness' in actually identifying the least favoured group.[2] Here we take up the challenge. Having in mind our definition of disadvantage, we suggest that the least advantaged are those who experience a clustering of the six most important disadvantages (which we have named, although we recommend that governments practice this exercise of finding the most important functionings), where being disadvantaged is defined in terms of low or insecure functioning.

We believe that focusing on the least advantaged is political theorists' urgent obligation. In contemporary Western societies economic gaps are growing. Interestingly, the larger inequality gaps are, the more important policies of redistribution become, as no other means will help the disadvantaged to survive. However, the more important policies of redistribution are for diminishing social and economic gaps, the more outspoken the critics of these policies become, and the more antagonistic the better-off's attitude towards redistribution.

Moreover, the least advantaged are often excluded groups[3] such as Muslims immigrants in France, African-Americans in the USA,[4] and Arabs in Israel. So not only is there no economic will to help them but also very little political will. These groups are often marginalized to the extent that other people care less and less about them. They often live in segregated communities and towns,[5] they participate less than other groups in the democratic process, and they 'bear a disproportionate share of environmental risks'.[6] By turning attention towards, rather than away from, the least advantaged, such a theory as ours is timely and in place.

(iii) *Relevance to real life.* Third, our theory sheds light on inequality in real life and the effect social policies can have in addressing inequality. By concentrating on such practical issues we hope we can shift the focus of the discourse on inequality. We believe some of the dichotomies around which this discourse has been engaged have led to significant theoretical achievements, but at the same time they lead the discussion to a dead end in terms of influence on policy. Such is, for example, the apparent tension between prioritarianism and equality that, we have argued, when it comes to actual policies, fades away. Another example is the contrast between the idea of the state supplying functionings on the one hand and opportunities on the other. As we have argued (see Chapter 4), in practice and in normal circumstances most goods that a government can legitimately (that is, without forcing people) offer are opportunities. In addition, and in line with trying to shift the discussion to a more policy oriented focus, we have also criticized the intensive discussion of opportunity and responsibility in terms of choice and identification. We have argued that while in ideal circumstances of equality these two concepts, or views, seem plausible candidates for a theory of opportunity and responsibility, when we step outside such circumstances and enter the real world these concepts are quite implausible, being either too harsh or too soft in their consequences. Instead of focusing on the circumstances which lead people to be (or not to be) responsible for their disadvantages, we suggest that the question whether it is reasonable to hold people responsible requires a consideration of the costs of various courses of action that are available to them.

(iv) *Including disadvantaged voices.* Fourth, because our theory is practice oriented, we develop a method of research which takes into account the voices of the least advantaged themselves, as well as experts who work with them, such as social workers, nurses, people who work with asylum seekers, and so on. We are not alone here. Recently more projects have lent their ears to the poor, the elderly, the unemployed, and so on.[7] However, critics of this new method have suggested that it might be counter-productive. For example, when it comes to listing basic needs, poor people tend to list fewer needs than the better off, apparently because they are used to lower standards. A similar worry arose when we interviewed disadvantaged people about which functionings were most important, and while almost everybody mentioned bodily health, the disabled interviewees did not since, they claimed, one could live a good life without being able to move freely and so on. Nevertheless, our approach can meet this challenge. We do not simply listen and write down what we are told. Instead, we applied the *dynamic public reflective equilibrium* approach, in which the discussion takes off with what these people have to say, and the philosopher enters a conversation that involves interpretation of these intuitions and theories. By this method, we hope, we can reach a mixing of participatory and theoretical measures.

(v) *Justification for focusing on the least advantaged.* Fifth, our contribution goes beyond definitions and mechanisms for policy makers. We also suggest that the justifications for abandoning the least advantaged are morally wrong. There are two popular arguments why the state does and probably should turn a blind eye to the least advantaged: a typical right-wing argument is that it is their own fault that they find themselves in such a terrible situation; indeed, disadvantaged people should learn to take responsibility and not rely on the goodwill of the state to solve their problems. We answer this by pointing to how disadvantaged people have to sacrifice certain functionings in order to sustain or secure other, more basic functionings such as not being hungry. Attempting to overcome disadvantage for oneself can lead to great risks, and hence on our view greater disadvantage. We claim that if this is the case people cannot be left alone to take responsibility, as they lack *genuine* opportunities for secure functionings.

A second argument why the state should not rush to help the least advantaged is supported by some on the political left as well, and it is that in a context of scarcity it is too expensive and inefficient to help the least advantaged; it is more efficient to help those whose functionings are not that insecure, or in other words those who could secure their functionings with very little help. We point to several examples of how more imaginative and creative thinking could overcome the so-called problem of inefficiency, and to other cases in which helping the least advantaged would also benefit the entire community. As an example of a more imaginative approach by the state, think of what can be learnt by focusing on clustering of disadvantages and corrosive disadvantage. As we argued in Chapter 9, lack of affiliation is corrosive and damages the security of 'control over environment', health, and in extreme cases the lives of those who lack affiliation. In order to provide affiliation, the government could invest in clubs, social activities, and sustaining communities. This is not necessarily enormously expensive, and it works to benefit other people as well. Thus even if the worst off end up not benefiting from this policy, it couldn't be argued that resources were wasted. If they do benefit – and assuming that affiliation is indeed a fertile functioning – then by investing a relatively small amount of resources, governments can secure many functionings for these people. In addition, such a policy does not stigmatize the least advantaged and therefore works towards social equality. But in order to know which policy to take up, further research is needed towards finding which are the most fertile functionings and corrosive disadvantages.

***

We believe that, together, the chapters of this book establish a powerful understanding of disadvantage, and a clear framework for trying to overcome disadvantage with social policy. We would like to suggest that following the general programme set out in this book is the best any government can do at the present time if it accepts the project of creating a society in which each person can regard him- or herself as one equal among others. Progress may be slow, and all must be ready to learn from failure, but without something like the type of action plan set out here, societies are destined to continue to reinforce patterns of entrenched privilege and disadvantage, widening gaps between rich and poor, and perpetuation of disadvantage. And who, these days, would admit to wishing for this?

APPENDIX 1

Interviews Conducted for this Research

The interviews for this project, which we have mentioned and relied upon at several points in this book, were conducted in Britain and Israel between July 2004 and January 2005, with the help of three research assistants. A second series of interviews was conducted in Israel in December and January 2006. The latter was carried out in order to double-check the results of the first series of interviews, and indeed we found that the results were largely consistent. However, nearly all the interviews we cite in the book are from the first series of interviews.

In the first round we interviewed thirty-eight adults (about two-thirds in Israel and a third in England) on both sides of welfare services, i.e. social workers who take care of unemployed people and unemployed people; doctors at hospitals and patients; teachers and students on state stipends; people who worked at asylum seekers centres and refugees; and so on. In the second round we interviewed about sixty people – so altogether we interviewed nearly 100 adults.

Needless to say, when we decided to interview 'disadvantaged' people in order to improve our understanding of the essence of disadvantage, we faced a methodological dilemma. We had to approach some people whom we thought were disadvantaged but only then, and on the basis of what they told us, did we come to our final conclusion of the meaning of disadvantage. In order to bypass this catch we conducted a series of pilot interviews, with colleagues as well, about whom we could be sure were disadvantaged. On the basis of these initial interviews we decided whom to interview to complete the series of interviews.

The interviews in the first round were semi-structured, in the sense that the interviewee could talk as long as he or she wanted to, about any subject that they thought was related to the interview. We taped them and considered everything they said as an input to our analysis, using our method of *public reflective equilibrium.* In that sense these meetings were not simple interviews but rather discussions with these people, in which we learnt from them, but also asked them to reflect upon our thoughts. At the same time, we insisted that they tried to answer the questions we posed to them, even when they said that this was extremely difficult.

As a preliminary the interviewees were first told about our project. The first phase concerned our attempt to produce a statement of the categories of functioning which contribute to individual advantage and disadvantage. Their first task was to name what they thought the basic categories for essential functionings. They were asked to reflect about each and reason why they mentioned this or that category. Next, they were shown a card with a list of fourteen such categories, which included Martha Nussbaum's list plus four other categories (see below). They were asked to take their time and comment. Only then did we introduce limits (budget, time, energy) and asked whether they had views about priorities, and why. To conclude this part of the interview they were asked to name the three most important categories among their new list, and to say whether there were areas in which the government should spend more than it currently does, whether there were areas in which the government should spend less, and why. We also asked them whether the showcard failed to mention any category they found important.

All second round interviews were conducted in Israel. Unlike the first round, these were not taped, but the results were written up by Avner, who conducted most of the interviews, some assisted by his graduate students in his seminar on equality. One batch consisted of about twenty interviews, following a less structured pattern than the first phase. A second batch, involving about forty subjects, was conducted after a ninety-minute meeting and deliberation about our research with students of social work who have already had experience of practice as social workers. They were given the questions and asked to answer them in writing. Interestingly, the results of these additional interviews, whether they were conducted as regular interviews or following the above-mentioned deliberation, supported the results of the initial round. There was no significant difference.

A question might be raised here about why we started with Martha Nussbaum's list, or to be more precise with a revised and extended version of her list. Perhaps the main drawback of Nussbaum's list is that it considers categories which might appear too broad. Indeed, as we show in the book, sometimes part of the 'trading' in functionings, when disadvantaged people sacrifice one functioning to sustain another which becomes insecure, happens between sub-categories within Nussbaum's categories. For example, disadvantaged people sacrifice balanced and healthy diet to secure satiation, but both of these appear under the same functioning in Nussbaum's list. However, we had to start somewhere, and it seems to us that Nussbaum's list is both intuitive and well argued, and that it is comprehensive enough. As a matter of fact, while our interviewees had some queries about why this or that functioning was on the list, in general they accepted the list as a reasonable one.

A further phase of the interview was designed to allow us to see how to define the 'least' advantaged in each category, or what it means to be disadvantaged in each category. The interviewees were asked to relate to their specific sphere of disadvantage, as they saw it. With those working with disadvantaged people this was easy: most of them were in charge of a particular project or disadvantage, e.g. homelessness, unemployment, elderly people, and the like. It was more tricky with the disadvantaged themselves, as they had to decide first on their main problem, whether, for example, it was unemployment or being chronically ill, and sometimes they wished to address both, to which we agreed. However, we wanted our interviewees to refer to their 'own' sphere, and name the three most important indicators or measures of doing badly. If they found it difficult to answer this, we offered examples with regard to another sphere. Finally, we asked the interviewees to reflect about policy in his or her area.

Interviewees were not paid, but were each promised a copy of the book. We also promised not to reveal their names or any fact that might expose their identity.

A few methodological comments are needed. First, why did we interview people rather than use a larger-scale survey instrument? As we explain in the text, we use the interviews as a major input into our research, as a stage in the process of *public reflective equilibrium*. So we wanted people to theorize, not only to offer their first gut feelings or unreflective intuitions. Large-scale surveys, on the other hand, must be based on closed questions with multiple-choice answers. This would not allow for such reflections. The notion of disadvantage is vague and problematic and large-scale surveys face the danger of oversimplifying or giving misleading results. We should note that the interviews were not conducted simultaneously, and this gave us the option to revise questions according to the answers or the emerging information we gathered in the initial series of interviews.

Second, it is possible that a person's status and location affected what they perceived to be the most and least important functionings.[1] This, it might be claimed, would yield a biased set or weighting of functionings. But this did not disturb us, as we were not looking to generate an objectively true list based on a statistical survey. Rather, we wanted to discover the range of representations current among our survey group, looking for affinities and differences in their own subjective understandings about what makes life go well and badly. As long as they could reason about their intuitions, we were content.

Third, we cannot claim that the interviews bear any statistically meaningful information. The entire empirical part of this research is intended to introduce and demonstrate a method, rather than take it to the point of completion, which would require a huge budget. Ours is empirical research that is meant to inspire rather than conclude. As explained when we discussed the *public reflective equilibrium* model, it is a springboard from which to philosophize and theorize. However, at the same time there is a lot that can be learnt from it, provided that we keep in mind that statistically this data should be taken with a pinch of salt.

Finally, we are also aware of the potential problem of translating between English and Hebrew. It might be the case that those reading the showcard in English and those reading it in Hebrew interpreted some of the concepts differently; however, we tried to overcome this problem by allowing the interviewees carefully to discuss with us the various concepts listed on the showcard before they started answering. It was not a survey, but a semi-structured interview.

All the details of the interviews are on tape. If the reader has any query regarding these tapes and the particular interviews, please address your request to Avner at msads@mscc.huji.ac.il.

The following is the showcard we showed to the interviewees:

Dear Sir/Madam,

Below is a list of 14 categories in one's life, which might seem vital for any person's flourishing. They can be described as things which one would like to do or be. Please go through them and comment on them. In particular we would like to know how you would consider failing to achieve each of them.

1. **Life**: Being able to live to the end of a human life of normal length.
2. **Bodily health**: Being able to have good health, including reproductive health; to be adequately nourished, to have adequate shelter.
3. **Bodily integrity**: Being able to move freely from place to place; being able to be secure against assault, including sexual assault, child sexual abuse, and domestic violence; having opportunities for sexual satisfaction and for choice in matters of reproduction.
4. **Sense, imagination, and thought**: Being able to imagine, think, and reason – and to do these things in a way informed and cultivated by an adequate education. Freedom of expression, speech, and religion.

5. **Emotions**: Being able to have attachments to things and people outside ourselves; to love those who love and care for us.
6. **Practical Reason**: Being able to engage in critical reflection about the planning of one's life.
7. **Affiliation**: Being able to live with and toward others, to recognize and show concern for other human beings, to engage in various forms of social interaction. Having the social bases of self-respect and non-humiliation. Not being discriminated against on the basis of gender, religion, race, ethnicity, and the like.
8. **Other species**: Being able to live with concern for and in relation to animals, plants, and the world of nature.
9. **Play:** Being able to laugh, to play, to enjoy recreational activities.
10. **Control over one's environment**: Being able to participate effectively in political choices that govern one's life. Being able to have real opportunity to hold property. Having the right to seek employment on an equal basis with others.
11. **Complete independence**: Being able to do exactly as you wish without relying on the help of others.
12. **Doing good to others**: Being able to care for others as part of expressing your humanity. Being able to show gratitude.
13. **Living in a law-abiding fashion**: The possibility of being able to live within the law; not to being forced to break the law, cheat, or to deceive other people or institutions.
14. **Understanding the law**: Having a general comprehension of the law, its demands, and the opportunities it offers to individuals. Not standing perplexed facing the legal system.

NOTES

Notes to the Introduction

1. This story describes a true case, but the names have been changed.
2. Indeed, while this is not the focus of our book, it is clear that women form a majority among the disadvantaged, and that often women experience particular disadvantages that men do not have to face. This is one of the reasons we open this book with Leah's story.
3. Dworkin, Ronald, 'What is Equality? Equality of Welfare', *Philosophy and Public Affairs*, 10 (1981), 185–246; and Dworkin, Ronald, 'What Is Equality? Equality of Resources', *Philosophy and Public Affairs* 10 (1981), 283–345, both reprinted in Dworkin, Ronald, *Sovereign Virtue* (Cambridge, Mass.: Harvard University Press, 2000). For wide views of Dworkin's project see Burley, Justine (ed.), *Dworkin and His Critics* (Oxford: Blackwell, 2004). See also Cohen, G. A., 'On the Currency of Egalitarian Justice', *Ethics* 99 (1989), 906–44; Arneson, Richard, 'Equality and Equal Opportunity for Welfare', *Philosophical Studies* 56 (1989), 77–93 and Nagel, Thomas, 'Equality', in his *Mortal Questions* (Cambridge: Cambridge University Press, 1979), 117–19. For the priority position see Parfit, Derek, 'Equality and Priority', *Ratio* 10 (1997), 202–21. For a discussion of the sufficiency position see Frankfurt, Harry, 'Equality as a Moral Ideal', *Ethics* 98 (1987), 21–43. Finally, for very good general reviews of the literature and the debate see Arneson, Richard, 'Equality' in Goodin, Robert and Philip Pettit (eds.), *A Companion to Contemporary Political Philosophy* (Oxford: Blackwell, 1993), 489–509; and http://plato.stanford.edu/entries/egalitarianism/ and Gosepath, Stefan http://plato.stanford.edu/entries/equality/.
4. Cohen, 'On the Currency of Egalitarian Justice', 906.
5. The relational view is expressed in the classic works of British socialism, such as Tawney, R. H., *Equality* (London: George Allen and Unwin, 1931). More recently it has been advocated by feminist theorists, e.g., Young and Phillips. See Young, Iris Marion, *Justice and the Politics of Difference* (Princeton: Princeton University Press, 1990), and Phillips, Anne, *Which Equalities Matter?* (Cambridge: Polity, 1999). However, this position has been advanced by other political theorists such as David Miller and Richard Norman. See Miller, David, 'What Kind of Equality Should the Left Pursue?' in Franklin, Jane (ed.), *Equality* (London: Institute for Public Policy Research, 1997), 83–100, and Norman, Richard, 'The Social Basis of Equality' in Mason, Andrew (ed.), *Ideals of Equality* (Oxford: Blackwell, 1998). It reasserted itself as a criticism of what has become to be called 'luck egalitarianism'. See Wolff, Jonathan, 'Fairness, Respect and the Egalitarian Ethos', *Philosophy and Public Affairs*, 27 (1998), 97–122, Anderson, Elizabeth, 'What is the Point of

Equality?' *Ethics* 109 (1999), 287–337, Scheffler, Samuel, *Boundaries and Allegiances: Problems of Justice and Responsibility in Liberal Thought* (Oxford: Oxford University Press, 2001) and Scheffler, Samuel, 'What is Egalitarianism?', *Philosophy and Public Affairs* 31 (2003), 5–39.

6. Tawney, *Equality*, 291.
7. Notice that often even with material goods this is the case. Providing some welfare services by taxing the middle class often results in the middle class using these services more than anybody else. See the interesting figures in Frank Field, *Inequality in Britain: Freedom, Welfare and the State* (Glasgow: Fontana, 1981), 129–35. So much so that some egalitarians have turned against free access to services. Shlomi Segall meets their challenge. See Segall, Shlomi, 'Bringing the Middle Classes Back In: An Egalitarian Case for Truly Universal Public Services', *Ethics and Economics* 2 (2004). See http://mapage.noos.fr/Ethique-economique/html_version/SEGALL.pdf.
8. For the distinction between being homeless and 'rough sleepers' see the Homeless Link, http://www.homeless.org.uk/db/20020802224222.
9. Miller, David and Michael Walzer (eds.), *Pluralism, Justice and Equality* (Oxford: Oxford University Press, 1995); Miller, David, *Principles of Social Justice* (Cambridge, Mass.: Harvard University Press, 1999); Walzer, Michael, *Spheres of Justice: A Defence of Pluralism and Equality* (Oxford: Blackwell, 1983).
10. Klinenberg, Eric, *Heatwave: the Social Autopsy of Disaster in Chicago* (Chicago: University of Chicago Press, 2002). See also 'Dying Alone: An interview with Eric Klinenberg', http://www.press.uchicago.edu/Misc/Chicago/443213in.html.
11. See http://www.haaretz.com/hasen/spages/598232.html.
12. We should make clear, however, that we do not wish to argue that ours is the only legitimate approach to political philosophy.
13. For this observation see Nozick, Robert, *Anarchy, State, and Utopia* (Oxford: Basil Blackwell, 1974), x.
14. We owe this way of putting the point to a lecture by Bernard Williams in London some time in the late 1980s.
15. We fully appreciate that these are not all novel projects and that others are trying to forge similar connections. A significant number of philosophers – enthusiastically following the lead of Amartya Sen – have been trying to provide a more realistic account of human well-being and suffering. See The Capability Approach Internet site: http://www.fas.harvard.edu/~freedoms/bibliography.cgi?page_builder=cap_app/; the Equality Exchange site (http://aran.univ-pau.fr/ee); and the Priority in Practice series of seminars (http://www.homepages.ucl.ac.uk/~uctyjow/PiP.htm). In Britain several leading political philosophers have been addressing real-life issues combining theory with empirical research. See Miller *Principles of Social Justice*. For his reasoning for this approach see especially Chapter 3, 'Social Science and Political Philosophy', 42–61. Similarly researchers in social policy areas as diverse as public health (Marmot, Michael, *Status Syndrome* (London: Bloomsbury, 2004); Daniels, N., Light, D., Caplan, R., *Benchmarks of Fairness for Health Care Reform* (New York: Oxford University Press, 1996); Daniels, N.,

Buchanan, A., Brock, D., and Wikler, D., *From Chance to Choice: Genes and Social Justice* (Cambridge: Cambridge University Press, 2000); Daniels, N., and Sabin, J., *Setting Limits Fairly: Can We Learn to Share Medical Resources?* (New York: Oxford University Press, 2002)) and public transport (see, for example, Tyler, Nick, *Justice in Transport Policy* (London: School of Public Policy, University College London, 2004, http://eprints.ucl.ac.uk/archive/00001354/01/2004_47.pdf) are looking to theories of social justice for guidance in priority setting. Here we attempt to provide one systematic account of the way in which the pieces can be put together.

16. See Daniels, Norman, *Justice and Justification: Reflective Equilibrium in Theory and Practice* (Cambridge: Cambridge University Press, 1996).
17. For more about *public reflective equilibrium* see de-Shalit, Avner, *Power to the People: Teaching Political Philosophy in Skeptical Times* (Lanham: Lexington Books, Rowman and Littlefield, 2006), chapter 3.
18. Dworkin, *Sovereign Virtue*.
19. Smilansky, Saul, 'Responsibility and Desert: Defending the Connection', *Mind* 105 (1996), 157–63.
20. For more details see the introductions to each of the three parts of this book.
21. For two recent examples see Lister, Ruth, *Poverty* (Cambridge: Polity, 2004), and Hills, John, *Inequality and the State* (Oxford: Oxford University Press, 2004).

Notes to Chapter 1

1. In general we will avoid using the terminology of 'justice' and 'injustice'. In our view society has an obligation to address many forms of disadvantage, whether or not they are injustices, strictly speaking. Hence to concentrate only on injustice would be to risk imposing an unhelpful restriction on our subject matter.
2. Scanlon, Thomas, 'Preference and Urgency', *Journal of Philosophy* 72 (1975), 655–69.
3. This example is originally due to Arrow, but was also importantly used by Dworkin, 'What is Equality?'.
4. Cohen, 'On the Currency of Egalitarian Justice'.
5. Dworkin, 'What is Equality: Part 1, Equality of Welfare', Cohen, 'On the Currency of Egalitarian Justice'.
6. See also O'Neill, Onora, 'The Power of Examples' in her *Constructions of Reason* (Cambridge: Cambridge University Press, 1990).
7. For a detailed attempt to solve this problem see Binmore, Ken, *Playing Fair* (Cambridge Mass.: MIT Press, 1994). For a more sceptical discussion see Hausman, Daniel, 'The Impossibility of Interpersonal Utility Comparisons', *Mind* 104 (1995), 473–90 and Hausman, Daniel and Michael McPherson, *Economic Analysis and Moral Philosophy* (Cambridge: Cambridge University Press, 1996), 84–8, 95–7.

8. For a leading view of this type see Dworkin 'What is Equality? Part 2: Equality of Resources'.

9. See also van der Veen, Robert, 'Basic income: Smart Policy or Instrument of Social Justice?', ALSP conference (Dublin, 2006). Some attempt to define a third relation 'on a par' or 'rough equality'. This does not affect the main argument of this chapter, but for discussion see the essays in Chang, Ruth, (ed.), *Incommensurability, Incomparability and Practical Reasoning* (Cambridge, Mass.: Harvard University Press 1997).

10. It may well be that goods of different types can be compared in some cases. We will see examples of how this may be so shortly.

11. Rawls, John, *A Theory of Justice* (Oxford: Oxford University Press, 1973), 40–5.

12. Although how income and wealth are to be compared is a further question, given that not all wealth is income bearing.

13. We interviewed close to 100 people on both sides of the welfare services, i.e. social workers, educators, people who work with asylum seekers, doctors, nurses on the one hand, and elderly people, refugees, homeless people, health patients, and so on, on the other. Details are set out in Appendix 1. They all mentioned five to fifteen different spheres of disadvantage, but they all added that ultimately these disadvantages were not reducible to a single category. Interestingly, these people did not seem to be making a metaphysical claim by saying that disadvantages were 'different from each other', but rather they mentioned two justifications: first, that they could not compare them, saying which is worse to have; and second, that in terms of rectifying them, policies would have to be rather different, and even that rectifying one disadvantage might clash with rectifying another. We return to this topic in Chapter 2.

14. A useful attempt at clarification is Robert Goodin's distinction between 'means-substitution' compensation and 'ends-displacement' compensation. See Goodin, Robert, 'Theories of Compensation', *Oxford Journal of Legal Studies* 9 (1989), 56–75; reprinted in Frey, R. G. and Christopher Morris (eds.), *Liability: New Essays in Legal Philosophy* (Cambridge: Cambridge University Press, 1990), 267–86. For doubts about this distinction and an attempt to replace it with a continuum, while remaining within the spirit of Goodin's suggestion, see Wolff, Jonathan, 'Addressing Disadvantage and the Human Good', *Journal of Applied Philosophy* 19 (2002), 207–18, 209.

15. We thank Mike Otsuka for pressing this point and others in this chapter.

16. This seems a reasonable assumption. Even if money will not compensate for a high risk of death, the reason for this is not that we become too easily saturated with money.

17. Dworkin seems to assume as much in discussing health care provision. See Dworkin, Ronald, 'Justice in the Distribution of Health Care' in Matthew Clayton and Andrew Williams (eds.), *The Ideal of Equality* (New York: St. Martin's Press, 2000), 203–22.

18. Cohen, for example, writes: 'If [someone] could not have avoided [their disadvantage] but could now overcome it, then he can ask that his effort to

overcome it be subsidized, but, unless it costs more to overcome it than to compensate for it without overcoming it, he cannot expect society to compensate for his disadvantage'; 'On the Currency of Egalitarian Justice', 920. This argument trades on the idea that it can be more cost-effective to change people's 'internal resources' than to provide them with compensating external resources.

19. Of course forms of monism which do not accept that money has value will be immune to this criticism. However, such a view has not been proposed outside, perhaps, very austere religious theory. But this is why we restricted the scope of this argument to 'plausible' forms of monism.

20. This continues to assume that we are operating within a range where money has not reached a saturation point.

21. Excluding, as before, high risk of death cases.

22. In Chapter 10 we will discuss this type of case in more detail. For reasons we will explain there, we call this type of action a 'status enhancement'.

23. For the purposes of this argument we need to exclude third-party effects, although in real policy cases this must be included. This too will be discussed in Chapter 10.

24. Some, no doubt, will see a worrying paternalism here. Once more we will return to this issue in Chapter 10.

25. It may be thought that the response to this is to move to some notion of 'idealized preferences'; that even if there is reason to override people's preferences, this is a reason not for giving up preference theory, but to incorporate an idea of what people's preferences ought to be. But the same issue arises. If, with ideal preferences, I refuse to accept cash compensation, this is to deny substitution monism. If, on the other hand, ideal preferences merely make me raise the price I need for compensation, this seems just as implausible as a lower price.

26. Anderson, 'What is the Point of Equality?'.

27. This we call a 'targeted resource enhancement'.

28. For those who are not convinced, the remainder of this book can be read in 'conditional mode': i.e. how to deal with the indexing problem and implementing appropriate policies on the assumption that disadvantage is plural. Those who are attracted to monism because it can solve the indexing problem may find its appeal diminished when they come to understand how such issues can be handled within a pluralist approach.

29. Rawls, John, *Political Liberalism* (New York: Columbia University Press, 1993), 7.

30. In 'A Kantian Conception of Equality', in Rawls, John, *Collected Papers* (New York: Columbia University Press, 1999), Rawls remarks: 'I also suppose that everyone has physical needs and psychological capacities within the *normal range*, so that problems of special health care and how to treat the mentally defective *do not arise*. Besides prematurely introducing difficult questions that may take us beyond the theory of justice, the consideration of these hard cases can distract our moral perception by leading us to think of people

distant from us whose fate arouses pity and anxiety. Whereas the first problem of justice concerns the relations among those in the normal course of things who are full and active participants in society and directly or indirectly associated together over the course of a whole life.' (259, emphasis added). For further, related, comments see Rawls, John, 'Social Unity and Primary Goods' in Amartya Sen and Bernard Williams (eds.), *Utilitarianism and Beyond* (Cambridge: Cambridge University Press, 1982), 168.

31. Of course, if elected they may be able to do something to end such discrimination, but that is not the question. It is whether these extra liberties on their own will compensate for the lack of other liberties.

32. We return to such issues in Chapter 10.

Notes to Chapter 2

1. Sen, Amartya, *On Economic Equality* (Oxford: Clarendon Press, 1973, 1997 expanded version); Sen, Amartya, *Resources, Values and Development* (Cambridge, Mass.: Harvard University Press, 1984); Sen, Amartya, *Inequality Reexamined* (Oxford: Clarendon Press, 1992); Sen, Amartya, *Development as Freedom* (Oxford: Oxford University Press, 1999); Sen, Amartya, 'Gender Inequality and Theories of Justice' in Nussbaum, M., and Glover, J (eds.), *Women, Culture and Development* (Oxford: Clarendon Press, 1995) 259–273; Drèze, Jean and Amartya Sen, *Hunger and Public Action* (Oxford: Clarendon Press, 1989); Nussbaum, Martha and Amartya Sen (eds.), *The Quality of Life* (Oxford: Clarendon Press, 1993); Sen, Amartya, *The Standard of Living* (Tanner Lectures on Human Values, Salt Lake City: University of Utah Press, 1986); Sen, Amartya, 'Equality of What?' in *The Tanner Lectures on Human Values*, ed. S. M. McMurrin, Salt Lake City: University of Utah Press, 1980), reprinted in Sen, Amartya, *Choice, Welfare and Measurement* (Oxford: Blackwell, 1982); Nussbaum, Martha, *Women and Human Development* (Cambridge: Cambridge University Press, 2000); Alkire, Sabina, *Valuing Freedoms: Sen's Capability Approach and Poverty Reduction* (Oxford: Oxford University Press, 2002). About the differences between Sen's theory and Nussbaum's theory and more about what capabilities and functioings are, see Crocker, David, 'Functioning and Capability: The Foundations of Sen's and Nussbaum's Development Ethics', *Political Theory*, 20 (1992), 584–612. For a review of Sen's work and its application see Agarwal, Bina, and Jane Humphries, (eds.), *Amartya Sen's Work and Ideas: A Gender Perspective* (London: Routledge, 2005), and Robeyns, Ingrid, and Wiebke Kuklys, 'Sen's Capability Approach to Welfare Economics', in Kuklys, Wiebke (ed.), *Amartya Sen's Capability Approach: Theoretical Insights and Empirical Applications* (Berlin: Springer Verlag, 2005), 9–30.

2. Nussbaum, *Women and Human Development*, 71, emphasis added.
3. Alkire, *Valuing Freedoms: Sen's Capability Approach and Poverty Reduction*, 4.
4. Sen, *Inequality Reexamined*, 40.
5. Robeyns, Ingrid, 'The Capability Approach: An Interdisciplinary Introduction', http://www.ingridrobeyns.nl/Downloads/CAtraining20031209.pdf/, 2003, p. 11.
6. Alkire, *Valuing Freedoms; Sen's Capability Approach and Poverty Reduction*, 19.
7. See Alkire, *Valuing Freedoms*, table 2.12, 78 – 82.
8. Robeyns, 'The Capability Approach: An Interdisciplinary Introduction' 23–6.
9. Nussbaum's premise is that for some functionings there are better ways of doing them or being them. By better we mean more human, or what Nussbaum calls, following Marx, 'not merely an animal way' of doing things. (See Nussbaum, *Women and Human Development*, 72). Marx offers the example of eating food. The starving person not only enjoys worse nutrition than the affluent person; s/he eats in a way which is not fully human: this person does not have the social and aesthetic experiences, associations, and enjoyments that other people do. In other words, eating for this person is never dining. As Nussbaum writes: '[Marx's core idea] is that of the human being as a dignified free being who shapes his or her own life in cooperation and reciprocity with others, rather than being passively shaped or pushed around by the world in the manner of a "flock" or "herd" animal. A life that is really human is one that is shaped throughout by these human powers of practical reason and sociability.' (Nussbaum, *Women and Human Development*, 72) For an interesting parallel discussion of human well-being and its relationships with nature that is inspired by Aristotle and Marx, see O'Neill, John, *Ecology, Policy and Politics* (London: Routledge, 1993), especially chapter 1, 1–7.
10. Nussbaum, Martha, 'Capabilities as Fundamental Entitlements: Sen and Social Justice', *Feminist Economics* 9 (2003), 33–59, p. 40.
11. Rawls, John, *Political Liberalism*, 133–72; Nussbaum, *Women and Human Development*, 76.
12. Some people would prefer to convey this idea using the term 'autonomy'.
13. This entails, Nussbaum writes, protections against discrimination on the basis of race, sex, sexual orientation, religion, caste, ethnicity, or national origin.
14. Alkire, *Valuing Freedoms*, 165.
15. Sen, Amartya, 'The Standard of Living' in G. Hawthorn (ed.), *The Standard of Living* (Cambridge: Cambridge University Press, 1987), 109; and Sen, Amartya, 'Capability and Well Being', in Nussbaum and Sen (eds.), *The Quality of Life*, 41. For a profound discussion of Sen's use of the term see Robeyns, 'The Capability Approach: An Interdisciplinary Introduction'.
16. One might wonder whether what we mean when we use the language of secure functionings, is that people have *rights* to certain levels of functionings. While we believe that if people should have *secure* functionings then this implies that they have a right to this level of security, in the sense that the state should guarantee it, we also think that at the same time this raises

philosophical and political complications, which make an already rather complex theory even more complicated. Thus we'll leave the question of whether our theory can be restructured in terms of rights and hopefully return to it in later works. See also Ingram, Attracta, *A Political Theory of Rights* (Oxford: Oxford University Press, 1995).

17. This may be one reason why Sen always leaves his lists open-ended. See Sen, *Development as Freedom*, 76–8.
18. Daniels, Norman, *Justice and Justification* (Cambridge: Cambridge University Press, 1996), 2.
19. Rawls, *A Theory of Justice.*
20. Miller, *Principles of Social Justice*, 54.
21. Walzer, Michael, *Interpretation and Social Criticism* (Cambridge, Mass.: Harvard University Press, 1987); Walzer, Michael, *The Company of Critics* (New York: Basic Books, 1988); Walzer, Michael, *Thick and Thin: Moral Agreement at Home and Abroad* (South Bend, Ind.: University of Notre Dame Press, 1994).
22. Walzer, *Interpretation and Social Criticism*, 1–33.
23. Walzer, *Thick and Thin*, 42.
24. Walzer, *Thick and Thin*, 52–3.
25. Walzer, *Thick and Thin*, 52–3.
26. See the Report of the Commission on Poverty, Participation and Power, *Listen Hear: The Right to Be Heard* (Bristol: Policy Press and the UK Coalition Against Poverty, 2000).
27. We would like to thank Ingrid Robeyns and Shivi Greenfield for discussing these matters with us.
28. In Nussbaum, Martha, *Poetic Justice: The Literary Imagination in Public Life* (Boston: Beacon Press, 1996), Nussbaum claims that being ethical starts with being able to empathize with the other. Nussbaum promotes the study of literature in order to develop what we can term the 'capability to be empathetic'. See also Nussbaum, Martha, *Cultivating Humanity* (Cambridge, Mass.: Harvard University Press, 1997), 101.
29. Gilligan argues that the ethics of care is feminine. Men focus on how to distribute evenly, whereas women have an instinct of care, seeing that nobody is left alone, and the like. See Gilligan, Carol, *In a Different Voice: Psychological Theory and Women's Development* (Cambridge, Mass.: Harvard University Press, 1982).
30. O'Neill, Onora, 'Justice, Gender and International Boundaries' in Nussbaum and Sen (eds.), *The Quality of Life*, 303–23; p. 311.
31. This is an Aristotelian idea. (See Aristotle, *Nicomachean Ethics*, Book 9.)
32. In the *Poverty and Social Exclusion in Britain* survey 'visiting friends and family at hospital' came fourth on the list of needs, with 92% defining it as a necessity. Being able to attend weddings and funerals also came high on the list (80% defining it as a necessity). Also, Richard Wilkinson, in *The Impact of Inequality* (London: Routledge, 2005, 259) reports the research finding summarized in the title of their paper by Brown, S., R. M. Nesse, A. D. Vinokur, and D. M Smith, 'Providing Social Support May be More Beneficial Than

Receiving It: Results From a Prospective Study of Mortality', *Psychological Science* 14 (2003), 320–7.

33. Narayan, Deepa, et al., *Voices of the Poor: Can Anyone Hear Us?* (Oxford: Oxford University Press and the World Bank, 2000), 39.

34. Narayan et al., 44–5.

35. Poverty is often linked to social exclusion. See Hills, John, Julian Le Grand, and David Piachaud (eds.), *Understanding Social Exclusion* (Oxford: Oxford University Press, 2002).

36. Notice that the laws most likely to be broken in this category are those without immediately identifiable victims. Benefit fraud, tax evasion, and buying stolen or counterfeit goods, do not damage an identifiable person in the way a burglary or street robbery does. Thus such action is consistent with a general respect for law insofar as it expresses a moral code of acceptable behaviour in relation to other individuals.

37. Alkire, *Valuing Freedoms*, table 2.5, 64.

38. The following possible functioning was suggested to us by colleagues, philosophers and political scientists, but surprisingly was not mentioned in the interviews. It is the functioning of one's culture and identity being recognized. This raises a question: is recognition an advantage? Can one be disadvantaged if one's culture is not fully recognized? This is an important question in contemporary philosophy, as well as politics. It is sometimes alleged that there is a tension between redistribution and recognition. (See Fraser, Nancy and Axel Honneth, *Redistribution or Recognition: A Political-Philosophical Exchange* (London: Verso, 2003)). Understanding whether this is so clearly bears on the question whether there is any functioning that has to do with recognition. But again surprisingly recognition did not come up as a functioning in the interviews we conducted and for this reason we have provisionally not included it in our current list of functionings.

39. Randian, rather than Nozickian, centering on the moral importance of independence and self-reliance.

40. See also Narayan et al., *Voices of the Poor: Can Anyone Hear Us?* 36–7.

41. As noted earlier, some people would refer to 'autonomy'.

42. We do not, by these comments, intend to endorse Maslow's particular suggestion about a hierarchy of needs or functionings. We return to such questions in Part 2.

43. http://www.normemma.com/armaslow.htm. Also see Twenge, J. M., Catanese, K. R., and Baumeister, R. F., 'Social Exclusion Causes Self-Defeating Behavior', *Journal of Personality and Social Psychology* 83 (2002), 606–15.

44. Maslow, Abraham, *Toward a Psychology of Being* (New York: Van Nostrand, third edition, 1998 (1962)).

45. http://web.utk.edu/~gwynne/maslow.HTM.

46. See Sen, Amartya, *Poverty and Famines* (Oxford: Clarendon Press, 1981). Sen refers to Adam Smith's work (p. 18; and Sen, Amartya, 'Capability and Well Being' in Nussbaum and Sen (eds.), *The Quality of Life*, 37) See also Alkire's discussion, *Valuing Freedoms*, chapter 5 section 1).

47. Smith wrote: 'By necessaries I understand, not only the commodities which are indispensably necessary for the support of life, but whatever the custom of the country renders it indecent for creditable people, even the lowest order, to be without.' (Smith, Adam, *The Wealth of Nations* (London: Modern Library Edition, (1776) 1937), Book 5, Part II, Article 4, 821–2). Smith went on to discuss a linen shirt as an example: in the times of the ancient Greeks this was not a necessity, whereas in Smith's time a day labourer would be ashamed to appear in public without it. See also the discussion in Quingley, William P., *Ending Poverty as We Know It* (Philadelphia: Temple University Press, 2003), 40f.

48. See, for example, the Workers' Education Association, a voluntary adult education movement: http://www.wea.org.uk/Contact.

49. Narayan et al. write: 'Myths and stereotypes that surround AIDS have caused sufferers of the disease to be cut off from social networks.' Narayan et al., *Voices of the Poor: Can Anyone Hear Us?*, 246.

50. For a further example see Masters, Alexander, *Stuart: A Life Backwards* (London: HarperCollins, 2005). Stuart Shorter, the subject of the book, who had been a 'chaotic homeless person', tells his MP that over the cold winter lives are at risk because there had been 'two litters on the street'. He goes on to explain that homeless people with dogs will not stay in the town's shelters which do not allow animals, and would prefer to stay with their dogs and take their chances in the cold than abandon them overnight. As the population of street dogs had recently increased many more people would be at risk unless the night shelters changed their animal policy. See p. 250. Similar concerns were reported during the flooding in New Orleans, where many residents refused to be rescued without their pets.

51. In an interesting interview with a social worker who works with elderly people, she suggested that 'independence' is not a functioning for most people – since people are so dependent on others and on their communities anyway that it does not make sense to really talk about 'independence' – but elderly people behave as if and believe that independence is a crucial functioning, and that losing it reflects a serious deterioration in one's situation.

52. See Narayan et al., *Voices of the Poor: Can Anyone Hear Us?*, 35. See also http://wbln0018.worldbank.org/dg/povertys.nsf/0/3ee9ddc1f9e883d7852568b2007af2c8?OpenDocument. Compare with McGee, Rosemary, 'Constructing Poverty Trends in Uganda: A Multidisciplinary Perspective', *Development and Change* Volume 35 (2004), 499–533.

53. For charity see Traa-Valerezo, Ximena, 'Social Assessment for the Guatemala Reconstruction and Local Development Project' (Washington: World Bank, 1997); http://wbln0018.worldbank.org/dg/povertys.nsf/0/d8272371674e11d7852568b2007abb08?OpenDocument.

54. Nussbaum, *Women and Human Development*, 78, fn 82.

55. See Narayan et al., *Voices of the Poor: Crying Out for Change*. In Israel there is a growing number of NGOs that offer legal services to laypersons. See http://www.haaretz.co.il/hasite/pages/ShArtPE.jhtml?itemNo=277100&contrassID=2&subContrassID=2&sbSubContrassID=0 (in Hebrew). See also one of these organizations' site: http://www.halev.org.il.

56. Recent changes to the legal aid system in the UK may make this more difficult in some cases.
57. We owe the term 'being verbally independent' to Yuval Elbashan (interviews).
58. Here is an example of an interview we conducted:

    Question: What do you think are the main necessities one's well-being?
    Answer: Yes, people want to live well.
    Question: Indeed, let's think about your children. What would you like them to do and be?
    Answer: My children do not have anywhere to go to.
    Question: Right. Can you tell me more about this?
    Answer: They have nowhere to go to in this town. There is nothing here.
    Question: So you think having places to go to – you probably mean places like a club, or the cinema, or a café – are one's necessities. Why? Is it because they can make friends there?
    Answer: My children have nowhere to go to, they just wander around.
    Question: OK, so you tell us you think having a place to go to is an important issue for one to feel good. What else would make one feel good?
    Answer: People should have places to go to. You see, my oldest son, he did not have anywhere to go to, so he moved to another city, and now he does not come to visit me, and if he comes he goes back immediately.
    Question: So you think good relations between children and parents are important?
    Answer: Yes, yes, like I said, he did not have anywhere to go to. (....)

59. Cano, Annmarie and Dina Vivian, 'Life Stressor and Husband-to-Wife Violence', *Aggression and Violent Behavior* 6 (2001), 459–80; Rogge, R. D. and Bradbury T. N., 'Till Violence Does Us Apart: The Differing Roles of Communication and Aggression in Predicting Adverse Marital Outcomes', *Journal of Consulting and Clinical Psychology* 67 (1999), 340–51.
60. Robeyns discusses this from a gender perspective. See Robeyns, Ingrid, 'Sen's Capability Approach and Gender Inequality: Selecting Relevant Capabilities', *Feminist Economics* 9 (2003), 61–92. See also Williams, Bernard, 'The Standard of Living: Interests and Capabilities' in Hawthorn (ed.), *The Standard of Living* 94–102, 100.
61. This goes hand in hand with Amartya Sen's use of the concept of functionings. See Sen, Amartya, *Inequality Reexamined,* 40–2. Indeed, if functionings were a list of goods, Sen would have to propose a list of functionings, which he constantly avoids doing.

Notes to Chapter 3

1. Indeed this may be true whenever the use of money and/or time is at stake. Other resources – such as education – can often be used to achieve several goals in a non-rival sense.
2. Sen, Amartya, *Development as Freedom*, 75.
3. More common, of course, are those who go on crash diets. These may cause health problems in extreme cases, but rarely malnutrition comparable to those who go hungry over a long period.

4. Sen, *Development as Freedom*, 146.
5. Sen, *Development as Freedom*, 8.
6. At this point we concede that it is also important to people *how* exposure to risks are distributed. Many might even agree to 'pay the cost' for society to progress, by exposing some functionings to greater risks than others do, provided that they were asked and consulted about this in a participatory manner. (We thank Dale Jameison and Sanjay Reddy for this comment. See also Schlosberg, David, 'The Justice of Environmental Justice: Reconciling Equity, Recognition, and Participation in a Political Movement', in Light, Andrew, and Avner de-Shalit (eds.), *Moral and Political Reasoning in Environmental Practice* (Cambridge, Mass.: MIT Press, 2003)). However, this is a different point, about the procedure of decision making.
7. We thank Miriam Cohen Christofidis for this argument.
8. Similarly, we can accept the feminist challenge that some women may consider themselves disadvantaged because they have not been *allowed* to take enough risks. This point is true, but has no bearing on this analysis.
9. See G. A. Cohen's discussion of 'being forced' and 'all other options being not reasonable', in Cohen, G. A., 'Are Disadvantaged Workers Who Take Hazardous Jobs Forced to Take Hazardous Jobs?' in Cohen, G. A., *History, Labour, and Freedom* (Oxford: Clarendon Press, 1988), 239–54.
10. The case where this is the *only* reasonable option is clearer, but rather rare. Still, even if this option is only the *most* reasonable one, if the gap between the reasonableness of this option and of the other ones is very big, as is often the case, suffice it to accept that the person was 'forced' to do this rather than that. We thank Steve Gardiner for this point.
11. Most environmental injustice cases can be described in terms of individuals or groups who are forced to take 'disproportionate risks', which other people do not have to take. See Shrader-Frechette, Kristin, *Environmental Justice* (Oxford: Oxford University Press, 2002), 3.
12. The Bedouin are Muslim tribes who live in Egypt, Jordan, and Israel. Those living in Israel are loyal to the state and many have even volunteered to serve in the army. However, their villages and towns are often not recognized by the state since they lack approval from Israeli planning committees. Many would argue that this disapproval is intentional and unfair.
13. The tragedy of political refugees and their frequent difficulties in assimilating in their new, often alien environments demonstrates this loss. In 1995 it was estimated that there were at least 25 million environmental refugees. They were defined by the UN as 'those people who have been forced to leave their traditional habitat, temporarily or permanently, because of a marked environmental disruption that jeopardized their existence and/or seriously affected the quality of their life'. 'Environmental disruption' here means any physical, chemical, and/or biological changes in the ecosystem or the resource base that render it, temporarily or permanently, unsuitable to support human life. As Derek Bell rightly argues, the essence of this tragedy is the loss of place and home. See Bell, Derek, 'Environmental Refugees: What Rights? Which Duties?'

Res Publica 10 (2004), 135–52. As for the importance of place, see Meyer, John, *Political Nature* (Cambridge, Mass.: MIT Press, 2001), chapter 6; Norton, Bryan and Bruce Hannon, 'Environmental Values: A Place Based Theory', *Environmental Ethics* 19 (1997), 226–47. But see also Sale, Kirkpatrick, *Dwellers in the Land* (San Francisco: Sierra Club Books, 1985); Ehrenfeld, David, *Beginning Again* (New York: Oxford University Press, 1993); and Sagoff, Mark, 'Setting America: The concept of place in environmental ethics', *Journal of Energy, Natural Resources and Environmental Law*, 12 (1992), 315–418. That is not to say that our sense of well-being is invariably bound to an attachment to 'place'. Empirically some people enjoy life when they move from place to place, and in fact believe it is good for them not to be attached to a single place. But these are exceptions, and most people's behaviour and attitudes shows that having a sense of place is crucial to their identity, and often their well-being.

14. This particular story ends rather happily. An NGO of students of law appealed to Israel's Supreme Court on behalf of the Bedouins and won their case against the state.

15. We could also state the problem in Nussbaum's terms of capabilities; this person will lose her capability to have control over her material environment, or more simply, she will lose her capability to find shelter.

16. This is named after a phenomenon in town planning. Suppose a major new road is under consideration. Property in the area that may be affected will be very difficult to sell until it is known with certainty whether or not the road will go ahead. Few purchasers will want to take the risk of a price crash – hence planning blight – but once there is planning certainty a new market price will be established.

17. See Blacksher, E., 'On Being Poor and Feeling Poor: Low Socioeconomic Status and the Moral Self', *Theoretical Medicine and Bioethics* 23 (2002), 455–70.

18. Burchardt, Tania, *Being and Becoming: Social Exclusion and the Onset of Disability*, CASE Report 21 (2003); http://sticerd.lse.ac.uk/case/. For a short report see http://www.lse.ac.uk/collections/pressAndInformationOffice/newsAndEvents/archives/2003/Disability_research.htm. This, in fact, ties in with what Sen calls the 'coupling of disadvantage' (see Sen, *Development as Freedom*, 88), which we will discuss in detail in Chapter 7 in the context of 'clustering' of disadvantages.

19. This is based on research conducted by the Brookdale Institute (Israel's leading institute for applied research on human services); http://brookdale-en. pionet.com/default.asp. For the full report, see http://brookdale-en1.pionet.com/files/PDF/445rr-foodsec-eng.pdf.

20. See http://www.adva.org/indexe.html.

21. Davis, Adrian, 'Inequalities of Health: Road Transport and Pollution' in Gordon, David, Mary Shaw, Daniel Dorling, and George Smith, *Inequalities in Health* (Bristol: Policy Press, (1997) 2002), 189.

22. Hanson, Meira, *Transport and Environment Policy in Israel—Where Are We Going To?* Israel Worldwatch Research Series No. 3 (Tel-Aviv: Babel and the Heschel Center for Environmental Learning, 2004) (in Hebrew).

23. The prospect of improving it is also important. This will be discussed in the next chapter.

Notes to Chapter 4

1. This is reflected in the title of Sen's book, *Development as Freedom*.
2. For an elaboration on this see Scanlon, T. M., 'Justice, Responsibility and the Demands of Equality' in Sypnowich, Christine (ed.), *The Egalitarian Conscience* (Oxford: Oxford University Press, 2006), 70–87.
3. Even compulsory vaccination can be evaded, safety regulations ignored, harmless products modified, and so on.
4. This 'common-sense' response to the criticism that capitalism gives the inheriting class a monopoly of private property is made by David Schmidtz. See his contribution to Schmidtz, David, & Robert E. Goodin, *Social Welfare and Individual Responsibility* (Cambridge: Cambridge University Press, 1998), 1–97.
5. For further difficulties concerning the way in which small unequal opportunities can accumulate, see Chambers, Clare, 'Each Outcome is Another Opportunity', paper presented at the ECPR conference, Granada, April 2005. See http:// mora.rente.nhh.no/projects/EqualityExchange/Portals/0/articles/chambers1.pdf/
6. Dworkin, *Sovereign Virtue*, 11–120.
7. Cohen, 'On the Currency of Egalitarian Justice'. See Dworkin's reply in Dworkin, *Sovereign Virtue*, 285–91, and in Burley (ed.), *Dworkin and His Critics*, 339–50.
8. Arneson, 'Equality and Equal Opportunity for Welfare', Arneson, Richard, 'Liberalism, Distributive Subjectivism and Equal Opportunity for Welfare', *Philosophy and Public Affairs* 19 (1990), 158–94; Anderson, 'What is the Point of Equality?',
9. See Arneson, Richard, 'Cracked Foundations of Liberal Equality', in Burley (ed.), *Dworkin and His Critics*, 79–99; Cohen-Christofidis, Miriam, 'Talent, Slavery and Envy', in Burley (ed.), *Dworkin and His Critics*, 30–45 for just two such views.
10. Saul Smilansky discusses these claims in light of the question of free will: 'If people lack the sort of self creating ability with which only libertarian free will might have provided them, then ultimately everything – including a person's choice – must be viewed as arbitrary, and cannot ultimately be seen as up to the person.' See Smilansky, Saul, *Free Will and Illusion* (Oxford: Clarendon Press, 2000), 119f. See also Smilansky, Saul, 'Choice-Egalitarianism and the Paradox of the Baseline', *Analysis* 63 (2003), 146–51.
11. Although originally drafted without any particular case in mind, in one of our interviews a single mother from a development town in Israel (towns designed in the 1960s to absorb new immigrants, mainly from North Africa) reported that she had to give up better job opportunities in

order to take care of her children, or else, she feared, they would be bored, leave school, and become attracted to crime.

12. For discussion of the question of whether 'luck egalitarianism' requires that mothers should pay the costs of their decision to look after children rather than work, see Mason, Andrew, 'Equality, Personal Responsibility and Gender Socialisation' *Proceedings of the Aristotelian Society*, 100 (2000), 227–46.

13. For empirical information about trends in factors influencing children's well-being in the USA, see Haveman, Robert, and Barbara Wolfe, *Succeeding Generations: On the Effects of Investments in Children* (New York: Russell Sage, 1995), 5–9.

14. We thank Michael Otsuka and Andrew Williams for pressing this point.

15. Anderson, 'What is the Point of Equality?'.

16. We owe this point to Simon Hampson.

17. On the other hand, some would say, it would allow her to sustain the functioning of affiliation, because working helps one feel part of the community. Nevertheless, we believe this is only partly true, because it very much depends on the type of work one is offered. It is often the case that those who take jobs such as cleaning public toilets, or working in slaughterhouses, eight hours in freezing temperatures, do not consequently sense more affiliation, but rather alienation.

18. This, of course, depends on the particular circumstances of the case.

19. See also the work of Brown, Alexander, 'If We Value Individual Responsibility, Which Policies Should We Favour?' *Journal of Applied Philosophy* 22 (2005), 23–44, who in many respects has a similar analysis of responsibility, and has helped influence the direction taken here.

20. Note, though, that there are other arguments against having rules that require investigation about whether or not people are responsible for actions and choices (see Wolff, 'Fairness, Respect, and the Egalitarian Ethos'). These issues will be discussed in Chapter 10.

Notes to Chapter 5

1. At this point we have to acknowledge that genuine opportunity may be more problematic since it can be harder to observe or define.

2. Michael Walzer, for example, argues that different spheres generate (or are governed, by) their own norms; Walzer, *Spheres of Justice*. David Miller claims that in different types of organization we apply different principles of justice. See Miller, *Principles of Social Justice*. See also Miller, David, 'Complex Equality' in Miller and Walzer (eds.), *Pluralism, Justice, and Equality* (Oxford: Oxford University Press, 1995), 197–225.

3. Elster, Jon, *Local Justice: How Institutions Allocate Scarce Goods and Necessary Burdens* (Cambridge: Cambridge University Press, 1992). Elster examines the ways in which different societies allocate scarce goods (or burdens), and he finds six categories: egalitarian principles, time-related principles, principles

based on status, principles defined by other individual properties (e.g. need), mechanisms of power, and what he refers to as mixed systems.

4. Swift, Adam, *How Not to be a Hypocrite* (London: Routledge, 2003).
5. Elster, *Local Justice*, 132.
6. We discuss these issues in more details in Chapter 7.
7. See Anderson, 'What is the Point of Equality?'.
8. Barry, Brian, 'Does Democracy Cause Inflation?' in Barry, Brian, *Democracy and Power: Essays in Political Theory* (Oxford: Clarendon Press, 1991), 61–100. It may be thought that this problem can be solved by 'index-linking' interest rates, salaries, and pensions, but this is not entirely the case. In any economy inflation rates for different goods vary, and index-linking will not pick up fine-grained variation. So those who hold assets that are inflating in value greater than the index will gain windfall profits, while others will find their assets, including cash assets, are dwindling in relative value. Indeed house prices, at least in certain economies, often do not even figure in the calculation of the index, given their volatility and the dominating effect they would have on the rest of the index.
9. See Arneson, Richard, 'Distributive Justice and Basic Capability Equality: "Good Enough" Is Not Good Enough,' in Alexander Kaufman, (ed.), *Capabilities Equality: Basic Issues and Problems* (London: Routledge, 2005). See http://philosophy2.ucsd.edu/~rarneson/capabilityandsufficiency1.pdf.
10. Crisp, Roger, 'Equality, Priority and Compassion', *Ethics* 113 (2003), 745–63. For a critique of Crisp's position see Brown, Campbell, 'Priority or sufficiency?. . . .Or both?' *Economics and Philosophy* 2004. See http://personal.bgsu.edu/~browncf/papers/PriorityOrSufficiencyOrBoth.pdf.
11. In this respect what we say has affinities with Anderson's theory of 'democratic equality'. See Anderson, 'What is the Point of Equality?'.
12. In a full account there would also be a second dimension for issues of risk and vulnerability of each functioning.
13. See Chakraborty, Achin, 'On the Possibility of a Weighting System for Functionings', *Indian Economic Review* 31 (1996), 241–50. See also Gordon, David, 'Census Based Deprivation Indices: Their Weighting and Validation', *Journal of Epidemiology and Community Health* 49 (suppl 2) (1995), S39–S44 (can be found also at http://www.bris.ac.uk/poverty/defining%20and%20measuring_ files/Census%20Deprivation%20Indices%201995%20paper.pdf. Gordon's claim is that 'over one hundred years of social science research has shown that different social groups have different probabilities of suffering from multiple deprivation; yet census based deprivation indices frequently assign equal weightings to each of their component variables. This becomes highly problematic when these indices are used as the basis for allocating resources to local and health authorities. In order to ensure fairness and accuracy in resource allocation these indices should be both weighted and validated.' His weightings are derived from the *Breadline Britain in the 1990s* survey to produce a census based deprivation index that estimates the percentage of poor households at electoral ward level. Saunders continued

and applied Gordon's method to smaller areas to give estimates of the number of deprived people living within them, producing a weighted index. See Saunders, J., 'Weighted Census-Based Deprivation Indices: Their Use in Small Areas' in *Journal of Public Health* 29 (1998), 253–60.

14. Hobbes was well aware of the limits of the ordinary person's time and attention, suggesting: 'And though this may seem too subtle a deduction of the Lawes of Nature, to be taken notice of by all men; whereof the most part are too busie in getting food, and the rest too negligent to understand'; Hobbes, Thomas, *Leviathan* (London: Pelican Classics, 1968 (1651)), 214 (part 1, chapter 15). Michael Walzer has made a claim about the need for philosophy due to the impossibility of all people spending so much time philosophizing and debating politics. They have other things to worry about. See Walzer, Michael, 'Philosophy and Democracy', *Political Theory* 9 (1981), 379–400. For a discussion of this position see de-Shalit, Avner, *Power to the People: Teaching Political Theory in Skeptical Times* (Lanham, Md.: Lexington Books, 2006).

15. We owe the analogy between decathlon scoring and social choice to Alfred Mackay, *Arrow's Theorem: The Paradox of Social Choice* (New Haven, Conn.: Yale University Press, 1980).

16. For a brief history of decathlon scoring see http://www.geocities.com/mdetting/sports/decathlon-points-history.html

17. We leave to one side whether it is possible to define a formal notion of weighting sensitivity. An intuitive understanding will suffice for present purposes.

18. Notice, also, that in such a society the practical disagreement between prioritarians and sufficientarians will diminish significantly.

19. Restricting the task further to naming the two most important functionings led to the result that interviewees said that they found it impossible.

Notes to Chapter 6

1. The differences could be a matter of a different stage in one's career: one could already have a decent income, but still be relatively poor in the sense that one lacks basic necessities; or one could have a decent income but be the family's sole breadwinner, and therefore lack basic necessities. For more about poverty measurements and its difficulties see Atkinson, A. B., *Poverty and Social Security* (New York: Harvester Wheatsheaf, 1989), chapter 1, 'How Should We Measure Poverty? Some Conceptual Issues', 7–25.

2. The notion of 'subjectively poor' was introduced to allow the voices of the poor to be heard also in the sense that they would define poverty. Bradshaw and Finch define those lacking four or more adult necessities because they cannot afford them, as 'necessities poor'. See Bradshaw, Jonathan and Naomi Finch, 'Overlaps in Dimensions of Poverty', *Journal of Social Policy* 32 (2003), 513–25, 515.

3. Bradshaw and Finch, 'Overlaps in Dimensions of Poverty'.

4. For this report see Gordon, D., Adelman, L., Ashworth, K., Bradshaw, J. et al., *Poverty and Social Exclusion in Britain* (Joseph Rowntree Foundation, http://www.jrf.org.uk/knowledge/findings/socialpolicy/930.asp, 2000).

5. The cumulative approach assumes that a person who is poor on all three dimensions is more likely to fall below the poverty line than a person who is poor on only one of the dimensions. Also, if George is poor on two he is more likely to be in poverty than Alex who is poor on one. In support of this approach comes the argument that we cannot rely on a single measure if we are in search of poverty (or being disadvantaged). Also many people think that poverty (or disadvantage) in several dimensions is more severe than in a single dimension, regardless of how severe poverty in that dimension is. The latter was revealed in the interviews we conducted.

6. Hills, Le Grand, and Piachaud (eds.), *Understanding Social Exclusion*.

7. Note that it will need to be modified to yield a continuous ordering rather than a series of thresholds. There are various ways of doing this, but it would be distracting to pursue the technical issue here.

8. In contrast to the York case this interviewee did not seem concerned that some people might report that they were in distress when they were not. Others, however, may want to see such reports 'backed up' by other evidence, which is in essence what our approach proposes.

9. Because, for example, it is reported in the news and the lawyers benefit from good public relations, and so on.

10. See, for example, Shrader Frechette, Kristin, *Risk and Rationality* (Berkeley: University of California Press, 1991); Douglas, Mary and Aaron Wildawsky, *Risk and Culture* (Berkeley: University of California Press, 1983).

Notes to Chapter 7

1. Ted Schettler et al present evidence that human exposure to some toxic chemicals can have intergenerational effects on human reproduction and development. See Schettler, Ted, Solomon, G. et al., *Generations at Risk: Reproductive Health and the Environment* (Cambridge, Mass.: MIT Press, 2000). For more about this research see http://psr.igc.org/gar-report.htm. In the USA, parents who worked at night were 2.7 times as likely to have a child who had been suspended from school than parents who did not have to work nights. See Heyman, Jody, 'Can Working Families Ever Win?' *Boston Review* 27 (2002), 1993–2005 http://www.boston review.net/BR27.1/hey-mann.html; quoted also in Barry, Brian, *Why Social Justice Matters* (Cambridge: Polity Press, 2005), 55. This figure is 'after controlling for other differences', so it is clear that parents' work during night is a causal factor for being suspended from school.

2. Figures can vary from 2,150 different words in an hour in professionals' families to 620 words in an hour in families that rely on welfare support. See Barry *Why Social Justice Matters*, 51. Barry cites Hart, Betty, and Todd Risley, *Meaningful Differences in the Everyday Experience of Young American Children*

(Baltimore: Brookes Publishing 1995), 193. The authors claim that large differences in children's abilities, especially verbal ones, exist from very early age, perhaps two years old.

3. We interviewed a kindergarten teacher who told us about children in her kindergarten, where the variety of verbal capabilities was wide and was reflected in these children's various social skills. For further research about transgenerational corrosive disadvantage see Atkinson, A. B., *Poverty and Social Security* (London: Harvester-Wheatsheaf, 1989) 81–5; Duncan, G. J., Hill, M. S., and Hoffman, S. D., 'Welfare Dependence Within and Across Generations', *Science* 239 (1988), 467–71. See also Stenberg, S., 'Inheritance of Welfare Recipiency: An Intergenerational Study of Social Assistance Recipiency in Postwar Sweden', *Journal of Marriage and Family*, 62 (2000), 228–39.

4. The figure for Israel, for example, is 79.1% of those who reported bad health also complained of not having good social relationships.

5. Hills, John, *Inequality and the State* (Oxford: Oxford University Press, 2004), 51–6.

6. Narayan et al., *Voices of the Poor: Can Anyone Hear Us?* 4, 31f.

7. Narayan et al., *Voices of the Poor: Can Anyone Hear Us?* 43–5. Narayan's account is an example of the most commonly applied definition of poverty in economically advanced societies, which sees poverty as exclusion from the life of the society owing to a lack of resources. See Nolan, Brian, and Christopher Whelan, *Resources, Deprivation and Poverty* (Oxford: Clarendon, 1996), 2. Attributed to Townsend, Peter, *Poverty in the United Kingdom* (London: Penguin, 1979). See also Hills, LeGrand, and Pischaud, *Understanding Social Exclusion*. Some definitions of poverty do not tie two or more disadvantages together. See Donnison, David, 'Defining and Measuring Poverty', *Journal of Social Policy* 17 (1988), 367–74.

8. Marmot, *Status Syndrome*; Wilkinson, Richard, *Mind the Gap: Hierarchy, Health and Human Evolution* (London: Weidenfeld and Nicolson, 2001); Marmot, Michael and Richard Wilkinson, 'Psychological and Material Pathways in the Relation Between Income and Health', *British Medical Journal* 322 (2001), 1233–6; Marmot, Michael and Richard Wilkinson, (eds.) *The Social Determinants of Health* (Oxford: Oxford University Press, 1999); Wilkinson, Richard, 'Social Corrosion, Inequality and Health' in Giddens, Anthony and Patrick Diamond (eds.), *The New Egalitarianism* (Cambridge: Polity, 2005), 183–200; Wilkinson, and Marmot (eds.), *The Social Determinants of Health: The Solid Facts*.

9. Klinenberg, Eric, *Heat Wave: A Social Autopsy of Disaster in Chicago* (Chicago: University of Chicago Press, 2002).

10. Marmot, *Status Syndrome*, 14–15.

11. Marmot, *Status Syndrome*, 78. Research conducted in Sweden examined the proportion of men aged sixty-four in 1990 who died in the period up to 1996, and analysed this according to their level of education. While the proportion of those with only elementary education was 15%, only 11% of those with secondary education died, and among those with a Ph.D. the

percentage was only 6%. See Erikson, Robert, 'Why Do Graduates Live Longer?' in Jonsson, J. O. and C. Mills (eds.), *Cradle to Grave: Life Course Change in Modern Sweden* (Durham: Sociology Press, 2001).

12. Marmot, *Status Syndrome, 81–2.*

13. Marmot, *Status Syndrome, chapters 4 and 5.*

14. Marmot, *Status Syndrome,* 248. Richard Wilkinson joins Marmot to argue that 'life expectancy is shorter and diseases are more common the further down the social ladder in each society'. So big are the gaps that a professional man's life expectancy is 78.5 years whereas the life expectancy of an unskilled man is 71 years. Wilkinson and Marmot (eds.), *The Social Determinants of Health: The Solid Facts 10.*

15. Wilkinson and Marmot (eds.), *The Social Determinants of Health: The Solid Facts,* 16.

16. Wilkinson and Marmot (eds.), *The Social Determinants of Health: The Solid Facts,* 20.

17. Elsewhere Richard Wilkinson names 'stress in early life' among the three most important categories of psychological risk for poor health, the other two being low social status and weak social affiliations. See Wilkinson, 'Social Corrosion, Inequality and Health', especially 185. According to Wilkinson, low sense of control is particularly relevant to social status and any such subordination which infringes one's sense of autonomy often leads to heart disease.

18. This is based on House J. S. et al., 'Social Relationships and Health', *Science* 241 (1988), 540–5. But see also Wilkinson, and Marmot. *The Social Determinants of Health: The Solid Facts,* 23.

19. Wilkinson and Marmot, 25

20. Klinenberg, *Heat Wave: A Social Autopsy of Disaster in Chicago.*

21. http://www.threestrikes.org/fbi_crimerates_ pg2.html

22. http://www.threestrikes.org/tslaw.html

23. Barry claims that in the USA 75% of drug users are white and around 15% are black, but blacks account for 35% of all drug arrests and 55% of all drug convictions. Barry cites Cole, David *No Equal Justice: Race and Class in the American Criminal Justice System* (New York: New Press, 1999) 50. But see also Kennedy, Randall, *Race, Crime and the Law* (London: Vintage, 1998) in particular Chapter 8, 'Race, Law and Punishment: the War on Drugs' 351–87.

24. Barry, *Why Social Justice Matters,* 99.

25. Barry, *Why Social Justice Matters,* 102.

26. See for example, Chang, S. M., Walker, S. P., Himes, J. and Grantham-McGregor, S., 'The Effects of Breakfast on Classroom Behaviours in Rural Jamaican School Children', *Food and Nutrition Bulletin* 17 (1996), 248–57. See also Simeon, D. T., and S. Grantham-McGregor, 'Effects of Missing Breakfast on the Cognitive Functions of School Children of Differing Nutritional Status', *American Journal of Clinical Nutrition* 49 (1989), 646–53. All these reports suggest that students who had a school-supplied breakfast often or sometimes had significantly higher maths scores than children who rarely or never ate a school-supplied breakfast. Also, students who increased their participation in the school breakfast program had significantly greater increases in their maths

grades and significantly greater decreases in rates of school absence and tardiness than children whose participation remained the same or decreased. Child and teacher ratings of psychosocial problems also decreased to a significantly greater degree for children with increased participation in the school breakfast program. See Murphy, J. Michael, Maria E. Pagano, Joan Nachmani, Peter Sperling, Shirley Kane, and Ronald E. Kleinman, 'The Relationship of School Breakfast to Psychosocial and Academic Functioning', *Archives of Pediatrics and Adolescent Medicine* 152 (1998), 899–907. See also Simeon, Donald and Sally McGregor, 'Nutrition and Mental Development', in *The Cambridge World History of Food* (Cambridge: Cambridge University Press, 2000), 1457–66. For further linkage between nutrition and mentality and mental abilities see also http://pubpages.unh.edu/~jel/intro/401-99intelligence.html.

27. Mayer, Susan, *What Money Can't Buy* (Cambridge, Mass.: Harvard University Press, 1997), 99.

28. See Fares, Amin, *The State Budget and the Arab Citizens in Israel* (Haifa: Mossawa Center, 2004), 32.

Notes to Chapter 8

1. Mayer, *What Money Can't Buy*, 1.

2. Mayer, *What Money Can't Buy*, 12.

3. Mayer, *What Money Can't Buy*, 8. In addition, Mayer argues that the 'good parent theory' does not work. According to this theory, higher incomes improve parents' psychological well-being, which in turn improves their parenting practices. Mayer argues (chapter 7) that the relationships between family income and parents' well-being are not proved. Brian Barry suggests that education is a key factor here, and that parents' social class predicts children's school success because of the different level of education at home. See Barry, *Why Social Justice Matters*, 15 and 46–69. Barry cites Lareau, Annette *Unequal Childhoods: Class, Race and Family Life* (Berkeley: California University Press, 2003).

4. Radio Address to the Nation on Welfare Reform, February 15, 1986 (Ronald Reagan).

5. This is based on Haveman and Wolfe, *Succeeding Generations: On the Effects of Investments in Children*, 52–79.

6. See our discussion about the need to belong.

7. Haveman and Wolfe, *Succeeding Generations: On the Effects of Investment in Children*, 78.

8. Mayer, *What Money Can't Buy*, Chapter 9.

9. Mayer, *What Money Can't Buy*, 114–15.

10. Notice that three of the examples we discuss are three dimensions of being autonomous and having control over one's environment. The first is straightforwardly about education. The second is about being able to use soft skills, a term commonly used by social workers, which refers to

autonomy and control over the environment, only it shifts the focus to common, everyday activities that are often ignored when people think of being autonomous in more abstract and political ways. The third example is also about control over one's environment, this time in relation to one's workplace.

11. Hills, *Inequality and the State*, 55.
12. Ruth Lister, for example, is quite cautious and refrains from saying there are no two ways about it. See Lister, Ruth, *Poverty* (Cambridge: Polity Press, 2004), especially 74–99.
13. Sen, Amartya, *Social Exclusion: Concept, Application and Scrutiny* (Manila: Asian Development Bank, 2000); http://www.flacso.org/biblioteca/sen_social_exclusion.pdf.
14. Sen, *Social Exclusion: Concept, Application and Scrutiny*, 6.
15. In their study of various neighbourhoods and how they cope with social changes, Ruth Lupton and Anne Power suggest that building the capacity of the community to self-manage would restore its members' sense of pride and should make a strong impact on other aspects of what we would call their functionings. See Lupton, Ruth and Anne Power, 'Social Exclusion and Neighbourhoods' in Hills, Le Grand, and Pichaud *Understanding Social Exclusion*, 118–41, 140.
16. The reason for this difference is probably related to the fact that in one of these neighbourhoods most of the residents arrived in Israel from the same country and shared a language of origin and culture, whereas in the other neighbourhood this was not the case.
17. Richardson, Liz and Mumford, Katherine, 'Community and Social Infrastructure' in Hills, Le Grand, and Piachaud (eds.), *Understanding Social Exclusion*, 202–26.
18. Richardson and Mumford, 'Community and Social Infrastructure', in Hills, Le Grand, and Piachaud (eds.), *Understanding Social Exclusion*, 208.
19. Haaretz, December 27, 2005.
20. Klinenberg, *Heatwave: A Social Autopsy of Disaster in Chicago*.
21. See also Jacobs, Jane, *The Death and Life of Great American Cities* (New York: Vintage, 1961).
22. Marmot, *Status Syndrome*; Wilkinson, *The Impact of Inequality*.
23. This research was conducted by Orit Nuttman-Shwartz and Rachel Dekel. We thank them for allowing us to refer to it. This research is not yet published.
24. Perhaps the first to point to this was Jean Piaget. See, for example, Piaget, Jean, *Judgment and Reasoning in the Child* (London: Routledge and Kegan Paul, 1968 (1924)); or Piaget, Jean, *Origins of Intelligence in the Child* (London: Routledge and Kegan Paul, 1953 (1936)); and Piaget, Jean, *Play, Dreams and Imitation in Childhood* (London: Heinemann, 1951 (1945)).
25. On top of the evidence we have from the physician we interviewed (see Chapter 7, section 3), there are several studies that support this thesis. For example, education helps people to take preventive measures and become

knowledgeable about health matters. See Rosenstock, Irwin, 'Prevention of Illness and Maintenance of Health' in Kosa, John and Irving Kenneth Zola (eds.), *Poverty and Health: A Sociological Analysis* (Cambridge, Mass.: Harvard University Press, 1975), 193–222. A wide survey and analysis of inequalities in health in Britain supports this thesis. Whitty et al. argue that based on a variety of studies 'education may be hypothesised as having both direct and indirect effects on health outcomes'. See Whitty, Geoff, Peter Aggleton, Eva Garmarnikow, and Paul Taylor, 'Education and Health Inequalities' in Gordon, David, et al., *Inequalities in Health* (Bristol: Policy Press, 2002), 138–47. Morris et al. argue that there is a clear correlation between social inequalities and educational attainment. See Morris, J. N., D. B. Blane and I. R. White, 'Levels of Mortality, Education and Social Conditions in the 107 Local Education Authority Areas in England', *Journal of Epidemiology and Community Health* 50 (1996), 15–17.

26. Data are even more shocking when a slicing is made according to gender. The chances of a woman with nine years of education finding a job within the formal economy are only 27% of the probability of a woman who has sixteen or more years of education. Flug, Karnit and Kasir Nitza, 'On Poverty and Work', working paper (2000), quoted in Ben-David Ran, 'Employment in Israel: International Perspectives', *Israel Economic Review* 50 (2003). We do not claim that these data generalize, but we have no reason to think that Israel is a special case.

27. The concept of a 'positional' good was introduced by Hirsch, Fred, *Social Limits to Growth* (Cambridge, Mass.: Harvard University Press, 1976). For a recent discussion of the complications positional goods create for egalitarianism see Brighouse, Harry, and Swift, Adam, 'Equality, Priority, and Positional Goods', *Ethics* 116 (2006), 471–98. For further complications with regard to education, see Koski, William and Rob Reich (forthcoming), 'When Adequate Isn't: the Retreat From Equity in Educational Law and Policy and Why It Matters'; http://www.stanford.edu/~reich/working_papers/Koski-Reich%20Equity.pdf.

28. Schmitt, John and Jonathan Wadsworth, Center for Economic Policy Analysis Working Paper April 2002; http://www.newschool.edu/cepa/publications/workingpapers/archive/cepa200206.pdf. In the USA unemployment dropped among the university educated to 57% of its 1992 rate; in the UK it dropped to 52.5% of its 1992 rate. Whereas among those with the lowest level of education unemployment dropped only to 65% of its 1992 level, in the USA and UK the decrease was very small: to 81.6% of its 1992 figure. That lack of education is a corrosive disadvantage in determining one's chances to be employed is the implication of yet another study, this time referring to data from all OECD countries. It analyses the participation of men aged 25–64 in the labour force according to level of education. In the thirty-one countries studied, employment rates for men in the labour force aged 25–64 were examined, dividing the sample into three groups: those with less than upper secondary education; those with upper secondary

education; and those with tertiary education. With the exception of just three countries (Iceland, Mexico, and Turkey) unemployment drops steadily and progressively with the years of education one has had. Source: http://www.adva.org/ivrit/eductionMen2000.htm. Based on *OECD Employment Outlook*, 2002, table D, 316–18. Figures for the UK and the USA differ from the previous table because in this table only men aged 25–64 are surveyed.

29. We thank Fran Bennet for discussing this matter with us. Soft skills are now widely acknowledged as highly important in many spheres of life. On January 29, 2005, it was reported that New York was expected to become the first state in the USA to issue 'a work-readiness credential to high school students who pass a voluntary test measuring their ability to succeed in entry-level jobs' because 'employers have complained for years that too many students leave high school without such basic skills', despite the battery of exams that New York requires for graduation; http://www.timeoutfromtesting.org/0129_article_ jobfitness.php. Many companies now offer soft skills training. See, for example: http://techrepublic.com.com/5100-6269-5055182.html.

30. See, for example, Warhurst, Christopher, *Between Market, State and Kibbutz*, (London: Routledge, 1999), and Sharabany, Ruth and Hadas Weisman, 'Close Relationships in Adolescence: The Case of the Kibbutz', *Journal of Youth and Adolescence* 22 (1993), 671–95.

31. Wilkinson, *The Impact of Inequality: How to Make Sick Societies Healthier*.

32. Wilkinson, *The Impact of Inequality*, 99.

33. Wilkinson, *The Impact of Inequality*, 307.

34. Wilkinson, *The Impact of Inequality*, 303–10.

35. To see if there are any effects on a small scale it would be very interesting to study the workers of the John Lewis Partnership in the UK, which from the outside looks like any other successful capitalist business, but is in fact wholly owned by its employees.

36. Lane, Robert E., *The Loss Of Happiness in Market Democracies* (New Haven, Conn.: Yale University Press, 2000). Robert Frank argues along similar lines. Frank, Robert, *Luxury Fever: Why Money Fails to Satisfy in an Era of Success* (Princeton: Princeton University Press, 1999). In addition, those examining 'reported happiness' claim that in very affluent societies the correlation between income and happiness is minimal. See Brittan, Samuel, 'What Makes Us Happy?' *Times Literary Supplement* 7/4/2000; http://www.samuel-brittan.co.uk/text36_ p.html/.

37. http://sticerd.lse.ac.uk/dps/case/CR/CASEreport21.pdf, 2.

38. Mayer, *What Money Can't Buy*, 145.

39. Parfit, 'Equality and Priority'. See also http://individual.utoronto.ca/stafforini/parfit/parfit_-_equality_and_ priority.pdf.

40. See Temkin, Larry, 'Inequality', *Philosophy and Public Affairs* 15 (1986), 99–121; and Temkin, Larry, *Equality* (Oxford: Oxford University Press, 1993).

41. Lack of affiliation, for example, seems to be a more important disadvantage in the UK. Perhaps this derives from differences in the degree to which the welfare state still functions in these two countries. In any case, the differences we have found are quite minor, but they imply that it could well be that in cultures that are more distinct from each other, differences will be more meaningful.

Notes to Chapter 9

1. We should distinguish between our question here and a more general question: who is owed justice, in the sense of what type of group is entitled to be considered (e.g. only adults, or children as well, perhaps animals and future generations too, etc)? We assume that this question has been answered, and now we want to discuss the weight of the claims of the least advantaged vis-à-vis other claims within that group. For the other questions see Vallentyne, Peter, 'Distribution to Whom?' in his (ed.), *Equality and Justice, Vol. 3* (London: Routledge, 2003), xi–xiv.
2. We would like to suggest reading David Miller's discussion of the triage, where he points out that the issue is *not* of efficiency but rather of justice, and that the relevant injustices are both the gaps between the least advantaged and those doing well, and also between the not so disadvantaged and those doing well. See Miller, *Principles of Justice*, 212–17.
3. For more about the balance between efficiency and priority to the least advantaged see Vallentyne, Peter, 'Equality, Efficiency and the Priority of the Worse Off', *Economics and Philosophy* 16 (2003), 1–19.
4. Pogge, Thomas, *World Poverty and Human Rights* (Cambridge: Polity, 2002), 8.
5. Clearly what counts as significant expenditure on such research is a contested question, but we would not want to excuse governments evading their responsibilities through token expenditure.
6. Unless one accepts that they benefit from political stability and lack of unrest, for which, it is argued, they would have been prepared to pay a great deal, if the proposition had been put to them in that form.
7. Rothstein, Bo, 'The Universal Welfare State as a Social Dilemma', *Rationality and Society* 13 (2001), 213–33.
8. See Segall, 'Bringing the Middle Classes Back In'.
9. We should add that we do not argue that the only forms of justified government action are those in the service of addressing disadvantage. For example, nothing we have said bears on the question of how much governments may spend to develop art and culture, or to preserve the natural environment, for their own sakes.
10. Elster, *Local Justice*.
11. No doubt such decisions are influenced by other considerations, e.g. progress in science and so on, but this goes beyond the scope of our book.
12. About the equality of status approach see, for example, the works of Anne Phillips, e.g. Phillips, *Which Equalities Matter?* and Phillips, Anne, 'Defending Equality of Outcome', *Journal of Political Philosophy* 12 (2004), 1–19.

Notes to Chapter 10

1. We also distinguished these questions from the question of who the government should be aiming its attention to, which we examined in Chapter 7.
2. For further elaboration on this debate see Kymlicka, Will, 'Left Liberalism Revisited' in Sypnowich *The Egalitarian Conscience: Essays in Honour of G. A. Cohen.*
3. Friedman, Milton, *Capitalism and Freedom* (Chicago: University of Chicago Press, 1962).
4. For a contemporary view (1968) of the effects of the Labour government's high tax policy, see http://www.time.com/time/magazine/article/0,9171,838185, 00. html.
5. For a typical account of the effects of security of tenure on the housing market, see http://www.landlordzone.co.uk/history.htm.
6. We thank Leif Wenar for very helpful clarification on this point.
7. Anderson, 'What is the Point of Equality?', 305. For a critique of Anderson's argument, see Segall, Shlomi, 'In Solidarity With the Imprudent: A Defence of Luck-Egalitarianism' (2005), http://www.filosofi.uu.se/filosofidagarna/ abstract5.htm. Segall argues that if luck egalitarians adopt a pluralist approach, according to which they also advance social solidarity, such letters would not be possible.
8. We thank Tom Christiano for this way of putting the point.
9. Wolff, 'Fairness, Respect, and the Egalitarian Ethos'.
10. See Eyal, Nir, *Distributing Respect* (D.Phil. thesis, Oxford University, 2003).
11. Segall, 'Bringing the Middle Class Back In: An Egalitarian Case For Truly Universal Public Services'.
12. Van Parijs, Philippe, *Real Freedom For All* (Oxford: Oxford University Press, 1995). See also Van Parijs, Philippe (ed.), *Arguing for Basic Income* (London: Verso, 1992); Robert van der Veen and Loek Groot (eds.), *Basic Income on the Agenda* (Ann Arbor: University of Michigan Press, 2000); see also the journal *Basic Income Studies*.
13. The remainder of this section draws on Wolff, Jonathan, 'Addressing Disadvantage and the Human Good', *Journal of Applied Philosophy* 19 (2002), 207–11. See also Wolff, Jonathan, 'The Message of Redistribution' (2003), http://www.catalystforum.org.uk/pubs/pub8.html.
14. Indeed Dworkin's view is that what you can legally do with a resource enters into the understanding of what that resource is, and how people will value it. See Dworkin, *Sovereign Virtue*, chapter 3. However we believe there are advantages in keeping these categories distinct.
15. See also Chambers, 'Each Outcome is Another Opportunity; Equality of Opportunity in Context'.
16. This, of course, is the debate between those who subscribe to the 'medical' model of disability and those who follow the 'social' model.
17. We thank Miriam Cohen Christofidis for discussion of this example.
18. Many people might find this proposal a threat to civil society. It is quite common among liberals and libertarians to promote a separation of civil

society from the state. This attitude is also common among many contemporary democrats, who think that an independent civil society is the key to a successful and vibrant democracy, where citizens can keep an eye on the government and the state. But here, they might argue, we seem to suggest questioning this separation because the state is asked to intervene in civil society by financing it. As the saying goes, he who pays the piper calls the tune. In reply let us say, rest assured, we do not suggest destroying or even diminishing civil society and its organizations. But it is also true that since non-governmental organizations owe their existence to private money, and since most of this money comes from affluent individuals, it is not always the case that civil society caters for the needs of the worse off. (See, for example, Talshir, Gayil, 'Citizenship Beyond Social Rights: The Ideological Battleground in Advanced Democracies' (forthcoming); Baker, Gideon, 'The Changing Idea of Civil Society: Models From the Polish Democratic Opposition', *Journal of Political Ideologies* 3 (1998), 125–47.) Thus we propose that the state should intervene to correct 'market failures' in the civil society, and subsidize such organisations, clubs, and so on that would not be financed, or would only be open to the wealthy, otherwise. Moreover, it can easily be legislated that while the state should finance these NGOs, it will not be allowed to run them or intervene in their conduct. There are many examples of such arrangements that already function, e.g. public universities, although this also illustrates that the danger of government over-intervention is a real one, and that appropriate structures and safeguards are needed too.

19. For this reason, collective resource enhancements are a form of status enhancement.
20. For a detailed application of these ideas to the case of disability, see Wolff Jonathan, 'Disability Among Equals' in *Philosophy and Disability*, ed. Brownlee, K. and A. Cureton (Oxford: Oxford University Press, forthcoming).
21. See Gaffkin, Frank and Mike Morrissey (eds.), *City Visions: Imagining Place, Enfranchising People* (Cambridge: Pluto Press, 1999).

Notes to the Conclusion

1. Of course we refer here to Rawls's restriction of his theory to society's basic structure. See Rawls, *A Theory of Justice*, 7–11, and his defence of this view in Rawls, *Justice as Fairness: A Restatement* (Cambridge, Mass.: Harvard University Press, 2001), 8–12. Gerald Cohen has been this view's most powerful critique. See for example Cohen, G. A., 'Where the Action is: On the Site of Distributive Justice', *Philosophy and Public Affairs* 26 (1997), 3–30.
2. Rawls, *A Theory of Justice*, 98.
3. Walker, Robert, 'Opportunity and Life Chances: The Dynamics of Poverty, Inequality and Exclusion' in Giddens and Diamond (eds.), *The New Egalitarianism*, 69–86.
4. See Barry, *Why Social Justice Matters*, 57–9, 95–103.

5. See Harvey, David, *Justice, Nature and the Geography of Difference* (Oxford: Blackwell, 1996); Portugali, Juval, *Implicate Relations: Society and Space in the Israeli-Palestinian Conflict* (Dordrecht: Kluwer Academic, 1993).

6. Shrader-Frechette, *Environmental Justice: Creating Equality, Reclaiming Democracy*, 74. See also Bullard, Robert (ed.), *Unequal Protection: Environmental Justice and Communities of Color* (San Francisco: Sierra Clubs Books, 1994).

7. See: Bennett, Fran, 'Poverty and Exclusion', paper delivered at the Priority in Practice conference, University College London, 2004. See http://www.jrf.org.uk/knowledge/findings/socialpolicy/334.asp; Lister, Ruth, 'A Politics of Recognition and Respect: Involving People With Experience of Poverty in Decision Making That Affects Their Lives', *Social Policy and Society* 1 (2002), 37–46. See also Cornwall, Andrea and John Gaventa, 'Bridging the Gap: Citizenship, Participation and Accountability', *PLA Notes* 40 (2001), 32–5; and The Commission on Poverty, Participation and Power, *Listen Hear: The Right to be Heard*.

Index

abortion 10
Adelman, Laura 209 n. 4
advantage and disadvantage; *see* disadvantage
advice centres 180
affiliation 6, 8, 39, 44, 45, 50, 54, 56, 67, 69, 105–6, 109, 113–14, 119–28, 138–42, 144, 159, 162, 168–72, 179–80, 185, 191, 206 n. 17, 211 n. 17, 216 n. 41
'affluent faster' example 64–5
Aggleton, Peter 214 n. 25
African-Americans 183
see also USA, imprisonment of black people in
Agarwal, Bina 197 n. 1
alcohol and alcoholism 58, 60
alienation 54, 126, 160, 172
Alkire, Sabina 37, 38, 48, 197 n. 1 198 nn. 3, 6, 7, 198 n. 14, 200 nn. 37, 46
Anderson, Elizabeth 31, 170, 174, 176, 192 n. 5, 196 n. 26, 205 n. 8, 206 n. 15, 207 nn. 7, 11, 217 n. 7
anger 39
animals; *see* species, other
anxiety 39, 68, 115, 148
Arabs in Israel 183
see also Bedouins, Palestinians
Aristotle 38, 198 n. 9, 200 n. 31
Arneson, Richard 76, 192 n. 3, 206 nn. 8, 9, 208 n. 9
Arrow, Kenneth 194 n. 3
Ashworth, Karl 210 n. 4
assault 38
assimilation 109
asylum seekers 48, 60, 145
Atkinson, A. B. 208 n. 1, 210 n. 3

attitudes, *see* social attitudes
autonomy 58, 114, 123, 144, 168, 169, 179–80, 198 n. 12, 200 n. 41, 211 n. 17, 212 n. 10
in the workplace 146–7

Baker, Gideon 218 n. 18
Bangladesh 65
bank account 146
see also income and wealth, savings
Barry, Brian 126, 207 n. 8, 209 nn. 1, 2, 211 nn. 23, 24, 25, 212 n. 3, 218 n.4
basic income, unconditional 172
Baumeister, Roy 200 n. 43
Beatles, the 147
Bedouins 67, 203 n. 12, 204 n. 14
see also Arabs in Israel
"before and after" argument 30
belonging, *see* affiliation
Bell, Derek 203 n. 13
Bennett, Fran 217 n. 30, 221 n. 7
bias, intellectualist 40, 53–4
Binmore, Ken 194 n. 7
Blacksher, Erica 204 n. 17
Blane, David 214 n. 25
blindness 114
body, the 52
bodily integrity; *see* integrity, bodily
Bradbury, Thomas 202 n. 59
Bradshaw, Jonathan 110–11, 208 nn. 2, 3, 209 n. 4
Brighouse, Harry 214 n. 27
Brittan, Samuel 215 n. 36
Brock, Dan 194 n. 15
Brookdale Institute 204 n. 19
Brown, Alexander 206 n. 19
Brown, Campbell 207 n. 10
Brown, Stephanie 199 n. 32
Buddhism 58

Lightning Source UK Ltd.
Milton Keynes UK
15 January 2011

165779UK00004B/2/P

9 780199 278268